PAUL RICOEUR

CRITICS OF THE TWENTIETH CENTURY
General Editor: Christopher Norris,
University of Wales,
College of Cardiff

A. J. GREIMAS AND THE NATURE OF MEANING
Ronald Schleifer

CHRISTOPHER CAUDWELL
Robert Sullivan

FIGURING LACAN
Criticism and the Cultural Unconscious
Juliet Flower MacCannell

HAROLD BLOOM
Towards Historical Rhetorics
Peter de Bolla

F. R. LEAVIS
Michael Bell

POSTMODERN BRECHT
A Re-Presentation
Elizabeth Wright

DELEUZE AND GUATTARI
Ronald Bogue

ECSTASIES OF ROLAND BARTHES
Mary Wiseman

JULIA KRISTEVA
John Lechte

GEOFFREY HARTMAN
Criticism as Answerable Style
G. Douglas Atkins

INTRODUCING LYOTARD
Bill Readings

EZRA POUND AS LITERARY CRITIC
K. K. Ruthven

PAUL RICOEUR

S. H. Clark

London and New York

First published 1990
by Routledge
11 New Fetter Lane, London EC4P 4EE

Simultaneously published in the USA and Canada
by Routledge
a division of Routledge, Chapman and Hall, Inc.
29 West 35th Street, New York, NY 10001

Phototypeset
and printed in Great Britain by
Redwood Press Limited, Wiltshire

British Library Cataloguing in Publication Data
Clark, S. H. (Stephen H)
Paul Ricoeur.
1. Philosophy of religion. Ricoeur, Paul
I. Title II. Series
200.1

ISBN 0–415–02309–2

Library of Congress Cataloging-in-Publication Data
Clark, S. H. (Stephen H.)
Paul Ricoeur / S. H. Clark.
p.   cm.—(Critics of the twentieth century)
Includes bibliographical references.
ISBN 0–415–02309–2
1. Ricoeur, Paul—Contributions in hermeneutics.   2. Ricoeur, Paul—
Contributions in literary criticism.   3. Literature—Philosophy.
4. Hermeneutics—History—20th century.   I. Title.   II. Series:
Critics of the twentieth century (London, England)
B2430.R554C35   1990   90–32232   CIP

Contents

Contents

List of abbreviations

BI   *Essays on Biblical Interpretation* (1980)

CI   *Le conflit des interprétations. Essais d'herméneutique* (1969) (published in English as *The Conflict of Interpretations: Essays in Hermeneutics*)

DCCT *Dialogues with Contemporary Continental Thinkers* (1984)

FM   *Philosophie de la volonté. Finitude et Culpabilité. I. L'homme fallible* (1960) (published in English as *Fallible Man*)

FN   *Philosophie de la volonté. I. Le volontaire et l'involontaire* (1950) (published in English as *Freedom and Nature: The Voluntary and the Involuntary*)

FP   *De l'interprétation. Essai sur Freud* (1965) (published in English as *Freud and Philosophy*)

GMKJ *Gabriel Marcel et Karl Jaspers. Philosophie du mystère et philosophie du paradoxe* (1948)

H   *Husserl. An Analysis of His Phenomenology* (1967)

HHS   *Hermeneutics and the Human Sciences. Essays on Language, Action and Interpretation* (1981)

HT   *Histoire et vérité* (1955) (published in English as *History and Truth*)

IT   *Interpretation Theory: Discourse and the Surplus of Meaning* (1976)

IU   *Lectures on Ideology and Utopia* (1986)

KJ   *Karl Jaspers et la philosophie de l'existence* (1947)

PS   *Political and Social Essays* (1974)

RM   *La métaphore vive* (1975) (published in English as *The Rule of Metaphor. Multi-Disciplinary Studies of the Creation of Meaning in Language*)

SE   *Philosophie de la volonté. Finitude et culpabilité. II. La symbolique du mal* (1960) (published in English as *The Symbolism of Evil*)

TN   *Temps et récit* (1983–6) (published in English as *Time and Narrative*)

Acknowledgements

This study was undertaken while on a British Academy postdoctoral fellowship at Queen Mary and Westfield College, University of London. My thanks also to Jeffrey Rodman and John Wood for both their criticisms and their support throughout the project.

1

Introduction

> Today we are in search of a comprehensive philosophy of
> language to account for the multiple functions of the human act
> of signifying and for their interrelationships.... We have at our
> disposal a symbolic logic, an exegetical science, an anthropol-
> ogy, and a psychoanalysis, and, perhaps for the first time, we
> are able to encompass in a single question the problem of the
> unification of human discourse. The very progress of the afore-
> mentioned disciplines has both revealed and intensified the
> dismemberment of that discourse. Today the unity of human
> language poses a problem.
>
> (*FP*: 3–4)

With characteristic modesty, Ricoeur immediately disclaims the title
of 'philosopher of integral language' who might be able to achieve
such a 'comprehensive philosophy'. And yet his work possesses an
acute and immediate relevance throughout the human sciences: concerning their epistemological value, on the problem of the subject, in
the philosophy of language, and in all spheres of interpretation
theory. Ricoeur is a genuinely interdisciplinary thinker, with distinguished and original contributions in a host of different areas – in
addition to those listed above, hermeneutics, historiography, literary
criticism, phenomenology, political theory, semiotics, structuralism,
theology. And without ever giving the sense of some glutinous composite, always addressing himself attentively to the question in hand
with a courteous rigour. This points to a central paradox. Ricoeur, the
explorer of the volitional, of human fallibility, of the semantics of
desire, never fails to conduct his investigations with a lucid concise-
ness and unfaltering commitment to 'the tradition of rationality that
has animated philosophy since the Greeks' (*CI*: 6). Yet the reason

1

for which he speaks is relative and constrained. Its authority is validated not through edict and proclamation but through disavowal and self-curtailment. There is 'ascèse' at the heart of his intellectual enterprise, a sustained exercise of humility.

The proclaimed rationalism and the overt theological commitment in Ricoeur's thought would appear to distance him from the constellation of Barthes, Derrida, and Foucault. So un-Parisian, one might say: so unchic, sober and collaborative, propelled by the internal momentum of his own preoccupations, an inconspicuous and almost humdrum figure. And yet the question may fairly be asked: on what major intellectual issues of the past forty years has Ricoeur *not* written with distinction?

Some biographical detail may here be helpful. Born in Valence in 1913, Ricoeur was educated in the 1930s in a general climate of existential and phenomenological thought. Captured early in the Second World War, he was allowed access to German philosophy; and over the next five years acquired a detailed familiarity with the works of Husserl, Heidegger and Jaspers. The results of this immersion appeared in his work during the immediate post-war years: *Karl Jaspers et la philosophie de l'existence*, co-written with Mikel Dufrenne, was published in 1947; *Gabriel Marcel et Karl Jaspers: philosophie du mystère et philosophie du paradoxe* in the following year; and in 1950, his translation of and authoritative commentary on Husserl's *Ideen* (the first volume in Sartre's and Merleau-Ponty's *Bibliothèque de philosophie*) established him as a leading expert on phenomenology. Subsequent essays providing a scrupulous and comprehensive commentary of the German philosopher's work have been collected together in *Husserl* (1967).

In 1948, he was awarded the Chair of Philosophy at Strasbourg: the sustained re-reading of the philosophical tradition that this entailed detached him from existential phenomenology. He now sought to develop a reflective philosophy concerned with establishing the ultimate grounds of authentic subjectivity; and in this to define human freedom in terms of a sustained negotiation with necessity rather than through the Sartrian moment of transcendent choice. This emphasis is apparent in *Freedom and Nature* (1950), an application of Husserl's strict analytic method to the affective and volitional spheres of human life. Although dealing with themes of the body, situatedness, decision, the book is devoted to a recognition of the constraints within which consciousness operates, and the necessity of a detour through the data of the empirical sciences in an arduous and indirect progress towards self-understanding. A collection of essays, *History and Truth*, appeared in 1955, distinguished by an attempt to situate an ethic of social intervention, 'praise of the word which reflects efficaciously and acts thoughtfully' (*HT*: 5), within an eschatological fiction of the 'Last Day'. His next major work, the two-volume *Finitude and Guilt*, appeared in 1960. The first volume, *Fallible Man*, approaches the issue of human fallibility through the resources of transcendental reflection; the second, *The Symbolism of Evil*, turns to the primary symbols of guilt as an alternative source of insight, and thus represents a crucial point of transition from a phenomenology of the will to a broader consideration of problems of language and interpretation.

Ricoeur's work quickly took up the challenge presented by the newly-ascendent disciplines of the 1960s: structuralism and psychoanalysis, both in their way reactions against the subject-centred discourse of Sartre and Merleau-Ponty. This admirably independent engagement produced such seminal essays as 'Structure, word, event', and what is still probably his best known book, *Freud and Philosophy* (1965). The hermeneutic theory enunciated in this text (more prominent in the French title, *De l'interprétation*) is more extensively developed in the 1969 collection of essays, *The Conflict of Interpretations*. Here it is argued, in an impressive variety of contexts, that the process of understanding involves a double movement of the recovery of meaning and of an exercise in demystification: opposing perspectives which complement each other in an open-ended and productive contest. Subsequently, there is a continued interest in the dynamics of metaphor and symbol (most notably in *The Rule of Metaphor* (1975)), which increasingly draws on Anglo-American linguistic analysis; but this is now situated within a broader engagement with the hermeneutic tradition, and more general problems of written language, text. The best brief summation comes in *Interpretation Theory: Discourse and the Surplus of Meaning* (1976). The positions here expounded are, however, substantially reworked in subsequent essays, in particular their implications in the sphere of practical reason and what Ricoeur calls the social imaginary of ideology and utopia. His most recent work, the three-volume *Time and Narrative*, deals with the relation of narrative, both fictional and historiographic, to the fundamental temporality of human existence.

Ricoeur is still comparatively little known in Britain. Eagleton's *Literary Theory*, for example, makes no direct reference to his work: *Freud and Philosophy* is listed, none too precisely, in the notes amongst 'other works in the tradition of hermeneutical phenomenology' (1983:

220), cited in the bibliography under psychoanalysis, and omitted from the index altogether. In the US, however, where h: has held a part-time professorship at Chicago since 1973, his reputation as a theologian has been high since the early 1960s, and over the past ten years his influence has been rapidly spreading in literary thought. One indication of this can be seen in his omission from Frank Lentricchia's influential survey, *After the New Criticism* (1980); and his inclusion, five years later, as an undisputed contemporary classic, in Hazard Adams' *Philosophy and the Literary Symbolic* (1985).

I think Ricoeur should have greater currency, be more widely discussed and debated with. Not out of some absolute standard of fair play, giving merit its due, but because sustained consideration of his work clarifies and compels redefinition of the current state of literary theory. Ricoeur never picks a fight. One of the most impressive traits of his work is his respectful, almost grateful, assimilation of criticism: there is nothing in his work remotely comparable to Derrida's altercation with Searle. At times we may lament the absence of 'blistering refutations' (*RM*: 6), but these would run counter to the values that Ricoeur's whole intellectual enterprise seeks to promote: humility, mutual respect, the truth of charity. But the force of his quiet implicit retorts to his more vociferous contemporaries should not be underestimated. In the midst of their rhetorical bravura, Ricoeur's calm and patient diligence appears almost stolid by comparison. He speaks as the professional, circumscribed, making no attempt to conceal or subvert his own situatedness, an emphasis present from the early existential writings. But there are currently enough prophets among us to make us appreciate this painstaking, vocationally unembarrassed, proponent of 'thinking, that is to say elaborating concepts that comprehend, and make one comprehend, concepts woven together, if not in a closed system, at least in a systematic order' (*CI*: 296). This might seem to imply closure, fixed vantages, dovetailed arguments yet it thrives on impasse and hiatus: the necessary detour, the acknowledged aporia, the secondariness of judgement to life, force, act. Ricoeur does not simply announce a commitment to openness. His is a rationality genuinely inclusive, kinetic, in constant internal evolution: the Socratic inheritance in its most positive form. Intellectual positions are never either finally formulated or completely abandoned: they are there to be reoccupied, reargued. (For example, recent essays on psychoanalysis such as 'The question of proof in Freud's psychoanalytic writings' (*HHS*: 247–73; see also *TN* 1: 60–2) move away from his previous concern with the status of the oneiric symbol, and now treat the metapsychology as a subordinate phase of explanation, and stress the importance of the production of a successful personal narrative within the analytic situation.) And in this continuous self-criticism Ricoeur's thought is more genuinely exploratory than many apparently more radical interventions.

Foucault implicitly denies the power of reference to discourse. Language is a self-sustaining system in which word bears no necessary relation to thing: hence, in *The Order of Things*, no kind of motivation is offered for the diachronic shifts between alternate states of the system or epistemes. His texts convey a pervasive illusion of coherence serenely oblivious to any external demand for verification. Lacan moves from Freud's insight that the unconscious can only be known through language to the premise that the unconscious is 'structured like' a language. This permits the technical terms of infra-linguistic analysis to be elevated to governing laws of the human psyche: most notably in the equation of condensation to metaphor and displacement to metonymy. The justification of his own notoriously hermetic exegesis of Freud would appear to be that its fissures and striations allow these relations to emerge in a kind of surface tension of signifying chains (see, for example, Bowie, 1987: 105). (The argument is, of course, self-defeating. If Lacan's style intentionally mimics the disruption of the unconscious, then it in fact represses its actual presence through a controlled simulacrum.) For Derrida, language is both vertiginous and yet ultimately closed. There are no boundaries to language because this would imply the violence of the inside/outside demarcation. But language cannot transcend itself, make new meaning: a circumscription that remains based on the premise of the closed synchronic system. Therefore the self, because it inheres in language, must endure a destiny of interminable deferral, always subject to the internal substitutions of morpheme, phoneme, and lexeme. In all three cases, what appears to be a subversive response remains conditioned by and to a large degree dependent on a series of restrictive and unstated premises derived from structuralism.

Ricoeur is post-structuralist in the sense of having heeded, absorbed, and utilised. He decisively states the major objections to a Saussurian linguistics: first, its idealist tendencies – a Kantianism without a transcendental subject; secondly, the reduction of history to the motiveless transitions between states of the system; thirdly, its exclusion of the referential and purposive aspects of language, the saying of something about something; and finally its absolutising of language without acknowledging its own methodological complicity

in constructing it as an object. But there is also a generous appreci-
ation of its achievements and an explicit incorporation of its techniques. In Ricoeur's work in the 1970s, it is retained as a powerful
component of the legitimate moment of formal explanation in the
hermeneutic arc. And in so doing, it takes us beyond a sterile antimony between positivist reduction and rampant indeterminacy, and
offers us new options on the far side of this debate.

For better or worse, the Anglo-American tradition has never been
seduced by the structuralist combination of quasi-scientific procedure with a Platonising celebration of form within form. There has
been an assimilation of the subsequent sceptical reaction without its
ever having been suffered as an oppressive orthodoxy. And this
cultural cross-pollination has acquired a self-perpetuating momentum of its own: the acclaimed Derridean free-play, *jeu*, chance, gam-
ble, is transformed in trans-Atlantic crossing into an anarchic
libertarianism, a comfortable disenfranchisement from value (though
one should be wary of any too credulous acceptance of the myth of the
fall of deconstruction into a host of parasitic imitators). Here it is
worth quoting Jonathan Culler, caught off guard:

> The more we know of critical theory the more interest we are
> likely to take in accurate discriminations, and the more we will
> smile with derision at those who, in reducing criticism to a
> simple moral scenario, abandon all pretence at discernment.
> The restaurateur who tells us he has two kinds of wine, red and
> white, does not impress us as a connoisseur.
>
> (Culler, 1983: 19)

Is it 'reducing' criticism to see it as necessarily implying some form of
cultural praxis, or is all morality inherently 'simple', some crassly
staged 'scenario'? Does this supposed emancipation entitle us to
'smile with derision' at the non-initiate? There is a symptomatic
progression from the 'interest' in 'accurate discrimination' to a 'dis-
cernment' opposed to any kind of ethical or political commitment,
which in turn shades into the sanctimonious detachment of the 'con-
noisseur': the critic as 'restaurateur', a vendor of commodities whose
raison-d'être is now solely to 'impress us'.

Such outright aestheticism would, I suppose, be harmless, if it were
not allied to the powerful post-structuralist critique of the constraint
and repression enforced by discipline boundaries. I would not wish to
undervalue the achievement of deconstruction in validating the application of sophisticated rhetorical exegesis to texts previously con-

signed to other domains, and conversely exposing literary works to greatly increased conceptual scrutiny. To the extent that it has been able 'to restore the complexities of reading to the dignity of a philosophical question' (de Man, 1983: 110), it makes it impossible to speak of the merely literary, and for that we must be duly grateful. But does this suddenly render more traditional demarcations completely obsolete? Should critical theory be celebrated as a liberating *mélange*, exalted for its very absence of grounding?

I would stress the disproportionate influence in Derrida's work of what Ricoeur calls 'vengefulness' (*RM*: 295). A theory of intertextual dependence that demands intimate cohabitation with past writings combines with ostentatious gestures of severance, a stylistic scorched-earth policy. If he cannot be the subject of his own discourse, he'll still have the trickiest text in town: a baroque, apocalyptic prose seasoned with a mincing self-righteousness. Yet when reinserted into the context of critical philosophy, Derrida represents not rupture and abolition but vigorous renewal. Onto-theology, in the more restricted sense of rationalist theodicy, was refuted by Kant (1933; 2:3:7 A632:525); Nietzsche's *The Genealogy of Morals* delighted in the exposure of faked and duplicitous origins; Husserl's *Logical Investigations*, far from positing a transparent self-presence, establish a complex dialectic between intuitive fulfilment and signification; and 'The task of Destroying the history of Ontology' is announced at the very beginning of Heidegger's *Being and Time* (1962: II, 6). It requires an ingenuous literalism to regard his proclamation of the death of philosophy as anything other than a profoundly orthodox generic trait. Here a particularly salutary comparison can be made with Ricoeur, ever respectful of the autonomy of different fields of thought, their modes of internal cohesion, their specifically appropriate expertise and methods of validation. This is genuinely cross-disciplinary thought, full of startling leaps, juxtapositions, *rapprochements*, but always proceeding with conciliation and respect. His work testifies to the continued possibility of constructive and relevant dialogue.

So if Derrida tends to merge back into the pack, distinguished only by his absence of generosity towards a past history of error, what of de Man? Certainly within the Anglo-American tradition, his work seems more targeted and hence more formidable. After all, it's easy enough to feel profoundly unconcerned by the fate of metaphysics. But if you are in any way attached to the literary text as embodying a form of knowledge unavailable to positivist description, then it is impossible not to be shaken by de Man's sinuous analyses. So neat a reversal to preserve the cognitive status of the text: its failure represents the higher honesty, the inevitability of disappointment. What is covert and undeclared in de Man is the absolute standard by which success is to be gauged. Language fails to give access to being: we listen but nothing is heard. And so the ontologist *manqué* must seek his consolation in the ruthless exposure of illusion: a negative transcendence in depriving the self of even a factitious stability. There seems no compromise possible between succumbing to this elegiac charisma or repudiating it wholesale as a *trahison des clercs* which can only culminate in a fatalistic quiescence.

Ricoeur offers an equally rigorous interrogation of any naive pretension to unmediated truth in language, and would, I think, be greatly sympathetic to de Man's imperative of self-understanding. He offers a philosophy of reflection applicable to many fields, and yet may legitimately be deemed an exponent of the absent centre: his thought is immediately obliged to move away from the realm of ontology, subsist and define itself on some more verifiable terrain. Ricoeur introduces an element of indefinite postponement into a broadly Hegelian teleology. As in *Fallible Man*, happiness is defined as always about-to-be, final resolution is always to be worked towards. For Derrida, this would be the site of différance, the 'absurd play of errant signifiers' (*HHS*: 217); for de Man, a bleak revelation of time as purely erosive, blank anonymous duration. And there is no easy consolation in Ricoeur (when will he write on the symbolism of bliss?). One is struck by the flimsiness of the putative moment of appropriation, of return. There is no arrival at certitude, merely an endless resumption of the search for a beginning. Ricoeur at this point reinstates the themes of existential decision and struggle towards self-consciousness. Thought is a 'task' that must acknowledge its own situation of fall, exile, and alienation, and direct itself towards 'reconstruction'. But the prefix is misleading. The excavation through the 'sedimented' levels of the concept does not allow the 're'-discovery of original wisdom. Meaning emerges not through nostalgic regression, but in the space opened by commitment to the 'act' of interpretation. And this is arguably the crucial issue in his work. Is the positive side of the dialectic essentially sacramental, a vindication of hierophany, a warning against 'forgetting the signs of the Sacred, losing hold of man himself, as belonging to the Sacred' (*CI*: 288); or does Ricoeur succeed in utilising all the resources of post-modernist scepticism in order to prompt a new beginning, a 'second naïveté' on the far side of the 'hermeneutics of suspicion'?

It is certainly possible to regard his work as 'the philosophical buttressing of a Christian synthesis' (Spiegelberg, 1960: 568), but this is by no means uncharacteristic of the existential tradition. Even such a robustly atheistic sentiment as Sartre's engagement can be traced, via Heidegger's resolution, back to Christian fortitude; similarly choice and authenticity can be seen as transmutations of conscience. Connections can be made in Ricoeur's thought between plurality and charity, respect for the other and love of the neighbour, the surplus of meaning and the future abundance of the Kingdom of God, though generally these remain implicit and unobtrusive. His work has obvious affinities with Jürgen Moltmann on the theology of the promise, Rudolf Bultmann on the necessity of demythification, and Karl Barth on the founding moment of choice that grounds any project of thought. The contemporary debate between theologies of the event and of the word is replayed in a variety of guises: the event (whether verbal, historical, political) is never fully subsumed into discourse. It remains prior, testifies, witnesses to something beyond itself. Yet it can only be known through its linguistic mediations: hence the necessity of indirection, the interminable detours of exegesis. Ricoeur repeatedly insists that his work as a philosopher be judged in separation from these debates; indeed perhaps what is most striking in this respect is his scrupulous refusal to activate the theological resonances of this vocabulary. Ultimately, however, we might feel obliged to demur, and see even the distant horizon of a fundamental ontology as an unacceptable closure. But Ricoeur might well reply that this shows an immature preference for chaos over order, despair over hope; and we can find the resources within his work for a stinging retort to joyous nihilism. At the very least, his work provides a salutary reminder that disbelieving means giving something up rather than the unproblematic prelude to instant and total emancipation. The issue remains, however, of whether Ricoeur's search for meaning-generating capacity in language is ultimately reliant on a model of communion, *kerygma*; and whether his conclusions are therefore vitiated for those of us who do not share his faith.

Within the constraints of space of an introductory volume, certain exclusions must be declared. Ricoeur's specifically phenomenological studies will only be discussed in much abbreviated fashion, and large areas of his thought – for example, his writings as theologian, educationalist, and social commentator – will remain virtually untouched. There will be an inevitable foreshortening of his early career, and a highly selective treatment of his numerous important articles;

though this will still, I hope, respect the major contours of his career. There is also the question of the relative availability of material in English, although this is sometimes better – the collection of essays on *Husserl* have only recently been published in book form in French as *A l'école de la phénoménologie* (1986), and *Ideology and Utopia*, lectures offering a detailed commentary on Marx and Althusser, given in 1975 at Columbia University, are presently unavailable in that language. Unlike many commentators, I shall emphasise the large-scale orchestration of his books over the trenchancy and compression of individual essays. From my perspective, that of a background in literary criticism, the major works are *The Symbolism of Evil, Freud and Philosophy, The Conflict of Interpretations, Hermeneutics and the Human Sciences, Interpretation Theory, The Rule of Metaphor,* and *Time and Narrative.*

With a thinker so bewilderingly diverse, there is no obvious teleology to adopt, despite a certain degree of inclusiveness in the final volume of *Time and Narrative*: a sense of signing off. Ricoeur has repeatedly protested his own sense of discontinuity in his work, which he presents very much in terms of the haphazard pragmatism of the intellectual bricoleur (see, for example, *HHS*: 32). There are no clear-cut segmentations or definitive statements. Articles criss-cross and overlap: there is no easy way of extracting fixed or conclusive positions from this series of mutually modifying debates. He displays an insatiable appetite for the interminable project: the third volume of the *Poetics of the Will* remains uncompleted, and we have been promised a detailed study of the German hermeneutic tradition and a collection of specifically theological essays. It is easy to see why the common fault of Ricoeur criticism, cowed by the sheer volume of production, has been to resort to reiterative paraphrase. Nevertheless I hope to be able to provide a compact and accessible summary of the major developments of his thought – existentialism, symbolism and mythology, psychoanalysis, text theory, metaphor, and narrative – and then to examine how these intersect with and clarify the current preoccupations of literary theory.

I would like to close by making a couple of points about Ricoeur's rhetorical practice. Is this an attractive, stimulating thought to encounter, or is its professionalism, its respectful enumeration of counter-arguments, its reliance on a disciplined and consecutive development, rather than rhetorical *coup de grâce*, actually a restoration of an oppressive sobriety overthrown by the mobility of deconstructive thought? One can take pleasure in Ricoeur's texts, though their rhetorical surface make little concession to anything less than studious attention. This is dense thought, difficult not out of any elitism or obscurantism or claims to self-reflexivity, but packed, compressed, ambitious in its expository deference. There is much more pressure in it than one at first realises. It seems to invite the reader into new domains of thought with a kind of weighty transparence; but then at a certain level of familiarity one realises that this very transparence is combative, a position staked on disputed terrain. There is no backing away from the necessarily conflictual nature of interpretation: and Ricoeur, we should remember, has held his own in uncompromising, at times vitriolic, debate with the major figures of the post-war period: Sartre, Lévi-Strauss, Althusser, Lacan, Derrida, Habermas. His reading against the grain is as dexterous and audacious a conceptual enterprise as anything in Derrida. I would particularly emphasise his fondness for eliciting the possibility of a counter-reading within the texts themselves – most notably perhaps in the complementary readings of *Freud and Philosophy* – but the nimbleness and elegance of the technique is prevalent elsewhere, for example the reading of Aristotle in the opening chapter of *The Rule of Metaphor* (9–43), or the treatment of Weber in *Ideology and Utopia* (197–215). His strict, almost ascetic, rationalism is situated within an overall conception of the hermeneutic field as fissured, warring and irreducible. The avowed faith in ultimate reunion amounts, in his local practice, to not disbelieving that rational debate can still be conducted. And the quality of argument offered by 'this tireless worker, so temperate and so honest' (*H*: 12) is such as to offer an unrivalled guidance through the intellectual debate of our time.

What, finally, from the perspective of literary studies as traditionally defined, is the value of Ricoeur's work? First, he situates it within the practice of interpretation in the broadest sense in the human sciences, and provides an almost inexhaustible supply of illuminating cross-connections and counter-perspectives between the French, German, and Anglo-American traditions. There is little or no reading of literary texts – an occasional review (e.g. 1952; 1954), some detailed work on scriptural parable (e.g. 1975d), and a series of diligent but unexceptionable analyses in *Time and Narrative*. Nevertheless, despite the more technical idiom, there is considerable overlap of concern with the English tradition: compare, for example, the close of Ricoeur's essay, 'Existence and hermeneutics' (*CI*: 3–24):

In this way ontology is indeed the promised land for a philosophy that begins with language and with reflection; but, like

11

Moses, the speaking and reflecting subject can only glimpse this land before dying.

(*CI*: 24)

with the final proclamation of Arnold's 'The function of criticism at the present time' on 'the true life of a literature':

> in an epoch like those, no doubt, the true life of a literature; there is the promised land, towards which criticism can only beckon. That promised land it will not be ours to enter, and we shall die in the wilderness: but to have desired to enter it, to have saluted it from afar, is already, perhaps, the best distinction among contemporaries...

(1962, III: 281)

It is worth stressing that Ricoeur's work has relevance not merely where it directly treats such issues as symbol, metaphor, and narrative, but also where its often highly technical discussions illuminate the conceptual heritage that lies behind much post-structuralist thinking. In the course of this book, for example, such major Derridean themes as the status of the trace, the alienation of the text, the centring of structure, and the latent power of concealed metaphor will be discussed in detail. Furthermore, if as de Man is prepared to concede 'however negative it may sound, deconstruction implies the possibility of rebuilding' (1983: 140; compare Derrida, 1973: 159), Ricoeur's persistent engagement with the full force of the hermeneutics of suspicion provides impressive testimony to the pledge that 'it is beyond destruction that the question is posed as to what thought, reason, and even faith still signify' (*FP*: 33). If 'superstition, like belief, must die', he has never ceased to enquire 'what remains when disbelief has gone' (Larkin, 1988: 98).

2

The existential heritage

EARLY INFLUENCES

It would be misguided to search for premature affinities between Ricoeur's work of the 1940s and 1950s and the current preoccupations of literary theory. This phase of his career, though impressively coherent on its own terms, shows little sign of the 'cooperation between phenomenology and literary criticism' through their 'combined use of the categories of sensation, consciousness, and temporality' that de Man found characteristic of the period (1983: 4). The obvious comparison is with Sartre, and Ricoeur's unassuming, often highly technical, mode of exposition inevitably seems overshadowed: there is less aphoristic verve, flair for empirical illustration, pace of innovation, but also less arrogance, repetition, and opportunism. In this chapter, I shall offer a comparatively brief overview of Ricoeur's existential affiliations, look at his relation to Husserl in rather more detail, and then seek to establish some points of contact with Derrida and de Man.

Ricoeur's 1957 article, 'Existential phenomenology' (*H*: 202–12), is careful to restrict existentialism to a subspecies of transcendental phenomenology: the attempt to relate 'the conditions of the appearance of things to the structure of human subjectivity' (*H*: 203). Rather than being a radical breakthrough or displacement it 'becomes a method and is placed in the service of a dominating problem-set, viz. the problems concerning existence' (*H*: 203). Elsewhere, Ricoeur comments:

> in many senses existentialism is a classical philosophy by its reflection on the limitations of knowledge revealed by the situation of the human existent; the importance of its discussion of the universal and the particular, essence and existence, and on

13

mystery and problem. The existentialist philosophy attempts a new possession of objectivity, the elaboration of a new form of intelligence and ... 'a new philosophical logic'.

(*HT*: 156–7)

Thus he insists that it in no way represents an abrupt break or even substantial mutation in philosophy: instead it holds onto and perpetuates the tradition. (Note the already hermeneutic emphasis: what for Rorty would be evidence of the inability of philosophy to deliver becomes for Ricoeur a sign of its capacity of self-renewal).

Ricoeur identifies three main strands in French existential phenomenology. The first is its concern with the lived body (*corps vécu*), stemming from Marcel's break with the anonymous epistemological subject and rerooting of the ontological mystery in concrete analysis. Merleau-Ponty's 'exorcism of standpointless thinking' (*H*: 209) also receives a sympathetic exposition, though considerable reservations are voiced about the breakdown of objective thought entailed by perspectivist doctrines. Ricoeur's own work explicitly engages with this issue in *Freedom and Nature*, with its analyses of the area of interchange between the voluntary and involuntary, and attempted reconciliation of first- and third-person understanding of the body, phenomenological intention and scientific fact.

The second is the theme of freedom, in which the ontological and existential are unified because 'the being of man consists in existing' (*H*: 210). Sartre is acknowledged to have 'inverted the ontological index of freedom' so that existence consists in being its own nothingness (*H*: 218). The opaque terminology conceals a basically simple reworking of an orthodox subject–object dualism. Consciousness, in a famous image, is like a doughnut: the emptiness at the centre (*pour-soi*) must be continually renewed through active repudiation of the inert given (*en-soi*). This is demonstrated in a 'phenomenology of nihilating acts' which 'manifests an abundance, a perspicacity and a force rarely equaled' (*H*: 210). Ricoeur objects, however, to the confusion of the sphere of objectivity with existential significations – there is nothing intrinsically destructive about formal negation – and more specifically to Sartre's 'hypostasis of the nihilating act into an actual nothingness' (*HT*: 319). This may seem a minor technical criticism, but in fact pinpoints the repeated elliptical transitions between negation as concept in Hegelian logic, and *négatités*, empirically observed psychological states. The terms are conflated into 'nothingness' and opposed to a correspondingly 'flimsy and already reified' concept of being-in-itself (*HT*: 319), a portmanteau term embracing phenomena as disparate as the object-world, the living body, and the remembered past. Ricoeur stresses the counter-possibility of Marcel's *disponibilité*: 'the decisive experience of freedom is to be found not in the moment of breaking away but rather in the moment of engagement which includes our whole involvement in situation' (*H*: 211).

> However radical a conversion can be imagined to be, it nihilates a dead past only to discover and stir up behind it a living past which the 'crisis' has liberated ... Thus I repudiate a past of myself only to assume another past.
>
> (*HT*: 322)

It could be said that Ricoeur replaces rupture with reinterpretation.

The third strand is the question of the Other. The attempt to progress methodically from cogito to community remains a perennial difficulty in Husserl's work. The reduction of the cogito to a monad in the fourth *Cartesian Meditation* raises the urgent problem of constituting the 'Other as another ego': the impasse is subsequently addressed through recourse to an analogical grasping of Otherness which 'creates as many problems as it solves' (*H*: 126). Sartre avoids the need to give any account of empathy or collaboration through reducing all forms of contact to relations of utter domination: the Other is only known in the form of the petrifying gaze, or 'as power of encroachment and of theft' (*H*: 212). Ricoeur's own work displays a variety of responses to this problem: to upgrade the faculty of sympathy; to cut the Gordian knot by the insertion of a Kantian principle of respect as a limit idea; and finally in his hermeneutic work simply to bypass the problem with the presupposition, there are texts. Put extremely briefly, the phenomenological account of intersubjectivity, despite its many problems, is seen as retaining constitutive role for the individual subject necessary that may curb the pretensions of the Hegelian philosophy of spirit. Indeed, the tension is never really satisfactorily resolved between the communitarian emphasis of his social thought, and the solipsistic tendencies of his philosophical mentor.

Contemporary French thought is here presented as 'situated at the confluence of the phenomenological method deriving from Husserl and the existential problem-set received from post-Hegelian philosophy' (*H*: 203); though existential thinkers will later be described as possessing no more than a loose family resemblance (e.g. Ricoeur,

1963b). To a considerable extent this may be regarded as Ricoeur's own philosophical ancestry. Hegel's *Phenomenology of Spirit* introduces the concept of the negative as the 'experiences of disappearance, contradiction, struggle and frustration which impart the tragic tone to his phenomenology' (*H*: 206). This was intended to provide a 'systematic cohesion' for the transitions between one cultural form and another which the logic of identity and contradiction had proved incapable of giving (in contrast to Sartre where the 'labour of the negative' is detached from any dialectical progression and subsists in its own right). Ricoeur's early work preserves a privileged experience of 'deficiency, non-being' in order to 'denounce as naive the pretensions of the subject to constitute himself' (*H*: 214). While the vantage of absolute knowledge is repudiated, the form of Hegel's logic remains evident. The projective teleology is most visible, as we shall see, in *Freud and Philosophy*, but works as far apart as *Freedom and Nature* and *Time and Narrative* preserve the framework of a kind of exoskeletal dialectic. Ricoeur's customary mode of argumentation posits a dual opposition which leads not to an asserted synthesis but to a fragile mediation, often to an aporia that provokes redefinition of the initial problem (see Ricoeur, 1976c).

This has evident affinities with the broken dialectic of Kierkegaard's work, which is praised for its concentration on 'the individual who emerges in sadness and solitude, in doubt and exaltation – and in passion', the irreducible existent 'whom the System does not include' (*H*: 206; see also 1976b: 57–87 for further discussion of anti-philosophy in this tradition). This would seem to preclude conceptualisation, but Kierkegaard provides an unparalleled analysis of the phenomenology of freedom: his 'almost sickly concern for self-justification' teases out the nuances of such concepts as dread, vertigo and seduction (*H*: 206). Ricoeur draws heavily upon this account of the anguish within freedom: the consciousness of being able to sin, 'the imminent possibility of degrading myself as a possibility of being free' (*HT*: 298). This influence is most powerfully manifested in *The Symbolism of Evil*: notably in the mutual eliciting of freedom and evil, the simultaneous existence of fallibility as state and moment of transition, and the declared impossibility of any final intellectual mastery of the issue (see Ricoeur, 1963b).

Nietzsche's work is categorised somewhat awkwardly as a critical phenomenology, larger in scope than the strict descriptive method: some rather tendentious parallels are drawn with Husserl such as the genealogy of the derived from the originary. In his first book, Ricoeur declares 'Nietzsche nous touche et nous éveille; sa philosophie même négative surtout négative, nous arrache au prestige de l'objet et à toute dogmatique de la Transcendence' ('Nietzsche stirs and awakens us; this philosophy, though negative, because negative, prises us away from the illusion of the object and any dogmatic belief in Transcendence' (*KJ*: 258). At this stage the value of his work is seen in its affirmation of human activity, and Ricoeur will continue to stress the priority of being as act over knowledge as representation. But this becomes equalled in importance by the 'ferocity' of disbelief, the ethic of *Redlichkeit* (*FN*: 119). The influence of this 'enormous enterprise of methodical disillusionment' and 'pitiless taste for unmasking the moral and spiritual falsehoods on which our culture is built' lies behind the hermeneutics of suspicion that Ricoeur sees as dominating contemporary thought. Such essays as 'The necessity of atheism' represent, I would argue, one of the most whole-hearted and coherent contemporary assimilations of his thought. But it must be stressed that Nietzsche is enlisted in an ascetic rather than a libertarian tradition, of struggle as its own reward; any such vitalism deemed is vacuous without the 'will to live' being 'justified as an ethical and political task' (*HT*: 13).

The tradition culminates in two contemporary thinkers. *Karl Jaspers et la philosophie de l'existence* (1947) offers an enthusiastic, even excited, account of the German philosopher. Though his work will later be harshly repudiated for its aestheticising of despair and decrial of religious consolation (see Ricoeur, 1957a), several concepts derived from his thought will be reworked throughout Ricoeur's career. The first is the absorption of the challenge of doubt, and a sympathy for, even fascination with, 'la foi qui sommeille dans la non-foi' ('faith which slumbers in non-faith') (*KJ*: 249): the role of 'le douteur, le mécontent, le soupçonneur' (*KJ*: 272) is regarded as a necessary stage of progession towards faith: 'qui n'a pas lutté contre Dieu ne l'a pas encore cherché' ('he who has not struggled against God is yet to search for Him') (*KJ*: 274). The second concept is the use of antimony as a form of dialectic that is 'concrète et non résolue' (*KJ*: 284): both thinkers share the desire both to refute and employ a Hegelian logic. The third is the theory of cyphers: 'le monde est le manuscrit d'un autre, inaccessible à une lecture universelle et que seule l'existence déchiffre' ('the world is the script of an Other, inaccessible to any single reading and which only existence deciphers') (*KJ*: 244); any attempt at 'une médiation directe' will be 'quasi impracticable' (*KJ*: 283). This sense of irreducible enigma only to be apprehended through indirection and virtual self-evacuation strongly prefigures Ricoeur's later work on symbol and text, though here there is no formal exegesis, only an ill-defined 'intuition'. The fourth concept is historicity, though in Jaspers' work this comes through as a rather vacuous commitment, unaligned in any meaningful way to the hermeneutic tradition, and with little sense of the formative power of social institutions, culture. Finally, the concept of a 'limit-situation', a moment of traumatic revaluation through which transcendence is paradoxically revealed, is employed as the ultimate rationale of both myth and narrative. Three major reservations are stated: whether this merely leads to a self-defeating subjectivism; whether the freedom so defined is self-sufficient or a testimony to some higher sense of being; and whether a philosophy that prides itself on culminating in paradox can ultimately be satisfactory.

This final point was taken up the following year in *Gabriel Marcel et Karl Jaspers: Philosophie du mystère et philosophie du paradoxe* (1948). Both are placed within a Christian tradition opposed to that of Heidegger and Sartre: typically, the pairing is announced as a 'dialogue communicatif et non point polémique'. Marcel's work is seen as having two major concerns: first, to define the nature of freedom in relation to the body and to history; secondly, to discover what its very limitations might reveal about the meaning of transcendence. Where Jaspers is concerned with choice as 'pouvoir de rupture', with freedom as 'déchirure' ('fissure') (*GMKJ*: 40), Marcel emphasises incarnation, 'un approfondissement de l'existence personnelle'. There is no break from the empirical self, but instead a stress on 'amorçage' ('on linkage') (*GMKJ*: 22), the anchorage of the subject in the density of its corporeal experience, and in its necessary and enhancing relation to the other. Marcel's philosophy offers 'un geste de réconciliation, en vue de renouer un pacte, de reprendre racine, de retrouver ses sources' ('a gesture of reconciliation, an attempt to renew a past, to reroot oneself, to recover one's origins') (*GMKJ*: 25). Despite the careful balance of the exposition, it is evident that Jaspers' influence is on the wane; that a certain note of histrionic self-dramatisation has been detected in his torrid accounts of *vertige* and *angoisse*, defiance and abandonment, and the journey through the night. His criticism of the Cartesian cogito for being insufficiently radical, for not doubting enough, has led to the suspicion that his broadly Kierkegaardian existentialism is no more than a final subtlety of idealism, a further exile within the self. Ricoeur is always supportive of, perhaps indulgent to, Marcel, his former tutor at the Sorbonne; and his distinction of problem and mystery, the positing of an underlying unity prior to subject–object relations, and stress on a positive ethical regard for the other leave a permanent mark on his thought. The concern with mystery in particular will continue throughout Ricoeur's work, subsumed into the symbol, and then phrased in more directly Heideggerian terms as the approach to being. But he is evidently vulnerable to the same objection of methodological deficiency as Jaspers, that his rejection of a totalising concept of reason leads to little more than a reassertion of fideism. The question remains, 'quel type de réflexion, quel type de pensée, peut avoir le rigueur et l'extrême lucidité que la philosophie requiert, sans réduire cette expérience précieuse?' ('what type of reflection, what type of thought, can possess the rigour and extreme lucidity that philosophy requires, without reducing this precious experience?') (*GMKJ*: 38). In the context of this demand, the attraction of the work of Edmund Husserl becomes apparent.

HUSSERL AND PHENOMENOLOGY

Ricoeur's early reputation was largely founded on his 1950 translation and commentary of Husserl's *Ideas I*, and subsequent essays cumulatively provide a comprehensive, one might say devoted, commentary. But the relation is by no means one of passive discipleship. Phenomenology is 'less a doctrine in its own right than a method capable of many exemplifications of which Husserl exploited only a few' (*H*: 4); Ricoeur insists on its openness and continued capacity for change. The two areas in which he will continue to draw heavily on Husserl are the basic intentionality of acts of consciousness and the susceptibility of this 'directed-towards' to analysis through the *noesis/noema* distinction (difficult concepts to translate, but roughly the difference between a thinking and what is thought. Note the impersonal usage. This does not refer to an individual subjectivity but an underlying constitutive structure.) The 'patient method of description' is admired not for its formal coherence, but rather for the 'ascèse' that it institutes (*H*: 232). All critical philosophy can claim to partake of such an impulse to some extent; to break free of naïve dependence on empirical appearances, and achieve a higher level of reflexive self-consciousness. With Ricoeur, this takes on an intensity sufficient to be regarded as a 'a sort of conversion which removes the ego from the centre of ontological concern' (*H*: 233).

This need not be identified with the famous Husserlian *epoché* or transcendental reduction, the bracketing of the question of the existence of the world in order to analyse how it appears to consciousness. (There are strong Platonic parallels to the project of shedding the merely contingent to reveal the essential.) This 'strait gate to phenomenology' (*H*: 176) enables a separation of transcendental subjectivity from empirical consciousness, the subject-matter of psychology. But this new 'science of appearances or of appearings' (*H*: 202) is pulled in two incompatible directions. In one version, it is merely a description of technique; in the other, it involves an ontological decision entailing a form of subjectivity completely constitutive of its world. As with the British empiricist tradition to which Husserl was so strongly drawn, there is a temptation inherent in seeking a perceptual basis to thought to slide from treating the world as 'being-for-me' to 'deriving-from-me'.

Freedom and Nature and *Fallible Man* explicitly employ the *epoché*; and the theme of imaginative variation – nothing resists the fiction that the world is not – will remain important throughout Ricoeur's later work on metaphor and narrative. But from the very beginning he is firmly committed to the Kantian precept of the limitations of a method defining its sphere of validity. 'Husserl *did* phenomenology: Kant *limited* and *founded* it' (*H*: 201). Kant's concept of the *dingansich*, the unknowable thing-in-itself, is used to preserve the ontological autonomy of the physical world; and the analogous postulate of the person as end-in-itself is employed to prevent the reduction of other minds to objects-for-me. (A parallel nowhere made explicit by Kant himself.) Interestingly, both elements diminish in the treatment of affectivity, which cannot easily be equated with either an 'appearing' or an *a priori* definition of the person (see Ricoeur, 1976d). A later essay, 'Phenomenology and hermeneutics' (*HHS*: 101–28), lists four other tenets as central to Husserlian idealism: its claim to radicality, to be self-founding prior to scientific discourse; the emphasis on intuitive fulfilment over deduction; the premise that all transcendence is doubtful, immanence alone indubitable; and the self-transparency of reflection. What is striking in retrospect is how little even Ricoeur's early work adopts these premises. There is no problem of evil or self-knowledge for the Husserlian ego: it doesn't feel guilt or sin; it doesn't suffer from self-occlusion or narcissism; it has no need of a painful struggle towards self-consciousness. Though Ricoeur remains committed to some variant of the transcendental ego, he offers a decentred self – first in relation to the data or signs of scientific investigation, later in relation to language – that will be obliged to constitute itself through a series of acts of interpretation.

It should be stressed that Ricoeur's theological concerns remain strictly segregated. His major criticism of the French assimilation of Husserl is its selective reading of his later work in a 'too quickly synthetic' manner, which tends to reduce every variety of experience to an 'indistinct existential monism' (*H*: 214–15). And from a comparatively early stage, pertinent misgivings are voiced about its tendency to endow analytic terms – project, motive, choice – with exemplary and exhortatory status. There's no logistic preference for its own sake in Ricoeur. But his debt to Marcel and continued fondness for 'ontological mystery' means that he preserves a higher investment in method as restraint. The postulate of affective participation in being must be stabilised by a rigorously analytic approach: 'in the early stages at least, phenomenology must be structural' (*H*: 215; compare Derrida, 1978a: 159).

Obviously one must show caution before attempting to map 'structural' onto structuralism. But the function is to some extent comparable: displacement, wounding, a decentring that matters less for itself than for its function as a necessary phase in the discovery of self. 'To recognise the task of testing the ordinary and scientific terminology of psychology' (*H*: 215) offers a *rapprochement* with empiricism opposed to Husserl's contestation of the priority of scientific discourse, in which he is explicitly followed by Derrida. The reciprocal movement is 'to discern through this corrected terminology the "essences" of subjective life' (*H*: 215): to understand myself as an object, as prestructured, as less than master.

Freedom and Nature is described as a continuation of Husserl's technique into 'affective and volitive subjective processes':

> Even in the obscure forest of emotions, even in the course of the blood stream, phenomenology gambles on the possibility of thinking and naming. It gambles on the primordial discursivity of each subjective process.
>
> (*H*: 216)

There is an obvious circle here, perhaps a tautology. That which is primordially non-discursive cannot presumably be spoken about so the discursive *per se* comes to be an operative definition of what is recognised as emotion. But at this stage the language in which such an investigation is conducted is regarded as largely unproblematic. The *noesis/noema* distinction is employed to break volition down into three

phases: decision, action, and consent. Unlike Sartre's 'eternally petri-
fied gesture' (*FN*: 135), choice is not unitary, absolute, the disruptive
and annulling emergence of freedom: it may be understood and
stabilised through reason, and this requires establishing the extent to
which freedom remains 'bound'. Each successive phase has its respective circumscription by the motives of the body (hunger, thirst, and so
on), its limitations of movement (capacity to act), and its necessary
biological horizons (birth and death). There is some degree of Hegelian ascension as an unstated governing presence: rather than standing in strict parallelism, the final stage of consent subsumes the
preceding two. It involves an acceptance of situation within the
world, an acknowledgement of brute contingency that compels a shift
into mythic alternatives: Promethean refusal, Orphic ecstasy, and
Stoic detachment (*FN*: 464, 469, 471). Indeed throughout the closing
stages of *Freedom and Nature* there is an uncomfortable oscillation
between stark acknowledgement of contingency and a somewhat
florid rhapsodic assertion. (The later insistence on preserving the
sobriety and boundaries of philosophical discourse perhaps represents a temptation kept in check with difficulty.)

The laboriousness of the overall construction is frequently matched
by the cumbersomeness of the style: see, for example, the extended
description of the 'evacuatory reflex' (*FN*: 112). Nevertheless there is
an impressive reconsideration of numerous classical mind–body
problems such as determinism and free-will, cause and motive, and
particularly fine discussions of need and lack, of the practical limitations imposed by the body, of the fundamental asymmetry of
pleasure and pain, and of the spontaneity of habitual conduct. These
give a salutary reminder of how thoroughly assimilated a Freudian
language of desire and repression has become. Ricoeur is concerned
with a comparatively desexualised body: passion, as distinct from
emotion, is displaced onto a virtually theological level as vanity,
dissimulation, and narcissism. (In one revealing aside it is suggested
that chastity (like hunger-strikes!) shows 'the truly human nature of
our needs' (*FN*: 86).) The relative absence of sexual desire allows
other facets to emerge more clearly: need, temperament, habit. Perhaps the showpiece of the book is the quite stunning account of the
phenomenology of birth, filiation, and hereditary, the 'bubbling,
trifling beginning consciousness' (*FN*: 433–43 (442)). Here Ricoeur is
obliged to forgo the resources of introspection, and depend wholly on
genetics and biology. There is no hostility to scientific fact but rather a
diagnostic relation towards it: a series of complex antimonies are

established between intentional analysis and the data of the empiricist and objectivist sciences. The cogito can only be known through the outward detour of interpretation.

The first question of phenomenology, Ricoeur never ceases to insist, is 'what does signifying signify?' (*H*: 203). Logic precedes language, but cannot adequately account for the wider field of signs; phenomenology is required to specify the criteria for a successful act of meaning, in accordance with its analysis of the intentional structure of all acts of consciousness. Language thus becomes an intermediary between the pristine clarity towards which it aspires and the mute elemental experience that lies beneath it: 'a medium, a mediation, an exchange between *Telos* and *Ursprung*' (Ricoeur, 1966: 208–9). Ideality is retained as the objective moment in interpretation, the reidentifiable content of a text. Nevertheless 'we have to discover that the idea of absolute and complete fulfilment is itself an ideal, the ideal of adequation; more than that, this ideal cannot be fulfilled' (Ricoeur, 1966: 213).

Does Ricoeur remain a phenomenologist? There is no simple answer. It remains a recurrent idiom: as late as *Time and Narrative*, for a hypothesis to be 'strict Husserlian orthodoxy' is very much in its favour (*TN* 3:169). Phenomenology is never brought into direct conflict with psychoanalysis; merely an 'approximation' is deemed sufficient (*FP* 3:1: 375–89). There remains a residual discomfort in the '*graft* of the hermeneutic problem into the *phenomenological method*' (*CI*: 3). By 1974, Ricoeur was prepared to concede the 'staleness' of the movement' (*HHS*: 101) but calls for its 'renewal' rather than its abandonment as a worked-out seam. We shall repeatedly see in his work the problems generated by attempts to remain attached to a phenomenological tradition while aligning it to more flexible linguistic models. In later essays he will vigorously insist upon a possible linguistic application of the *epoché*: 'we interrupt lived experience in order to signify it' (*HHS*: 114). Most striking is the redefinition of the *Lebenswelt* of Husserl's later genetic phenomenology: 'the life-world, for us who wakingly live in it, is already there, existing in advance for us, the "ground" of all praxis whether theoretical or extratheoretical' (Husserl, 1970b: 142). Ricoeur will later see the hyper-empiricism of this project, its attempt to uncover a genesis of meaning through unfolding the layers of constitution sedimented over raw, mute experience, as self-defeating, possessing a 'tragic grandeur': 'the *Lebenswelt* is never actually given but always presupposed. It is phenomenology's paradise lost. It is in this sense that phenomenology has undermined its own guiding idea in the very attempt to realise it' (1983a: 189; see also *H*: 205). Ricoeur's response is to resort to radical redefinition: it must 'not be confused with some sort of ineffable immediacy and is not identified with the vital and emotional envelope of human experience, but is rather construed as designating the reservoir of meaning, the surplus of sense in living experience' (*HHS*: 119). Hence what is most private, inward, elusive is also paradoxically open to history, demanding the interpretation of signs. These repeated attempts at reformulation are not without problems – how much baby remains after the bath-water has gone? But it will be helpful to move from Ricoeur's insistence that 'what hermeneutics has ruined is not phenomenology, but one of its interpretations, namely its idealistic interpretation by Husserl himself' (*HHS*: 101) to Derrida's treatment of the same issues.

DEFERRAL OR ESCHATOLOGY

The seminal essay on 'Différance' begins with some Hegelian play on the verb 'différer', which, Derrida observes, 'seems to differ from itself' in its alternative meanings of differ (in the order of the same) and defer (within a logic of non-identity) (1973: 129). Not for the first time an occurrence of polysemy is elevated into a metaphysical aporia. From here we move to 'différance', a purely typological coinage, that serves to emphasise the 'irreducibility of temporalising' (1973: 130). One may be amused by the appositeness of Derrida's whimsy, or irritated by its preciousness; certainly one could not have predicted the obsequious credulity with which it has been received. This serves as 'the *strategic* note or connection' between 'the thought of what has been conveniently called our era': Nietzsche, Freud, Levinas, Saussure, Heidegger. This '*assemblage*' (1973: 131) indicates a key vulnerability in Derrida's argument: its unargued use of analogy between different intellectual spheres. If the transposition is accepted, the trace is elevated into a virtual metaphysical origin in its own right: 'the movement of différance is not something that happens to a transcendental subject; it produces that subject' (1973: 82; see also Dews, 1987: 16–19, 25–31; and Habermas, 1987: 161–84). It is perfectly possible, however, simply to deny its initial legitimacy, and insist that such diverse conceptual fields cannot be collapsed onto each other.

The form of logical predication adopted by Husserl is subdivided into two categories: indication and expression. Only the second is meaningful. Indication, 'the *physical phenomenon* forming the physical side of the expression', remains devoid of meaning unless animated by expression, 'the acts which give it meaning and possibly also *intuitive fullness*' (Husserl, 1970a: 273). This conforms, as Derrida points out, to a theological dualism between the 'body of speech' and the 'living spirituality of the meaning-intention' (1973: 34, 38). Paradoxically, the paradigm of language use is not dialogue, but the animation of an imagined signifier within the sphere of a solitary mental life. The ideal status of meaning as a determinate sense through successive articulations depends on this posited moment of pure self-presence; even communication is a kind of fall into reliance on a material sign. Only the possibility of a future occurrence guarantees the stability of present meaning: hence 'ideality is the preservation or mastery of presence in repetition' (1973: 9–10). Thus it depends on what is not present, and so complies with Derrida's account of the trace as the 'constituting value' of an 'irreducible non-presence' (1973: 6). A simple enough point: an utterance must be repeated before it can be said to be the same. So far, so good, though one should note how the strictness of Derrida's criteria of identity and difference overrides Husserl's careful qualifications about the 'multiplicity of possible acts' contained within the 'ideal unity' of any given sense (Husserl, 1970a: 329–30).

Derrida uses this temporal element to pass from the issue of signification to the series of disconcerting aporias arising from the 'irreducibility of temporalizing' (1973: 130). The justification for this transition appears to be no more than the 'two related senses' of the word 'presence': 'the proximity of what is set forth as an object of the intuition, and the proximity of the temporal present which gives the clear and present intuition of the object its form' (1973: 9). The complexities of Husserl's concept of the triple present of 'longitudinal' intentionality will be expounded in greater detail in the final chapter: here the essential point is that the present is only present in relation to what has passed before, and so possesses a primordial differentiation. If consciousness manifests itself through the 'power of synthesis, an incessant gathering up of traces', it must depend upon a preceding moment out of which the 'traces' are constituted (1973: 147). Thus any attempt to establish the existence of an inaugural moment of consciousness must posit a simultaneous presence and non-presence: 'the living present springs forth out of its non-identity with itself and from the possibility of a retentional trace' (1973: 85). In the light of the extended analysis of 'The aporetics of temporality' in *Time and*

Narrative, it becomes clear that Derrida generates this daunting series of paradoxes through conflating two separate traditions. The demand for 'a point-like present, identical to itself, required by the intuitionist concept of the sixth *Logical Investigation*' is illegitimately imported into discussion of the play of retention and protention in which 'the presence of the perceived present . . . is *continuously compounded* with a nonpresence and nonperception, with primary memory and expectation' (1973: 64; see also 60–9). This invites the simple but effective retort, that 'nothing says the present reduces to presence'; and Ricoeur's own analysis will insist that it is treated as a '*time of initiative*' (*TN* 3: 208).

One cannot fault Derrida's adroit articulation of a declaredly omni-subverting principle. The meaning of meaning is non-meaning, or rather the transition between meanings motivated by 'the structured and differing origin of differences' (1973: 141). This will in turn be allied to the Saussurian concept of the linguistic field as a system of differential variations. It must be stressed, however, that these paradoxes are produced through strict adherence to a transcendental logic: 'precisely what is in question here is the requirement that there be a *de jure* commencement, an absolute point of departure, a responsibility arising from a principle' (1973: 135). Here, as with the supposed aspiration of 'the *present* or *presence* of thought to a full and primordial intuition' (1973: 5), Derrida is obliged to accentuate, even to caricature, the phenomenological postulate of return to primordial experience. His characterisation is at best only applicable to certain emphases in Husserl, and to the extent that it might be plausible cannot simply be transposed onto other modes of thought. It may be contrasted with Ricoeur's distinction between the application of a method and its pre-philosophical origin: the two questions are separate in kind and should be firmly segregated.

There is little point, however, in contesting the fact that the principle of deferral has been enshrined as one of the major interpretative paradigms of our time; objections directed against Derrida's original analyses of the trace have little relevance to the later assimilation of the concept. I would like to contrast this with a structure recurrent in Ricoeur's thought: a present of intervention situated within an eschatological horizon. In *History and Truth*, he seeks to extricate himself from the seductive embrace of the Hegelian system: to renounce the hubristic claim to a vantage of absolute knowledge, an eternal present comprehending a completed development, without rejecting any ascription of a degree of intelligibility to the historical process as merely a 'philosopher's contrivance' (*HT*: 294). To this end he invokes a 'hope with eschatological intention' to serve as a 'regulative feeling capable of purifying historical scepticism' (*HT*: 6):

> From one point of view, the concept of the Last Day works as a limiting concept in a Kantian sense, that is, as an active limitation of a phenomenal history by a total history that is thought but not known. The presence of this limitation shatters the pretension of philosophies of history to express the coherent meaning of all that has passed and all that is to come. I am always short of the Last Judgement. By setting up the limit of the Last Day, I thereby step down from my seat as the final judge.
>
> (*HT*: 12)

Faith is not expunged from rationalism but retained as a declaredly hypothetical goal while the investigation at hand proceeds with scrupulous elaboration. The postulate of the Last Day (self-confessedly 'incurably mythical' (*HT*: 6)) can be seen as a kind of riding the tiger, maintaining propulsive and dialectical elements while retaining a limit idea of indefinite postponement that effects a 'dethronement of rational supremacy' (*HT*: 13). Ricoeur talks of the book in terms of an 'unresolved tension' between 'desire for reconciliation' and 'emphatic distrust of premature solutions': 'what eschatological language calls hope is captured reflectively in the very delay of all syntheses' (*HT*: 11). A voluntary eschewal of certainty is advocated; there can only be totality at the cost of violence and closure. (This aspect of Ricoeur's thought is theologically Pauline in its exploration of the paradoxes of sin under the Law. Law sets an impossible standard that must be transgressed and so creates sin; and then provides the temptation of identifying with the Law for the sake of self-righteous domination (see *SE*: 139–50).) This movement will later be defined in terms derived from Jürgen Moltmann's *The Theology of Hope*, with its emphasis on the forward-directed promise over Hellenistic schemas of epiphany. History is less the experience of change than 'the tension created by the expectation of a fulfilment; history is itself the hope of history, for each fulfilment is perceived as confirmation, pledge, and repetition of the promise' (*CI*: 403; see also *DCCT*: 26).

But Ricoeur stresses not only the 'category of the not yet', but also the category of the 'from now on' (*HT*: 13). The myth of the Last Day is not so much the collapse of a Hegelian absolute (albeit one whose ambition remains an object of tantalising envy) as the retention of a forward-directed agency within perpetual deferral. The individual act, however contingent, does not lose significance through the ultimate fictiveness of its teleology. 'The truly therapeutic significance of French existentialism' lies not in its occasional 'penchant for the absurd' and leanings towards an apocalyptic fatalism but in its animation 'by a sort of courage before the uncertainty of meaning in history': the possibility of 'pure loss' is offset against 'trust in a hidden meaning' and 'a kind of vehemence to exist' that 'surges up at every offence' (*HT*: 297).

This invites comparison with the famous closing declaration of Derrida's 'Structure, sign and play in the discourse of the human sciences':

> Turned towards the lost or impossible presence of the absent origin, the structuralist thematic of broken immediacy is therefore the saddened, *negative*, nostalgic, guilty, Rousseauesque side of the thinking of play whose other side would be the Nietzschean *affirmation*, that is the joyous affirmation of the play of the world and of the innocence of becoming, the affirmation of a world of signs without fault, without truth, and without origin which is offered to an active interpretation.
>
> (1978a: 292–3)

There can be little doubt to which of these 'two interpretations of interpretation' Ricoeur would subscribe: 'the one' that 'dreams of deciphering a truth or an origin which escapes play and the order of the sign', and which 'lives the necessity of interpretation as an exile' (Derrida, 1978a; 292). This, it should be stressed, applies equally well to de Man, whose assimilation of an existential heritage displays numerous suggestive parallels to that of Ricoeur: a strikingly comparable conception of 'endless tension of a non-identity, a pattern of dissonance that contaminates the very source of the will, the will as source' (de Man, 1979: 99); an assiduous promotion of the 'asceticism that can lead to ontological insight' (de Man, 1983: 49); and the espousal of a 'highly seductive, highly attractive ... combination of nihlistic rigor with sacred revelation' (de Man, 1986: 79). For both thinkers, the poignancy of literature lies in its dual status as the realm where the most powerfully cherished illusions come nearest to substantiating themselves, and where personal authenticity demands that its blandishments be exorcised as 'what was believed in as the most reliable/ And therefore fittest for renunciation' (Eliot, 1969: 189).

The accumulation of epithets by which Derrida characterises this tradition need not necessarily be regarded as disparaging. 'Saddened': well, as Philip Larkin has observed, 'happiness in the sense of a continuous emotional orgasm' is impossible 'if only because you know that you are going to die, and the people you love are going to die' (1983: 66). '*Negative*': there's still a Hegelian resonance to this, a necessary moment in the development of the self. 'Nostalgic': I would insist upon Ricoeur's prospective emphasis on hope, striving without ultimate arrival. 'Guilty': the whole thrust of his early thought is to desynonymise, to use Coleridge's term, guilt and finitude. For Derrida to speak of a sign 'without fault' is a solecism; to say a world 'without fault' is a human untruth.

What precisely is being 'affirmed' in this passage? 'Without truth' applied to signs presupposes the structuralist postulate of the closed linguistic system; but falls, as we shall see, to Ricoeur's decisive demarcation between semiotics and semantics, the order of the sentence and that of the sign. The move from a 'world' to a 'world of signs' is surely illegitimate: not for the first time we see Derrida covertly importing a Saussurian premise in order to ground a Nietzschean gesture. Such an 'affirmation' undeniably possesses a certain grandeur in its primal anonymity, but the 'rupture' and 'annihilation of time and history' that it involves results in the utter annulment of any activity as such: 'in absolute chance, affirmation also surrenders itself to *genetic indetermination*, to the *seminal adventures* of the trace' (Derrida, 1978a: 292). Within the rhetoric of post-structuralism, 'the active production of meaning' is regularly, even monotonously, contrasted with the 'passive consumption of texts' of an earlier criticism. But in this key passage, 'active interpretation' is not only detached from the intervention of any specific subject, but also obliged to sit patiently until it 'surrenders itself to' (note the Eliotic resonance) or 'is offered' (a significant passive) an equally deracinated 'affirmation'. One must remain content, as in numerous other aspects of Derrida's thought, with an espousal of a transcendental principle that not merely resists translation into more immediate ethical and political concerns but proves intrinsically inimical to their very formulation. Deconstruction on this account should be defined not as 'an activity of thought that cannot be consistently acted upon' (Norris, 1982: xii) but as one specifically constituted by its move beyond any identifiable empirical intervention.

It is tempting, though undoubtedly facile, to make an *ad hominem* comparison and appeal in a straightforward manner to Ricoeur's exemplary record of ethical praxis (see for example 1957b; 1963a). More significant, however, is the presence of a comparable bifurcation in his own early work. On the one hand, primary affirmation, the vehemence to exist that stands prior to the potential absurdity of history, occurs on the ontological level: the fundamental positivity of being is asserted against philosophers such as Sartre (followed by de Man) who identify reflection with negation. On the other, less elevated, anthropological plane, man is not so much good as active: the individual is memorably defined as an unfinished task. Ricoeur's later work represents a concerted examination of the relation between 'the act whereby consciousness posits itself and produces itself and the signs wherein consciousness represents to itself the meaning of its action' (*CI*: 212). The act exceeds knowledge but can only be known through representation: its meaning must always be retrospectively inferred from its reverberations (textual or otherwise) in the world: 'we must endlessly appropriate what we are through the mediation of the multiple expressions of our desire to be' (*CI*: 222). The question of the ultimate validity of this unending affirmation within an open eschatological horizon remains to be debated: it is certainly arguable that its transcendental and ethical dimensions remain ultimately irreconcilable. But where Derrida delights in the paradoxes of their sundering, Ricoeur never flags in his conviction that the attempt to reunify them must be made.

3

Finitude and guilt

FALLIBLE MAN

The two main strands of Ricoeur's early thought, the existential and the rationalist, converge in his next major work, *Finitude and Guilt*, a study of the internally divided character of the human condition, or, put theologically, the enigma of original sin. In so far as an existential heritage can be said to exist, it is closely interwoven with Christian thought: Christ's parables on the end-time of decision, the Pauline account of conversion and rebirth, Gnostic speculation on the exiled nature of man, and Augustinian salvation through introspection. What is distinctive in Ricoeur is his commitment to methodological rigour in his approach towards his subject. Reason initially appears to be testing itself against the mystery of evil, extending its prerogative. But the first volume, *Fallible Man*, dramatises the failure of speculative reason to deal with the 'non-coincidence of man with himself' (*FM*: 1); in the second, *The Symbolism of Evil*, it is demanded that hermeneutic inquiry undergo a comparably humbling 're-enactment' of confession. To a certain extent the method is derived from genetic phenomenology, a patient excavation of the structures that constitute a given concept in pursuit of a more fundamental level of experience: to study original sin, 'to reflect on its meaning is in a certain way to *deconstruct the concept*, to break down its motivation, and by a kind of intentional analysis to retrieve the arrows of meaning which aim at the *kerygma itself* (*CI*: 270). (Ricoeur's usage of 'deconstruct' in a theological context, incidentally, dates from the late 1950s, preceding that of Derrida by several years.) The rationale is that the issue of evil above all others has been distorted by a false accretion of concepts: 'a juridical category of debt and a biological category of inheritance' (*CI*: 270). What is required is a preliminary '*defeat of knowledge*' to

31

enable the 'working toward the recovery of meaning' (*CI*: 270). This has particular relevance to *Time and Narrative*, where a comparable strategy is employed of exhaustive investigation revealing its own inadequacy. The process of argumentation may itself be read as a kind of trope, an allegory of the relation to the divine. The point at issue is not the dismantling of the theological superstructure, but the kind of value ascribed to the enigma that remains. The paradox is central to Ricoeur's whole treatment of the symbol: although it is endowed with rootedness in the mystery of being, this is precisely what it withholds. While a theological account of the symbol may appear to be concerned with access to the divine, its ultimate message is one of exclusion.

In *Fallible Man*, the bracketing of the 'empirics of the will' in *Freedom and Nature* (p. xli) becomes a tantalising holding off, an almost wilful deferral, in an ingenious narrative of non-definition. The reader is obliged to follow Ricoeur's dense argumentation through an ascending dialectic that finally announces that there will be no further progress without a methodological break and a move into hermeneutics. The break (*faille*), geological fault, between the possibility and the reality of evil, the leap 'from fallibility to the already fallen' demands this 'hiatus of method' (*FM*: 143). So Ricoeur finishes poised on the brink, having deduced the fundamental structures of fallibility, but with no immanent experience of fault. The final absorption into 'total comprehension' is never achieved 'because in man's precomprehension there is a wealth of meaning which reflection is unable to equal' (*FM*: 6). The strategy of the book might be dubbed 'hunt the surplus' or at least corner it; the twist is that it eludes a whole succession of methodologies. There always remains a 'residue of meaning' (*FM*: 6), a term which will crop up again and again, that prevents the coincidence of first-order symbol or text and second-order reflection.

Without a reasonable familiarity with the technical concepts deployed, it is difficult to gauge Ricoeur's overall direction, let alone the degree of his success, so a brief synopsis of this forbidding text will doubtless be appreciated. The model employed in *Fallible Man* is Kantian in two respects. Firstly, the three levels posited correspond to the faculties of theoretical, practical, and affective consciousness. Secondly, the mediation of understanding and sensibility by the transcendental imagination at the level of the theoretical consciousness is repeated in the analysis of practical and affective domains. (Though the extent to which these triads can be satisfactorily mapped onto each other is debatable.) The basic procedure is to reduce experience to a finite and an infinite aspect of the self at each level, and then trace the relation between these two aspects back to a third mediating category: Ricoeur refuses to posit a simple origin, but instead starts out with the dual, and the tension between two poles. In the concluding chapter, the three categories of fallibility are deduced from the triad of thinking, doing and feeling, and equated with the Kantian categories of reality, negation and limitation, which are relabelled originating affirmation, existential difference, and human mediation ('the fragile synthesis of man as the becoming of an opposition' (*FM*: 141)).

In the opening meditation, 'Pathétique of misery', the writings of Plato, Pascal, and Kierkegaard are accredited with an intuitive apprehension of the 'primordial conflict' of the 'polemical duality of subjectivity' within man's nature (*FM*: 82). There is an admirable account, for example, of Pascal's characteristic rhetorical movement: a 'system of tensions' in which a meditation on the disproportion of external space is abruptly internalised as an image of man's spiritual condition (*FM*: 8). But this mode of insight is limited through being '*undifferentiated*' (*FM*: 9): it requires the application of transcendental reflection ('a way of being understood that does not come from image, symbol or myth' (*FM*: 1)), to perform a labour of clarification and analysis.

The second chapter, 'The transcendental synthesis', is concerned with the impersonal subject in relation to the object, and 'the specific disproportion of knowing' (*FM*: 18): a stage of the argument described as 'necessary, although inadequate' (*FM*: 17). It provides a 'useful beginning'; because the synthesis occurs '*upon*' the object, there is no need to have recourse to self-consciousness (*FM*: 18). Kantian sensibility is equated with finite perspective: understanding with the 'infinite verb'. No one point of view is sufficient to the object: instead it appears through a sequence of profiles. From these can be inferred the vantage of an I or viewer. (There are some fine observations on the nature of hereness in relation to the body; and the contrast between origin and birth.) But recognising this finitude necessarily implies a transcendence of it: 'the transgression of the point of view is nothing else than speech as the possibility of expressing, and of expressing the point of view itself' (*FM*: 26). Therefore saying exceeds perception. This is explained by a slightly awkward borrowing from Aristotle: the verb both posits existence of the noun and allows a predicate to be ascribed to it. (Socrates is walking =

there is a walk that is said of Socrates.) In a slightly portentous manner, affirmation becomes the defining feature of the verb: the saying of yes and no which transcends the specific noun. The Husserlian distinction between verbal form and animating purpose is transposed onto the freedom-intention of the verb infusing the truth-intention of the noun. The copula is made to bear an ontological weight in a way strongly prefiguring the climax of *The Rule of Metaphor*: 'the transcendence of speech centered on the verb, and the verb revealed its soul of affirmation' (*FM*: 36).

The transition from 'I think' to 'I will' in the third chapter, 'The practical synthesis', involves change on two levels. First, the referent alters from things to human works; secondly, instead of a synthesis performed upon the object, it is directed towards a person, now defined as 'a projected synthesis which seizes itself in the representation of a task' (p. 69). Here Kantian respect acts as the mediating term serving the dual function of constituting one's own personhood, and according comparable rights to the other (with the bonus of bypassing the tortuous Husserlian progression from monadic individual to the interpersonal community). The analyses of affective perspective in *Freedom and Nature* are deployed as the pole of finitude (motive, habit, temperament) counterbalanced by an idea of happiness as unrestricted possibility (corresponding to the finite perspective and the infinite verb). In his strictures against eudaemonism, Kant relegates happiness to the level of desire and has it re-emerge as merit; Ricoeur's rejoinder is to see happiness as 'not given in any experience; it is only adumbrated in a consciousness of direction' (*FM*: 68). While sensory perspective provides a strong analogy to affective perspective (if only because what is responded to tends to be within a perceptual field), it is far more doubtful whether the impulse towards totality can be equated with the openness and liberation of language. Totality is perhaps unlikely to be achieved but statements can, after all, be made. The strength of Kant's moral formalism surely lies in the degree of specific prescription that it retains. To apply it to an open-ended project of existence is to risk lapsing into a limp and diffuse benevolence. Again one feels that the thrust of the argument is not so much to establish a mediating synthesis as to preserve the pole of the infinite against prejudgement and reduction.

'Affective fragility' is the core of the book, the section breaking most new ground and somewhat unexpectedly striking a strongly affirmative note. This comparatively upbeat quality lies in its sustained resistance to Kant's 'moral rigorism', and insistence that *'it is always "through"* the fallen that the primordial shines through' (*FM*: 144). Ricoeur's adoption of the Kantian triad of 'possession, domination, honour' involves both a move into social and interpersonal realms and, more importantly, an urge to 'restore the primordial state which is at the root of the fallen' (*FM*: 111). These 'fundamental quests' must be redeemed by 'the imagination of another empirical modality, by exemplification in an innocent kingdom' (*FM*: 112). The first is having: the very fact of possessions represents an elevation from the merely animal concern of self-preservation, continuous consumption. The second is power, a concept implicit in work, control over nature (though Ricoeur concedes that 'the State is linked to evil through the sanction of 'corrective violence' (*FM*: 119), and then offers a some-what desperate equation of non-violent power with the Kingdom of God (there and only there)). The third is honour, the legitimate quest for esteem and reciprocity: the mutual constitution of subjects through opinion. Yet 'the triple quest in which the Self seeks itself is never completed': it retains 'a note of indefiniteness and, along with it, the threat which clings to an endless pursuit' (*FM*: 126). The desire of desire has no end. 'Human action regenerates and nourishes itself, drawn forward by its insatiable quests' (*FM*: 127). Here the influence of Nietzsche comes to the fore with a crucial rehabiliation of the 'grandeur of passion' (citing Rastignac and Othello as examples): their 'transcending intention can only flow from the infinite attraction of happiness' (*FM*: 129). This section of the book concludes with an unexpected praise of abandon and restlessness as 'organizing force' and 'dynamizing action' (*FM*: 130).

This positivity also emerges from the account of emotion, as onto-logical affirmation and mode of knowledge. Ricoeur locates two levels: feelings with specific objects, equated with momentary pleasures, and ontological moods, characterised by a yearning for the infinite mediated by courage. Feeling is not a distraction from knowl-edge, but in certain respects stands prior to it; knowing gives structure to feeling which in turn endows it with motive and intention in a 'mutual genesis' (*FM*: 83). Boundaries between internal and external are dissolved as the same experience comes to 'designate a thing-quality, and, through this thing-quality, manifest, express, and reveal the inwardness of an I' (*FM*: 85); or, more concisely, 'by means of feeling objects touch me' (*FM*: 89). Three features are emphasised: feeling anticipates more than it gives and so represents promise over possession; its very formlessness indicates its openness to being; and it is the plane on which a 'clash between Anguish and Beatitude occurs' (*FM*: 106).

Strong reservations are stated about philosophies that identify reflection itself with negativity. This represents the ultimate extension of what Ricoeur sees as a characteristic conflation of guilt and finitude within existentialism. The fact and inevitability of death becomes a defeat, an active culpability. Limitation is perceived as a kind of imposition, punishment, turning guilt into an ontological characteristic of the human condition. Even Camus's attempt at mitigation can only claim that revolt might 'without claiming an impossible innocence . . . furnish the principle of a limited culpability' (1971: 16). This may be compared to Ricoeur's dictum: 'Man is the joy of the yes in the sadness of the finite' (*FM*: 140). But such a reformulation is not without its own problems. Ricoeur does a disservice to his own argument by importing the Marcellian idiom of 'loving participation' (*FM*: 103) in so undiluted a fashion. It is claimed that this relation can only be spoken of obliquely, though we surely speak relatively directly about emotion. Terms such as happiness and respect (even in the restricted Kantian sense) are elevated to a level where they cease to be emotions that could be empirically experienced and instead become concepts retrospectively inferred through protracted dialectical analysis. The handling of the concept of lyric remains awkward, even tendentious, in Ricoeur's later work, where it is manoeuvred into an implicitly assertive role (the concept of a lyricism of despair is not addressed). It is certainly an open question to what extent Ricoeur's recent work on narrative and metaphor has been coloured by its extensive debt to Aristotle's theory of tragedy. There is an underlying intimation, difficult to shake off, that all true stories are tragedies as all true symbols tell of guilt. The existential heritage cannot be buried quite so easily.

Ricoeur attempts to displace this gratuitous and debilitating fatalism by inserting a prior category of primary affirmation. The lineage for the concept is long and varied: Spinozan conatus, Leibnizian appetition, Fichtean self-positing, and Nietzschean will to power are all summoned to the cause. 'Negativity', Ricoeur argues, is better regarded as 'the privileged road of the climb back to foundation'; 'nihilation' is only 'the obscure side of a total act whose illuminated side has not been disclosed' (*HT*: 327). The 'experience of finitude' is said to imply an 'act of transcending itself in "denegation"' (*HT*: 315). Ricoeur insists on the body as openness-to; with saying always

36

surpassing the limitations of perspective. Signifying becomes a negativity, the summoning of the not-here: meaning is non-vision. There is no volition without nolition: even the positing of another's existence involves a not-I. Negative experiences are seen as implying a pre-existent positive: anguish becomes a loss of faith, pain a loss of health, and 'the vehemence of the Yes' is again summoned against the 'victorious march of negation' and overvaluation of 'rupture and isolation' espoused by Sartre (*FM*: 137). Participation thus overrides alienation, the will-to-live overrides being-towards-death.

One may distrust the assigning of relative priority to emotions, and feel that discursive convenience slides all too readily into a myth of origin. The Hegelian logic employed comes dangerously close to a dialectical sleight of hand. It is also unresolved how Ricoeur would meet the objections to Camus's similar concept of the act of revolt as an inaugural grounding moment: the dependence of his thought on an individualist gesture and a putative transcendence difficult to distinguish from sentimental self-aggrandisement. Nevertheless the argument here directed specifically against a Sartrian existentialism prepares an identification of being with act that will be sustained through the later work on linguistics, psychoanalysis and hermeneutics. The idea of lack and absence being constitutive will be converted into a necessary detour through interpretation of symbol and text.

'Mood' is an unfortunately slight term for what is at issue here. It provokes a move away from a perceptual, primarily visual bias, and definitions of knowledge as primarily what is represented, *Vorstellung*. The most influential statement of this critique comes in Heidegger's *Being and Time*, with its attempt to detach itself from dependence on *Bild*, image. On an anthropological level, Heidegger insists on feeling as a realm prior and irreducible to formal analysis – *Sorge, Unheimlichkeit*, the sombre tonalities of the existential world, which, as has often been observed, present a bleak landscape of quasi-stoic fortitude and unrewarded quest. It is a generally recognised strength of the existential tradition that it resists the customary philosophical reduction of the emotions to a secondary and usually obfuscating role. The cost exacted is a drift towards irrationalism, and a preponderance of somewhat morose states of mind. One way of seeing Ricoeur's work is as a series of progressively subtler refutations of this dichotomy, initially through scrupulous if somewhat laborious phenomenological description, later through taking the argument onto the terrain of language itself. The comparative flimsiness of the existential affirmation

37

lies in its resistance to verification. This seems to invite back the very opposition which has just been dismissed; but it takes us to a central paradox. In moving to language, to symbol and text, Ricoeur finds structure at the heart of non-cognitive modes of knowledge.

THE PRIMARY SYMBOLS

The shift onto language undertaken in the second volume of *Finitude and Guilt* represents a crucial methodological transition for Ricoeur. The need to introduce 'the dimension of evil into the structure of the will' occasions a 'fundamental change in the method of description': 'I could speak of purposive action without symbolic language, but I could not speak of Bad Will or of evil without a hermeneutic' (*RM*: 309). A certain caution, even trepidation, is later acknowledged about this move away from the disciplined limitation of a Kantian phenomenology in order to venture into the more turbulent arena of a general theory of interpretation. Some fairly wide-ranging distinctions need to be drawn between the two halves of *The Symbolism of Evil*, concerned with symbol and myth respectively.

The first is the more innovative and, in my opinion, by far the more satisfactory. Despite its postulate of manifestation underlying meaning, it remains primarily a semantic analysis of a linguistic field, whose constitutive symbols are regarded as primary with regard to both myth and reflection. There is a corresponding density in Ricoeur's commentary: a kind of elision occurs through which the symbolism of evil becomes inseparable from his own contemporary and existentially informed awareness: or, more complexly, his making present of an archaic awareness for our own time.

Two different claims, however, appear to be made at the same time: that a semantic analysis of the symbolism of evil is a local and even small-scale project, but that because it deals with the fundamental ontology of the human condition, its split and internally divided character, it can also claim priority as an enterprise in grounding the whole hermeneutic field. The issue emerges more clearly in Ricoeur's later theological writing where Biblical hermeneutics are simultaneously treated as both a regional study within the broader sphere of interpretation theory, and yet also as commanding privileged access to ultimate reality (compare Ricoeur, 1975c: 14).

It is, in fact, because evil is supremely the crucial experience of the sacred that the threat of the dissolution of the bond between

man and the sacred makes us most intensely aware of man's
dependence on the powers of the sacred.

(*SE*: 6)

This appears strongly reminiscent of Jasper's limit-situations, and is
surely open to the same charge that Ricoeur himself makes: that it
responds to the fact of suffering with an aestheticising lyricism. The
reiteration of 'sacred' cannot entirely occlude the paradoxical nature
of the argument: the breakdown of the 'bond' is the strongest testimony to its existence. The premise is, to say the least, unargued: on
Ricoeur's own terms, why should it not be taken as proof of the
inherent and unredeemable guilt of the human condition? To adapt
Kafka's phrase, there may be the sacred, but not for us.

Ricoeur begins by insisting on the necessity for a regressive movement back from the 'appearance of rationality' of the theology of
original sin through myth towards the primal avowals of symbols: 'it
is to the least elaborate, the most inarticulate expressions of the
confession of evil that philosophic reason must listen' (*FM*: 4). One
detects a perennial temptation to locate the authority of these symbols
in a merely chronological priority, rather than ordering the field of
study in terms of its own methodological coherence. There is also a
kind of inverted condescension in the insistence that thought must
'revert from the "speculative" expressions to the "spontaneous"
ones' (*SE*: 4). What's missing here is the later insistence on the
demand of the text for interpretation to release its plenitude; 'spontaneous' expressions surely require attentive exegesis no less than
sophisticated ones to activate their potential meaning. And it is
difficult to accept their intellectual priority over the texts of Plato and
Pascal analysed in *Fallible Man*. There is a perilously thin line dividing Ricoeur's own commentary from gnosis, the contamination and
arrogance of pseudo-philosophy. The charges that can be laid against
this tradition seem all too easy to transpose onto any secondary
interpretation whatsoever dealing with the 'philosophical problem of
fault'. There is an underlying sense of the presumptuousness of the
enterprise, a readiness to concede ground to hierophany and a pre-
critical naïvety, that is difficult to reconcile with his later repudiation
of the theological demand for 'a *sacrificium intellectus* where what was
needed was to awaken believers to a symbolic superintelligence of
their actual condition' (*SE*: 239; see also *BI*: 42–3).

The language of sedimentation tends irresistibly towards positing a
'stratum' of prelinguistic meaning 'at a lower level than any narration

or any gnosis' (*SE*: 6). This reneges on Ricoeur's customary commitment never to explain the complex by the simple: here he appears to posit a lost unity, which narrative somehow disperses and gnosis obfuscates and calcifies. Behind the myth of the fall lies the confession of sins, and 'this dimension of the symbol can only be recovered by the "re-enactment" of the experience made explicit in the myth' (*SE*: 7). It should be stressed that there is no recourse to the romantic hermeneutic ideal of empathy with the original creative impulse: here meaning is located not in an authorial psyche but in an objective structure. But the 'language of confession' itself is only a 'counterpart', a simulacrum, possibly a duplicitous substitute, of an 'emotional note' pushing out to receive 'objectification in discourse'. This is not without immediate problems. At what level is confession situated here: as an intention to confess or as something externally vouchsafed, a leading from above, a something given? If the coming to language allows the coherent articulation of what previously was a 'blind experience', where is this situated: in the penitent, the exegete, or the language that mediates between them? There is a whole series of elisions between speech, the speech of faith, and communion with the divine, all of which are reliant on the possibility of redemptive coincidence. It's the running paradox of the *The Symbolism of Evil* that the experience of fault is equated somewhat unproblematically with a language of 'symbolic richness' (*SE*: 26), restored plenitude. It is the original emotion that is 'equivocal, laden with a multiplicity of meanings': the polysemy of language merely 'elucidates' these 'subterranean crises' (*SE*: 8). Thus the symbol can be seen as a univocal expression of existential ambiguity. In this insistence on ontological correspondence, Ricoeur, perhaps surprisingly, comes close to de Man: in *Blindness and Insight*, for example, the premise that 'sign and meaning can never coincide' is confidently pronounced to be evidence of a 'failure . . . in the nature of things', and the 'true poetic ambiguity' of a Marvell poem is said to 'proceed' not from a playful lyric insouciance but 'from the deep division of Being' (1983: 17–18, 237).

The self-generating nature of the language of fault appears separate from the semantic innovation of any individual speaker. The 'linguistic inventiveness' (*SE*: 9) ascribed to 'Hebraic and Hellenic literatures' does not create new worlds: it uncovers a necessary and pre-existent pattern to which we must still adhere, and whose 'existential eruptions' (*SE*: 9) suggest an arbitrariness and a fatalism that cannot be brought under the control of a purposeful creativity. So is the experience of sin of equal profundity as primary affirmation? If so, could not 'blindness, scandalousness, equivocalness' themselves be seen as constitutive of the human condition (*SE*: 7)? The 'living experience of fault' (*SE*: 7) certainly invites comparison with the later phrase, 'la métaphore vive': instead of possessing a semantic dynamism that thrives with new meaning, new possibility, new hope, the fascination of the language of sin lies in the fact that the more it yields, the more it reveals of how thoroughly entrapped we are. To 're-enact the passage from defilement to sin and guilt' seems to imply not merely sympathetic imagination as a condition of understanding, but to continue to be bound by its imperatives; an injunction continued in the reference to symbols being 'our guide in the labyrinth of living experience' (*SE*: 9). There's a kind of capitulation to past wisdom here, a refusal of hermeneutic recreation in and for our own time, that comes dangerously close to a dogmatic archetypalism. Why, after all, should this 'language' still lying beneath the 'myths of evil' continue to be relevant for us, when Ricoeur himself will later acknowledge 'what counts as defilement, for a conscience that lives under its regime no longer coincides with what counts as evil for us' (*SE*: 26–7)? This is a fairly basic question, but still one that deserves an answer.

At this point, Ricoeur does not develop a detailed theory of interpretation; instead he prefers to resort to the virtual solecism of a 'spontaneous hermeneutics' (*SE*: 9), and move on to a different question: language is symbolic and therefore 'a philosophy that is concerned to integrate confession with the consciousness of self cannot escape the task of elaborating, at least in outline, a criteriology of symbols' (*SE*: 10). He proceeds to sketch 'the extent and variety of its zones of emergence': the three dimensions of the cosmic, oneiric and poetic are seen as 'present in every authentic symbol'. But in what sense can man be said to 'read the sacred on the world' (*SE*: 10)? It would be through treating it as the book of nature, perhaps, and so susceptible to systematic interpretation. But the emphasis is firmly on 'spoken symbolism' rather than a text, and thus legitimately vulnerable to a Derridean critique of voice and self-presence. This alludes to a pre-existent order, a 'hierophany' implanted in nature for the devout soul to 'refer back to'. The sacred is said to exist 'in' the object which in turn loses its status as 'fragment'; its 'concrete limits' dissolve to release 'innumerable meanings' that 'integrate and unify' an otherwise alienated consciousness (*SE*: 11). The putative plenitude of meaning is all directed to a single end of underwriting the presence of the divine: it is difficult to see how this can lead to anything other than a nostalgic irrationalism.

Ricoeur tries to break out of this blatant circularity by denying that 'symbols, in their cosmic aspect, are anterior to language or even foreign to it' (*SE*: 11): but it is still insisted that 'manifestation' occurs 'through the thing'. This serves as the finite and unitary pole of the opposition with the 'surcharge of inexhaustible meaning' (*SE*: 11). (The phenomenological parallel would be the infinite adumbrations which constitute the object.) There's an underlying distrust of dispersal in language which prompts the insistence on 'concretion' and 'condensation' (*SE*: 11), an attempt to stabilize meaning by locating it in a 'symbol-thing' outside language.

Taking the cosmic level of symbolism as paradigmatic leads to a denial of autonomy to the oneiric and poetic; instead they are presented as a reduplication of the same theological investment. This represents a rare failure of one of the characteristic strengths of Ricoeur's thought: the willingness to acknowledge discrepancy between different levels of the same phenomenon (for example, the later subdivision of guilt into different semantic spheres: ethico-juridical, ethico-religious, psycho-theological). The 'oneiric dimension' is simply an alternative outlet for the 'most fundamental and stable symbolism of humanity': 'to manifest the "sacred" *on* the "cosmos" and to manifest it *in* the psyche are the same thing' (*SE*: 12). There is here no painful self-knowledge, no possibility of conflict, involved in 'the way to a discovery, a prospection and a prophecy concerning ourselves' (*SE*: 13). The 'third modality of symbols: the poetic imagination' is similarly reduced to a 'complement'. This shows 'expressivity in its nascent state' (*SE*: 13); and is firmly distinguished from any psychologistic theory of the renewal of the past sensory image. But this 'welling up' of language is denied any genuine freedom or innovation. It merely offers further confirmation of the 'hieratic stability' of the cosmic and the oneiric; any deviation from this course would presumably render it unpoetic. The 'remarkable convergence' has been asserted rather than demonstrated: why should there be only 'one structure' and how could this primarily linguistic phenomenon be susceptible to a 'direct eidetic analysis'? Phenomenology stops here: a descriptive analysis detailing the structures common to all acts of symbolic understanding, the 'identical nucleus of meaning' which is achieved and reachieved through 'a more or less intuitive grasp' (*SE*: 13).

Now Ricoeur embarks on 'a series of increasingly close approximations to the essence of a symbol' (*SE*: 14), which are worth examining in detail. The initial proposition concedes the world of things to be necessarily mediated by the universe of discourse, though it retains a certain degree of priority. (This is also evident in the identification of dreams with 'nocturnal spectacles' that were no more than 'originally close to words' and poetic images with, somewhat perplexingly, 'essentially words' (*SE*: 14–15).)

> Thus, contrary to perfectly transparent technical signs, which say only what they want to say in positing that which they signify, symbolic signs are opaque because the first, literal, obvious meaning itself points analogically to a second meaning which is not given otherwise than in it.... This opacity constitutes the depth of the symbol, which it will be said is inexhaustible.
>
> (*SE*: 15)

It is this 'double intentionality' that provides the criteria for distinguishing the symbol from the sign. Meaning is still located firmly within an author/speaker rather than an auditor/reader, and operates within a positivist opposition of connotation and denotation; there is merely a special-case status for the symbol. ('Opacity', I think, is an unfortunate term because it comes so close to the terminology of stain and contamination with which the book itself is concerned.) Attention is directed to its capacity to be 'essentially *bound*, bound to its contents, and through its primary content, to its secondary content' (*SE*: 17). The term is by no means easy to fathom – 'bound' to what, to the human condition, to knowledge of the sacred, or simply to the literal meaning? Ricoeur insists on the necessity of the continued presence of both literal and secondary meaning, that the secondary intention only takes on its distinctive character through the continued presence of the first, and so cannot be translated into a meta-language. The immediate comparisons would be with Sartre's account of viscousness (1957: 600–15) and Bachelard's meditation on fire: attempts to ascribe objective meaning as intrinsic to certain kinds of phenomena. What we have in Ricoeur is a willingness to move from 'the idea of a quasi-material something that infects as a sort of filth'(*SE*: 25) to a series of explicit moral and theological corollaries. It's worth stressing that this is the practical application of the secondariness of reflection. To prevent the reduction of the symbol, a certain materiality of its primary reference must be preserved, and there must be an explicit lacuna between this and any conceptual equivalences to be established. There must be a continued disjunction, even a slight element of shock, in the conversion into the contemporary (whereas for all the psychoanalytic virtuosity of Kristeva's work on abjection (1982: 56–89) the correspondences suggested are surprisingly inflexible, even complacent). The comments on the 'indissoluble complicity between sexuality and defilement' are a good example of the way these equivalences may remain provocative; 'at the limit, the infant would be regarded as born impure, contaminated from the beginning by the paternal seed, by the impurity of the maternal genital region, and by the additional impurity of childbirth' (*SE*: 28–9). A meaning for us may not necessarily be a meaning readily acceptable to us. This kind of combination will be theorised in his work on the mixed discourse in Freud; but already there is a refusal to dissolve or transpose symbol into commentary. 'Ethics is mingled with the physics of suffering, while suffering is surcharged with ethical meanings' (*SE*: 31); with a slight adjustment this would become 'because of the metaphoric model of physics certain insights into suffering become possible' – fatalism, vulnerability, direct causality.

The tendency is to privilege etymology over usage, a return to the juncture of Hebrew and Greek sources: 'a bundle of concrete expressions each of which, in its own way, is the beginning of a figurative manner of a possible line of interpretation' (*SE*: 71). The rationale for sorting the bundle – missing the target, deviation from the path, and so on – is by no means clear; and images are treated in isolation rather than as parts of larger syntactical or textual units. 'Pardon', for example, is obviously not a symbol in the way stain or even wandering is; it requires a residual context, a telling.

Instead Ricoeur invokes the 'structure of signification, which is at once a structure of absence and a function of presence'. Symbolic logic accentuates the capacity to 'signifier à vide', to substitute signs for things: the symbol accentuates presence, the capacity of a 'full language' to summon forth a world (*SE*: 18). (There is no recognition that ordinary language and not just symbolic expression is irreducible to symbolic logic.) There are several immediate problems. At what point is the first level annulled to make way for the second; and how indeed is one to distinguish between them? Should the second be given automatic authority over the first through its application to 'a certain situation of man in the sacred' ('certain' has a perhaps fortuitous but certainly symptomatic doctrinal ring). Ricoeur then goes on to specify more precisely what it is 'to be like'.

While analogy is inconclusive reasoning that proceeds by fourth proportional – A is to B as C is to D – in the symbol, I cannot objectify the analogical relation that connects the second meaning with the first. It is by living in the first meaning that I am led by it beyond itself; the symbolic meaning constituted in and by the literal meaning which effects the analogy in giving the analogue.

(SE: 15)

Here there is a kind of capitulation in the refusal to 'objectify' which is seen as the prelude to a decision to 'live in' the first level of meaning. Interpretation seems in no way a rule-governed and intelligible activity; instead it demands an admission of failure and personalised leap of faith. The nebulous process of being 'assimilated to' a meaning is surely falsely opposed to the claim to 'master a similitude intellectually' (SE: 16–17). There is a linguistic voluntarism lurking here: anything less than axiomatic demonstration becomes the grounds for a passive deference.

The 'donative' status of the symbol is contrasted with allegory, where a 'relation of translation' exists between the two levels: the 'symbolic meaning' is here 'external enough to be directly accessible' so that the 'henceforth useless' primary term 'can be dropped'.

> To interpret is then to penetrate the disguise and thereby to render it useless. In other words, allegory has been a modality of hermeneutics much more than a spontaneous creation of signs. It would be better, therefore, to speak of allegorizing interpretation rather than of allegory. Symbols and allegory, then, are not on the same footing; symbols precede hermeneutics; allegories are already hermeneutic. . . .
>
> (SE: 16)

The ultimate dispensibility of the primary meaning is perhaps equally applicable to Ricoeur's own account of the symbol: to 'penetrate a disguise' may be regarded as a justification in its own right, serving as a liberation of potency or, in de Man's famous account, a kind of freedom through negative self-knowledge. 'Allegorizing interpretation' is transgressive, deflating: it refuses to defer to that which is said to 'precede' it, remain unviolated by its activity. In comparison the 'spontaneous creation of signs' appears an almost culpable naïvety. It is even suggested that 'symbolic and allegorical interpretations' could be regarded as 'two directions of interpretation bearing on the same mythical content' (SE: 18). Here we have a

45

proto-conflict of interpretations. But instead Ricoeur weights the balance towards symbols as 'more radical', because possessing 'analogical meanings which are spontaneously formed and immediately significant', whereas myths become 'symbols developed in the form of narrations', extended into 'fanciful history' (*SE*: 18). It is very difficult for such an emphasis to avoid relegating myth into a form of diffusion. So we see in Ricoeur's formal definitions potential for development towards a more dynamic model of the hermeneutic field consistently suppressed in favour of a comparatively static sacramental symbol. In fact what will be most distinctive in his subsequent work will be the way the relegated term of allegory will become dominant, and subject the status of the sacred to increasingly heavy pressure. Its vulnerability lies primarily in its dependence on a series of linguistic postulates that Ricoeur himself will reject after his encounter with the structuralist critique. (A comment such as 'in the sign there dwells the transcendence of the Logos of man' (*FM*: 27), for example, will become impossible.)

Ricoeur goes on to enumerate the contextual conditions of his own thought: the Greco-Judaic heritage of Western philosophy which limits and specifies a field of inquiry ('there is a moment when a principle of orientation becomes a principle of limitation'(*SE*: 22)). This recognition of contingency may seem to concede very little; but in the context of the Husserlian project it marks a crucial shift towards a hermeneutic inquiry, the full force of which has yet to be acknowledged: to be historically situated, to recover and renew a cultural tradition, to enter into dialogue with declared presuppositions. The Nietzschean lesson of genealogies, the mystification and authority of origins, has been fully learned, for example in analysing the Torah (*SE*: 132–5) or the penal rationality of the Greeks (*SE*: 109–18), but this is regarded as a method of comprehension rather than grounds for their rejection.

Ricoeur claims that 'to be able to perceive this internal dialectic of guilt, one must set it in a vaster dialectic, that of three moments of fault: defilement, sin, guilt' (*SE*: 100). Defilement is a quasi-material contagion, an objective necessity of chastisement; awareness of sin represents an ontological insight into the real situation of man before God; guilt is equated with the subjective moment of appropriation of that knowledge. This move away from the communal guilt to individualisation involves a subtler discrimination of degrees of responsibility. However the 'complete substitution of guilt for sin never appears': instead there is an equilibrium between 'the absolute measure, represented by the sight of God, who sees the sins there are, and the subjective measure represented by the tribunal of the conscience, which appraises any guilt that becomes apparent' (*SE*: 104). The self-consciousness of both these later phases, however, seems flimsy compared to the 'ineradicable' symbolism of defilement. There's an impasse at the very heart of *The Symbolism of Evil*: self-knowledge does not bring freedom from the archaic, but a fuller awareness of servitude:

> the more historical and less cosmic symbolism of sin and guilt makes up for the poverty and abstractedness of its imagery only by a series of revivals and transpositions of the more archaic, but more highly surcharged, symbolism of defilement. The richness of the symbolism of defilement, even when this symbolism is fully interiorised, is the corollary of its cosmic roots.
>
> (*SE*: 12)

The historical is here equated with 'poverty and abstractedness', though the vantage from which the cosmic may be understood ahistorically is never discussed. The Hegelian *Aufhebung* seems remarkably unproductive: it is perceived almost solely in terms of loss rather than the creation of a second-order vocabulary and hence an enlargement.

The implicit Hegelian schema is difficult to reconcile with the neutralised observer of descriptive phenomenology. Where does absolute reason stand in the context of guilt? Are the 'movement of rupture and ... of resumption' archetypal, structural, hypothetical (*SE*: 100)? And is the guilty man acknowledging his own corruption will such an inspiring conclusion? The 'servile will' is offered as the endpoint of the study: 'the final symbol indicates its limiting concept only by the taking up into itself all the wealth of the prior symbols' (*SE*: 152).

> The paradox of a captive free will – the paradox of a *servile will* – is insupportable for thought. That freedom must be delivered and that this deliverance is deliverance from self-enslavement cannot be said directly; yet it is the central theme of 'salvation'.
>
> (*SE*: 152)

The 'dimension of freedom' that these symbols are said to denote seems severely curtailed. There is an underlying supposition – one might almost say complacency – that guilt follows from transgression concealed from oneself: it is ultimately appropriate, deserved. 'Why should the suppliant beg to be *released* from what he has *committed* if he did not know obscurely, if he did not know without knowing, if he did not know enigmatically and symbolically, that he has put upon himself the bonds from which he begs to be released?' (*SE*: 153) Guilt has been dissociated from finitude only to re-emerge as omnipresent responsibility. It is said to have three constituents: it has positive existence (against traditional definitions of sin as nothingness); it is an external seduction, not merely brought about, but already there; it is an infection proceeding from within. At this point this appears to be an asserted fiat or utopian horizon rather than any genuine disputing of the symbolism of guilt: 'however *radical* evil may be, it cannot be as *primordial* as goodness' (*SE*: 157).

So 'the primary symbols' achieves a peculiarly eloquent blend of the sermonic and the hermeneutic: an intense personal involvement in a more generalised moral and theological discourse, yet capable of meticulous historical contextualisation. The initial restriction of being situated within the Greco-Judaic heritage becomes the outstanding strength of the book: the making present of archaic modes of thought in such a way as to blend with modern existential preoccupations. Particularly fine examples of this quality come in the pages on ethical terror, a kind of ethnology through Kierkegaard (for example, the meditation on dread (*SE*: 63–70), and the uncharacteristically bullying dichotomy, 'the pure and simple alternative, God or Nothing' (*SE*: 103)); the numerous powerful analyses of anticipated chastisement, whether as theological taboo or social deterrence; and that on the 'abolition of fear' as the 'eschatological future of human morality' through its transformation into demand for love rather than coercive sanction (*SE*: 44–5). This in turn exemplifies the appropriate relation of philosophic commentary to primary symbols. One may have lingering reservations about the status of the proposed model, its presumed teleology, and in particular its privileged insight into an ontological realm of human existence; but it could scarcely be denied that Ricoeur offers a cogent and powerful analysis of a complex and enigmatic aspect of human experience.

MYTHOLOGY

The second half of the book, 'The world of myth', opens with the premise that the isolation of primary symbols is itself 'an abstraction that has uprooted them from the rich world of myths' (*SE*: 161): these in turn have now been 'disassociated' from history and therefore become a source of 'embarrassment'. It is suggested that this offers an opportunity to understand 'myth as myth' and conquer 'the mythical dimension' (*SE*: 162). Here Ricoeur appears to invite having his own argument, in 'Preface to Bultmann' (*CI*: 381–401), turned against him: that nothing is really lost in the moment of scepticism; it merely serves as the prelude and the justification of an ascribed plenitude. This is borne out in the tendentious distinction between demythisation, the abandonment of myth, and demythologisation, the removal of 'pseudo-knowledge, the false logos of the myth' (*SE*: 162):

> the myth can no longer be an explanation; to exclude its etiological intention is the theme of necessary demythologization. But in losing its explanatory pretensions the myth reveals its exploratory significance and its contribution to understanding, which we shall later call the symbolic function – that is to say, its power of discovering and revealing the bond between man and what he considers sacred. Paradoxical as it may seem, the myth, when it is thus demythologized through contact with scientific history and elevated to the dignity of a symbol, is a dimension of modern thought.
>
> (*SE*: 5)

The yielding up of ground to scepticism is more apparent than real. The kind of mythic knowledge which is conceded no longer to have relevance competes with the hard data of the physical sciences, the sphere of explanation; understanding, the arbiter of the human sciences, is not only left unchallenged, but also claimed to provide access to the 'sacred'. Presumably that which undermines or denies the existence of such a 'bond' is no longer included within the 'symbolic function'; no challenge to its 'dignity' is to be permitted. The sacred is never really under threat, never itself an object of demythologisation; the myth viewed in this way becomes little more than a form of predictable reassurance – an odd conclusion given what is later conceded to be an 'inexhaustible source of violence' within the mythical canon (*TN* 1: 47). And this version of modernity can only be preserved through a convenient omission of the masters of suspicion: Marx, Freud, Nietzsche. Passages such as this are significant in the context of Ricoeur's later work because they show how much he is there prepared to stake on the conflict of interpretations: it is a wager that can be lost. According to his own later terminology, the moment of explanation is not here formalist enough: existential significations are imported prematurely, and so represent a closure of interpretation rather than a further extension of meaning.

The capacity of myth to serve as a vehicle of 'totality', capable of grasping human reality 'in a whole', is supported by no more than a vague invocation of its resources of 'reminiscence and expectation' (*SE*: 6); and this awareness of temporal structuring in broadly Husserlian terms makes little impact on the wholly dehistoricised nature of the truth supposedly revealed. Lévi-Strauss's account of myth as mediation of contradiction posits a purely formal reconciliation. Ricoeur, in contrast, wants to preserve a 'primordially dramatic structure of the world of myths' for which 'the narrative form is neither secondary nor accidental, but primitive and essential' (*SE*: 170). This, however, remains an undifferentiated category: the whole issue of what exactly mythic narration adds to primary symbolism is left unexplored – it appears secondary but without the claim to intelligibility of philosophic commentary. Viewed retrospectively through *Time and Narrative*, one can say that myth is here treated without a rigorous investigation of narrative.

Ricoeur's insistence on myth-narration spares him the need to postulate 'living participation' in unfallen consciousness as 'an indivisible plenitude, in which the supernatural, the natural, and the psychological are not yet torn apart' (*SE*: 167). He insists that this 'intuition of a cosmic whole' is 'not *given*, but simply *aimed* at': 'it is because he himself has lost that wholeness that man re-enacts and imitates it in myth and ritual. The primitive man is already a man of division' (*SE*: 167). There is an unqualified refusal to project an idealised state back into prehistory; this innocence can only be a promise, a horizon, something to be worked towards. Nevertheless, there is something dismayingly quantitative about the treatment of mythology; despite the explicit support for Bultmann's project of demythification, Ricoeur's actual analyses adopt the neutralisation of belief urged by the phenomenology. Throughout the compendious (and at times laborious) taxonomy, there is not a single instance of rejecting a myth. If Ricoeur resists one common failing of myth-criticism, the projection of an unfallen consciousness into a sentimentalised prehistory, he does not altogether escape the somewhat dreary equalisation that archetypalism can be prone to, the assumption that each and every myth not only partakes of indispensable vision, but also that its insights are somehow more valuable because repeated to the point of banality.

Ricoeur lists three working premises: that myths of evil 'embrace mankind as a whole within one ideal history'; that they endow the 'universality of man' with a 'concrete character'; and that they possess an 'ontological bearing' in their narration of 'the leap and the passage, the cut and the suture' between the essential being of man, innocence, and his fallen historical existence (*SE*: 162–3). The myth centres on the world of fault while remaining irreducible to allegory. There are correspondent limitations that Ricoeur does not choose to go into: the insistence on the hero as everyman denies plurality, character, alternative stories; while narration is seen as release from confinement to an absolute present, it still only operates between the absolute poles of perdition and salvation, beginning and end; and in covering over the break of fault could be said to offer a mystificatory consolation. Most importantly, the possibility that something in the myths themselves invites the pretension of gnosis, hardening into knowledge, is not addressed. The aetiological element falls to demythologisation perhaps; but this commits us to reading the core of the myth rather than its entirety. These arrogant demarcations between true and false elements might themselves seem a form of gnosis: only the check of hermeneutic good faith separates Ricoeur's own text from the 'greatest explanatory ravings' (*SE*: 165) prompted by the disjunction between the destination of man in innocence and his actual situation.

Ricoeur's stress on the 'dynamics' of myth is continually undercut by the 'statics of classification' apparent in his 'morphology of the principal images' (*SE*: 172). There is no Jungian celebration of myth *per se*, but the elaborate taxonomic arrangement has a similar effect: one is invited to inhabit and admire but not raise the question of ultimate belief. Four categories are offered: the drama of creation in which the origin of evil lies in the chaos with which the creative god struggles; the fall as an irrational event in an already completed creation; a tragic theology of a god who tempts, blinds, leads astray, in which freedom is equated with understood necessity; and the myth of the soul as exiled in a fallen body. The gap between myth and commentary seems larger than between symbol and commentary, despite the fact that secondary and tertiary stages should be closer. The phenomenology of confession remains in continuous contact with the semantics of religious language: Babylonian creation myths, sadly, seem considerably more estranged. Certainly it is an uncomfortable translation of the strife of Tiamat and Marduk to say 'this promotion of the divine at the expense of the primordial brutality' suggests 'negatively, that man is not the origin of evil; man finds evil and continues it', and 'positively, that evil is the oldest of beings' (*SE*: 178). The commentary is too abrupt, too condensed: to say

'Violence is inscribed in the origin of things, in the principle that establishes while it destroys' says both too much and too little (*SE*: 182–3).

Ricoeur openly declares the 'pre-eminence' of the Adamic myth for its subordination of original sin to the doctrine of salvation; for the duty of understanding incumbent upon the Christian believer; and more debatably because it subsumes within itself the truths of other myths (*SE*: 309). Three aspects are stressed: Adam's essential human character as ancestor of the whole race; the origin of evil as separated from the origin of good (i.e. creation precedes fall); the story as focused not on a single character but involving Eve and the serpent. There is an interesting backtracking to establish the presence of the tragic within the Adamic myth itself; the 'underlying peccability' of Adam which cannot be reduced to the pre-existent evil of the serpent, and provides the basis for the dogma of original sin. It is nevertheless difficult to see how 'the tragic myth saves the Biblical myth only insofar as the latter resuscitates it' (*SE*: 323–4). Despite the supposed 'irreducibility' of the tragic, Ricoeur provides an unembarrassed exegesis in terms of malign predestination. This sounds a little odd, but in fact provides quite a neat summation of the theme of absurdity in existential thought and necessity in Freudian or Marxist perspectives. The punishment that is perceived as both necessary and unjust undermines the imposing façade of theodicy: 'the figure of the just man suffering, image and type of unjust suffering, constituted the stumbling block against which the premature rationalisations of misfortune were shattered' (*SE*: 32).

Yet it is claimed that 'explicit formulation of the tragic theology would mean self-destruction for the religious consciousness' (*SE*: 226). It is never made clear why a 'tragic vision' that cannot be restated in speculation can be embodied in a 'spectacle': surely theatrical form is equally capable of being 'unmasked' as a 'warning and an invitation'. The whole investigation into the symbolism of evil might equally well approach the category of an '*insupportable* revelation' (*SE*: 212–13). And the final conclusion is disappointing: after an explicit confrontation with the conceptual implications of a tragic theology, a purely aesthetic reconciliation is invoked. Nevertheless the challenge to the Adamic myth is sufficiently powerful to force it to ground itself firmly on eschatological postulates that have to be imported as protection from the impasse of anguished scepticism to which the study of tragedy led. And the future direction of Ricoeur's thought becomes visible in the reduction of the taxonomy of myths to an opposition between tragedy and faith.

THE RECREATION OF LANGUAGE

The final section continually espouses a hermeneutics not necessarily exemplified in the body of the text. There should be nothing particularly surprising about this kind of telos in a work by Ricoeur; instead of amplification and verification of an initial proposition, there is a dialectical progression that subsumes and to some extent discards its earlier stages. Just as *Fallible Man* brought pure reflection to the point where it was obliged to acknowledge its own incapacity, *The Symbolism of Evil* pushes descriptive phenomenology to the point where it in turn is displaced by a more dynamic and self-implicating concept of the hermeneutic field.

> The world of symbols is not a tranquil and reconciled world: every symbol is iconoclastic in comparison with some other symbol, just as every symbol, left to itself, tends to thicken, to become solidified in an idolatory. It is necessary then to participate in the struggle, in the dynamics in which the symbolism becomes a prey to a spontaneous hermeneutics that seeks to transcend it.
>
> (*SE*: 354)

It is fair to say that this struggle is just what has been precluded by the phenomenological ordering of the book; it has seemed all too possible to operate within a comfortable eclecticism; the sacred has never had to occupy the position of 'prey' to a hostile hermeneutics. Ricoeur is still insistent on 'the hiatus between pure reflection on fallibility and the confession of sins' (*SE*: 347). A third and mediating term is still sought, which would allow the reintroduction of reflection enriched through recourse to symbolic language. The proposed solution resides in the maxim, 'le symbole donne à penser', usually translated as 'gives rise to thought', but this omits the strong connection with the donative, the gift. 'It is necessary to renounce the chimera of a philosophy without presuppositions and begin from a full language'; but the very selection of the subject has restricted the 'full language' to a 'theologically-charged symbolism'. 'The symbol gives; but what it gives is occasion for thought, something to think about' (*SE*: 349): it must not be endowed with the spurious priority of a sentimental archaism:

> The beginning is not what one finds first; the point of departure must be reached, it must be won.... The illusion is not in looking for a point of departure, but in looking for it without presuppositions. There is no philosophy without presuppositions. A meditation on symbols starts from speech that has already taken place, and in which everything has already been said in some fashion: it wishes to be thought with its presuppositions. For it the first task is not to begin, but from the midst of speech, to remember; to remember with a view to beginning.
>
> (*SE*: 348–9)

So far so good. The pre-existent fact of language provides a starting-point whereas the Cartesian dream of reason will continue to regress forever in search of absolute origin. But Ricoeur extends this:

> The historical moment of the philosophy of symbols is that of forgetfulness and restoration. Forgetfulness of hierophanies, forgetfulness of signs of the sacred, loss of man himself insofar as he belongs to the sacred. The forgetfulness, we know, is the counterpart of the great task of nourishing men, of satisfying their needs by mastering nature through a planetary technique. It is in the age when our language has become more precise, more univocal, more technical in a word, more suited to those integral formalizations which are called precisely symbolic logic, it is in this very age of discourse that we want to recharge our language, that we want to start again from the fullness of language.... It is not regret for the sunken Atlantides that animates us, but hope for a re-creation of language. Beyond the desert of criticism, we wish to be called again.
>
> (*SE*: 349)

We should not underestimate the complexity and ambivalence of Ricoeur's sense of modernity (evident for example in the subtle analysis of 'mondialisation' in his social essays). Modernity provides the tools of new understanding – philology, exegesis, phenomenology of religion, psychoanalysis – and in the midst of an eloquent pledge of faith there is due recognition of the material progress that makes possible the search for the means of renewal. The 'philosophy of symbols' can only come into being at this specific 'historical moment'; it demands a wholesale 'forgetfulness' to allow its belatedness to fructify into a project of 'restoration', and the Bloomian term is not at all inappropriate here. The text has 'always been said'; the task is to 'recharge our language'. The concomitant of modernity is the reduction to sameness, the emptying out of language, the 'desert of criticism'. The problem with Ricoeur's response is encapsulated in the phrase 'loss of man himself as far as he belongs to the sacred'; other sources of social alienation are apparently relegated to the inconsequential, and the sacred becomes rather too easily synonymous with the 'essence of man'. And the proposed solution of a 'recreation of language' immediately raises difficulties: whose language, for whose benefit, how might the kerygma operate in contemporary society; the concluding passive 'to be called again' is both disarming and faintly ominous. Ricoeur's hope for meaning beyond demystification involves an uncompromising insistence on the sacral dimension of the act of interpretation, but any criticism that wishes to accord value to its privileged texts above social documentation will be obliged to advance similar claims. (One thinks of the closing pages of Hartman's *Criticism in the Wilderness*; but the practice of canon-formation in both Leavis and the New Criticism is similarly motivated). Here the problem for Ricoeur is that of an appropriate secondariness: 'an interpretation that respects the original enigma of the symbols, lets itself be taught by them, but beginning from there, promotes the meaning, forms the meaning in the full responsibility of autonomous thought' (*SE*: 349–50). One might retort that 'autonomous thought' requires sustained interrogation of the initial premise of dependence. Too much is accorded to the symbol too readily; and to ascribe an 'immediacy' to it is perhaps to restrict rather than to open up. This is quickly acknowledged: there is 'nowhere a symbolic language without hermeneutics':

> we are in every way children of criticism, and we seek to go beyond criticism by means of criticism, a criticism that is no longer reductive but restorative.... In every way, something has been lost, irremediably lost: immediacy of belief. But if we can no longer love the great symbolisms of the sacred in accordance with the original belief in them, we can, we modern men, aim at a second naïveté in and through criticism. In short it is by *interpreting* that we can *hear* again.
>
> (*SE*: 350–51)

Criticism, it should be noted, follows the Kantian ideal of a self-reflexive, non-naturalistic philosophy. As I have observed before, 'demythologisation' as 'the irreversible gain of truthfulness, intellectual honesty, objectivity' (*SE*: 350) is a kind of preliminary ground-clearing that in no way intervenes in the second stage of renewed contact with the sacred, the recovery of a once-present meaning as a 'remedy' for the 'distress of modernity'. Ricoeur's major themes of effort to be and primary affirmation have yet to be aligned with the task of interpretation: here this remains a regrettable necessity that must be undertaken because of the impossibility of regaining 'primitive naïveté'. It is on this issue that great advances will be made when he insists on the benefits and possibilities opened up by the very alienation of the text.

At this stage, however, a genuine moment of suspicion is lacking: the enemy is the desiccation of symbolic logic. The techniques of modernity are here seen as in the service of the retrieval of meaning once an initial pledge has been made to the 'fullness of language': the possibility of them providing a persuasive counter-exegesis is not explored. Ricoeur's next work, *Freud and Philosophy*, will take up the hitherto ignored challenge presented by the masters of suspicion.

4

Freud and philosophy

THE HERMENEUTICS OF SUSPICION

Ricoeur opens with the admission that 'this book deals with Freud and not with psychoanalysis. This means there are two things lacking: analytic experience itself and a consideration of the post-Freudian schools' (*FP*: xi). The object of study is not merely Freud, but a Freud granted his own internal coherence 'as a monument of our culture, as a text in which our culture is expressed and understood' (*FP*: xi). 'Monument' sounds faintly ominous, a bewhiskered old Victorian commemorated in a thousand nondescript town squares. Has a Freud thus regarded lost his radical edge, his capacity to shock and to threaten?

Given the nonreproducibility of the intersubjective context of analysis, it is inevitable that writings (whether case histories or not) should take precedence over analytic practice. What could not be predicted is the way that Ricoeur's own conflictual hermeneutic will restore potency on another level to Freud as text. The process of doubt is two-way: philosophy must seek to preserve its own realm of jurisdiction and privilege of situating alternative modes of thought, but in return it must risk itself, expect to be transformed in the encounter with its challengers. This dialectic is not restricted specifically to psychoanalysis: Freud joins forces with Marx and Nietzsche to found the modern hermeneutics of suspicion, of freedom through disbelief, through demystification. Though the sphere of validity of the psychoanalytic critique may at times appear quite sharply restricted, the ideal of critique itself is accorded an immense and unwavering respect.

Ricoeur gives us all the linguistic sophistication of what has been labelled French Freud; the insistence that the language in which

Freud articulates his discoveries cannot be translated into a terminology of theory and verification without fatal deformation of his thought. This emphasis should at least partially be seen as a result of coming to Freud late: there is, for example, no French equivalent to the English *Standard Edition*, and no comparably strong indigenous tradition of clinical practice. (As late as 1975, Luce Irigaray bases her argument in *Speculum: of the Other Woman* on a corrupt and abridged translation of Freud's famous lecture on femininity (Koffman, 1985: 14; see also 'Reinventing Freud in France', Turkle, 1978: 47–68).) The comparative crudity of Ricoeur's earlier analysis ('Freudianism has something fascinating for the feeble consciousness' (*FN*: 403)) also reflects this limited familiarity. His specific criticisms generally follow Sartre's attack on the bad faith of psychoanalysis (1957: 458–75). 'The naturalistic mythology' of Freudianism 'where the unconscious feels and thinks and where consciousness appears naively as a part, an effect, or a function of the unconscious' (*H*: 220) offers 'an explanation that rescues (us) from the charge of being free' and an opportunity 'to shift all responsibility to the ruses of that unconscious demon that I claim to bear within me' (*FN*: 403, 385).

In *Freud and Philosophy*, Ricoeur is prepared to accord a great deal more to Freud's deliberate tempo of argumentation, 'that strategy of lecturer and writer that keeps surprising the reader' (*FP*: 285), than a deconstructive reading, while coming very close to its premise of persistent self-undermining ('Freud was always a dualist: what kept changing was the distribution of the opposed terms and the nature of the opposition itself' (*FP*: 292)). But this is not deployed as testimony to the suppression of the radical implications of his own work (Lacan) or the capacity of différance to subvert any stable conjunction of mind, desire and language (Derrida): instead Ricoeur retains the vantage of the conscious interpreter, and presents the' oneiric dimension of the unconscious as an object constructed by rational interpretation. This is the crucial issue in his vexed debate with Lacan, who accuses him of not comprehending that 'the realism of the unconscious' is 'not the ambiguity of acts, future knowledge that is known not to be known, but lacuna, cut, rupture inscribed in a certain lack' (Lacan, 1977a: 153; see also Tort, 1966 for an extended if somewhat intemperate Lacanian critique). For Ricoeur, we produce the unconscious through a disciplined exegesis of its surcharged language – 'the unconscious is homogeneous with consciousness: it is its relative other and not the absolute other' (*FP*: 430). This in turn can be harnessed to an increased freedom of enhanced self-consciousness: recognition of these archaic determinants can be prospective, directed towards the future rather than a savage and foreclosed revelation of the absence of psychic mastery.

Ricoeur situates Freud as a figure of major stature within the Western philosophical tradition, and seeks to demonstrate that psychoanalysis possesses sufficient internal cohesion as a hermeneutic discipline to hold its own against either positivist or phenomenological critiques. He provides both a flexible and comprehensive working schema for the grouping and preliminary understanding of Freud's work: his three-tier synchronic model provides an admirable holding position. This may seem of merely pedagogic concern, but anyone attempting a sustained understanding of his thought will have to come to terms with its constant internal revision, its infuriating propensity never to maintain a stable position. As with neuroses, 'earlier phases of development are not simply replaced by succeeding ones, but conflicts arise between vestiges of the former and demands of the latter' (*FP*: 284).

One might have doubts about the extent to which the post-Freudians may be 'deliberately set aside', but the overall project of 'rigorous debate with the true founder of psychoanalysis' demands respect. The emphasis instead falls 'on the new understanding of man that Freud introduces' (*FP*: xii): an uncompromising allegiance to a humanist tradition usually perceived as permanently undermined by psychoanalysis. More specifically, attention is directed towards 'the texture or structure of Freudian discourse' (*FP*: xii). This synonymity may appear initially disconcerting, but, in the context of the work as a whole, will be magnificently justified. This is subjected to interrogation within the categories of epistemology, reflective philosophy, and dialectics: there remains a bottom line of intelligible discourse, and one of the triumphs of Ricoeur's book will be its assimilation of the sceptical challenge of Freud's work within this coherence.

The 'written work' of Freud is seen as detaching itself from the analytic context in a way that reveals its 'broadest aim' to be 'not only the renovation of psychiatry, but a reinterpretation of all psychical productions pertaining to culture, from dreams, through art and morality, to religion' (*FP*: 4). So the 'textual approach' while initially giving a 'truncated' version of psychoanalysis liberates its cultural ambitions, which, Ricoeur will emphasise, were present from Freud's earliest writings (*FP*: 4). He stresses the collectivity of its diagnoses, rather than regarding it as 'a form of individual psychology, tardily transposed into a sociology of culture' (*FP*: 5). Common to both is the

59

meditation on the relation between desire and language, for which the dream is the paradigm because of its 'disguised, substitutive, and fictive expressions of human wishing' (*FP*: 5). This can never be a direct object of study: rather the text of the dream account is replaced by another that seeks to articulate 'the primitive speech of desire' (*FP*: 6). Analysis moves from meaning to meaning: it addresses not un-mediated force but the 'semantics of desire' (*FP*: 6). And it is in posing the question of how desires achieve or fail to achieve speech that psychoanalysis makes its distinctive contribution to the philosophy of language.

For Ricoeur, the dream provides a working model of intelligibility that may be extended to widely different spheres. It is now posited that 'language itself is from the outset and for the most part distorted' (*FP*: 7), though this is immediately restricted to the 'region' of the symbol. This elevation of 'double-meaning expressions' to 'the privileged theme of the hermeneutic field' (*FP*: 8) is somewhat arbitrary; and the notion of text is also as yet somewhat unspecific. But in the context of the book as a whole the 'decision to mutually delimit the field of symbolism and interpretation' (*FP*: 9) is the prelude to a far more ambitious mapping. In *The Symbolism of Evil*, hermeneutics was an orientation, the pledge of continually available meanings within a cultural heritage, rather than a theorised rule-governed activity. Now with the acknowledgement of 'the showing-hiding of double meaning' (*FP*: 7), the phenomenology of religion is no longer exempted from sustained challenge.

Ricoeur proceeds to repeat the three modalities of symbolism set forth in *The Symbolism of Evil*, here with a greater stress on the common semantic structure of the cosmic, oneiric, and poetic usages of language. 'There must always be a word to take up the world and turn it into hierophany' (*FP*: 16); dreams are only intelligible as recounted; and the poet shows the birth of the word. Analogy, however, is reduced to merely one of the relations of latent and manifest meaning: if anything, its immediate sensory equivalence is deceptive. It presumes innocence, cannot account for the 'multitude of ruses and falsifications of meaning' (*FP*: 17). The crucial concept of 'disharmony' of interpretation is here introduced (*FP*: 18): even 'symbolic naïveté' is 'from the start moving toward interpretation by virtue of that transgression of meaning by meaning at the heart of the symbolic structure' (*FP*: 19). This necessarily involves 'an intellectual activity of decision, of finding a hidden meaning': instead of a revelation of the preordained order of the sacred, it becomes 'work, perhaps interminable' (*FP*: 19). Symbols do not pre-exist interpretation, but come into being as a result of the activity they elicit; and that activity includes resistance and doubt as well as the plenitude of assent.

Nietzsche and Freud are then equated with a new sense of interpretation that replaces truth and falsehood with error and illusion. This is said to point to a 'key difficulty' of modern hermeneutics, not arising from the problem of the symbol, but 'peculiar to the act of interpreting as such':

> There is no general hermeneutics, no universal canon for exegesis, but only disparate and opposed theories concerning the rules of interpretation. The hermeneutic field, whose outer contours we have traced, is internally at variance with itself.
>
> (*FP*: 26–7)

There is no attempt to provide a stable matrix for a 'complete enumeration of hermeneutic styles': instead Ricoeur opts to accentuate the dispersal and 'start with the polarized opposition that creates the greatest tension at the outset of our investigation' (*FP*: 27). The posited neutrality of the phenomenology of religion must be jettisoned; it is seen as involving an initial movement of belief that not only compromises its objectivity but renders it one extreme pole of the hermeneutic field. It must remain an open question whether 'the manifestation or restoration of a meaning' need ultimately be identified with proclamation and kerygma (*FP*: 28), or whether Ricoeur's thought provides the resources for a more moderate statement of the positive pole. There is no abandonment of the hope of rational thought, however; instead that rationality is aligned squarely with the 'reduction of illusion' (*FP*: 27). Our modernity consists of 'a double solicitation and urgency': we must

> on the one hand, purify discourse of its excrescences, liquidate the idols, go from drunkenness to sobriety, realize our state of poverty once and for all; on the other hand, use the most 'nihilistic', destructive, iconoclastic movement so as to *let speak* what once, what each time, was *said*, when meaning appeared anew, when meaning was at its fullest. Hermeneutics seems to me to be animated by this double motivation: willingness to suspect, willingness to listen; vow of rigor, vow of obedience. In our time we have not finished doing away with *idols* and we have

barely begun to listen to *symbols*. It may be that this situation, in its apparent distress, is instructive: it may be that extreme iconoclasm belongs to the restoration of meaning.

(*FP*: 27)

This is a dense and in many ways surprising passage. Notice how 'drunkenness' is put to the side of faith, whereas the nihilistic is equated with rigour and sobriety. There is a strongly penitential strain running through the 'state of poverty' and 'vow of obedience', but also a passionate identification with the 'extreme iconcoclasm'. We should not underestimate the consistent respect Ricoeur shows for the force of the human in itself, as opposed to a renewal both located in an estranged past and a hypothetical future. Nothing is guaranteed after the first stage of 'an ascesis of reflection whose first movement is to let itself be dispossessed of the origin of meaning' (*FP*: 27).

This is most eloquently articulated by the 'three masters, seemingly mutually exclusive' who 'dominate the school of suspicion: Marx, Nietzsche, Freud' (*FP*: 32). From the very phrasing something survives: the concept of the 'master', the outstanding individual by whom we may be schooled, who may be to our souls a singing-master. Ricoeur does not halt at their declared hostility towards the sacred, the 'expectancy of a new word', but finds a 'positive meaning' in their renewal of the 'problem of the Cartesian doubt', now turned against consciousness itself (*FP*: 33). Understanding now becomes hermeneutics: 'to seek meaning is no longer to spell out the consciousness of meaning, but to *decipher its expressions*' (*FP*: 33). Such a transposition onto a 'mediate *science* of meaning (*FP*: 34) would surely be unacceptable to a Marxist; and the denigration of the subsequent tradition might also be challenged. It is little short of caricature to claim that their respective disciples reduce Marx to 'economics and the absurd theory of reflex consciousness', Nietzsche to 'biologism and a perspectivism incapable of expressing itself without contradiction', and Freud himself to a 'simplistic pansexualism' (*FP*: 32–3):

all three, however, far from being detractors of consciousness aim at extending it. What Marx wants to do is liberate *praxis* by the understanding of necessity; but this liberation is inseparable from a 'conscious insight' which victoriously counterattacks the mystification of false consciousness. What Nietzsche wants is the increase of man's power, the restoration of his force; but the meaning of the will to power must be recaptured by meditating on the cyphers 'superman', 'eternal return', and 'Dionysus', without which the power in question would be but worldly violence. What Freud desires is that the one who is analyzed, by making his own the meaning that was foreign to him, enlarge his field of consciousness, live better, and finally be a little freer, and if possible, a little happier.

(*FP*: 34–5)

These are to a certain extent reduced versions of these thinkers: very much an early Marx of labour and alienation; a non-textualist Nietzsche, whose thought yields a definite core that may be paraphrased and debated; a Freud who seeks to 'enlarge the field of consciousness' rather than to wound and humiliate it. All three are seen as imposing 'the rude discipline of necessity' and 'the lesson of Spinoza: one first finds himself a slave, he understands his slavery, he rediscovers himself free within understood necessity' (*FP*: 35).

Now Ricoeur returns to the recurrent problem of how a philosophy of reflection' can 'nourish itself at the symbolic source and become hermeneutic?' (*FP*: 41). He proceeds to open out the cogito, reinterpreted as the more active Fichtean formulation of the thetic judgement: a self-positing that is simultaneously being and act. This proposition however remains 'as abstract and empty as it is invincible' unless outward directed. Consciousness is not a given but a task: its mere apperception of itself is a 'certitude devoid of truth' (*FP*: 44) without the appropriation of the effort to exist. Not only must we 'systematically cultivate the equivocal' (*FP*: 41), but also 'let ourselves be torn by the contradiction between these divergent hermeneutics' (*FP*: 54). This is certainly a perspective from which 'dispossession' appears anything but ludic; the constitution of the self through encounters with texts, ambiguous language, entails a commitment to the 'harsh hermeneutic discipline' (*FP*: 56). Ricoeur, however, retains the specific purposiveness of effort, a conscious directedness towards the future in the full awareness of present inadequacy. He talks of the 'recovery of the act of existing' obscured by a culpable forgetfulness, but I would prefer to emphasise the prospective and at times purely fictive nature of appropriation; the detour to which the self is condemned among the 'opaque, contingent and equivocal signs' of culture serves as an enlargement rather than the loss of a more rigorous ideal of critical thought. 'To be separated from ourselves, to be set off center' (*FP*: 55), to acknowledge that the 'home of meaning is not consciousness but something other than consciousness' is not to abandon the subject entirely: instead self-consciousness becomes an operative goal, always to be achieved.

The most radical question, however, that of the transition between demystification and restoration of meaning, remains open. Ricoeur gives us the possibility of the 'aporia rightly formed and rightly posed' (*FP*: 47). In deconstruction, the term has come to signify the subversive, even traumatising, revelation of a false pretension. Its appropriate mode of insight is the unmasking of error: it cannot risk statement because the very nature of conceptual language would condemn it to a repetition of the same blindnesses. For Ricoeur the equivocal nature of language involves forgoing a claim or a certain set of claims to certitude, to absolute grounding; but the converse of this is the opportunity presented for the productive competition of interpretations. The presence of aporia within the metapsychology and its numerous points of divergence from analytic practice become positive and enabling strengths. The fact that the arrogance of totality must be disavowed does not render the project of interpretation illegitimate, or rather naïvely futile. That there is a 'war of hermeneutics' is no cause for despondency: what is important is that one should risk oneself in this contest: a kind of rigorous but fallible good faith.

READING FREUD

The second section, 'How to read Freud', is offered as a complement to the more general positioning of psychoanalysis within the hermeneutic field that precedes it, and the eliciting of a teleological impulse that follows, where 'all opposition will be carried over into him' (*FP*: 60). I shall follow Ricoeur's arguments in this section in slightly laborious detail: the credibility of his project largely depends on the' quality of commentary that will emerge.

The first cycle, 'Energetics and hermeneutics', is devoted to the question of interpretation in psychoanalysis: Ricoeur seeks to demonstrate that the two strands of the mixed discourse of Freudianism – the connections of force and the relations of meaning – imply rather than exclude each other. The economics of cathexis appear to demand a naturalistic explanation over interpretation. Yet psychoanalysis is also a hermeneutics directed towards representations – dream-texts, illusions, culture. There remains a 'residual dissociation' (*FP*: 67): desire may move from force to language, but cannot be completely integrated within language. Ricoeur treats the energetics, Freud's language of mental dynamism, as a form of metaphorical model, but does not integrate this into the issue of the symbol, which increasingly appears both privileged and confined by its separation from ordinary language. Secondly, the status of interpretation must remain paradoxical: the conscious and directed intentionality of the analyst produces meanings grounded on a principle of cathexis that radically undermines its autonomy. The more convincingly it interprets, the less its authority.

Ricoeur first goes to the *Project* of 1895 for a statement of the constancy principle and the quantification of psychic energy in its most mechanistic form. Here the terminology of cathexis is adduced to neurology, all of which will take on an increasingly metaphorical sense: discharge, resistance, screens, and so on. He finds a number of interesting prefigurations, notably in the tension between the principle of inertia and that of constancy (*FP*: 74–5); and the discrimination between hallucinatory desires and perceptual mechanisms (*FP*: 78–9). In particular he stresses the resistance of the constancy principle to verification: the very absence of precise and verifiable measurement for cathexis is what allows its later transfer onto more elaborate topologies.

Anatomical reference has completely dropped out of the psychical apparatus of *The Interpretation of Dreams*: cathected ideas replace cathected neurons. There is a more sophisticated awareness of the figurative aspect of the model, combined with an explicit subordination of the explanation derived from topographic-economic premises to interpretation, which guides the construction of the system without being contained within it. The concrete work of both patient and analyst, however, remains outside 'schematic' transcription (*FP*: 88). The emphasis is placed firmly on the substitution of a clearer for an obscure text, with the recurrent analogy of translation. The equivocal 'effect-sign' can be contained within a 'general semiology' (*FP*: 89–90). But this operates at two levels: revealing what is fulfilled in the dream, whose content remains constant whether latent or manifest; and understanding the processes of the dreamwork. Here we get a concentration on the phenomenon of regression: the energetics as a mode of disclosure of the prior and, crucially, of an active barrier of repression. Ricoeur is very acute on the 'intersection of energy and force' (*FP*: 91). A phrase such as 'the fulfilment of the repressed' joins the ethical discourse of satisfaction with the physical discourse of repression: the term censorship implies both the imposition of blanks into a text and an expression of coercive power. Overdetermination implies an operation of meaning involving condensation and displacement which can be compared to 'rhetorical procedures' (*FP*: 93), but these same terms inhabit the discourse of force as compression and transference of power. Ricoeur switches the emphasis from sexual symbolism to regard for representability, in order to avoid getting ensnared in Freud's own extremely restrictive definition of the symbol. There is very little respect for the oneiric *per se*: it is the raw material rather than the productive source of creativity: 'dreams make use of a symbolism, they do not elaborate it' (*FP*: 100). Thus analysis is sharply distinguished from symbolic interpretation; and the interesting problematic will arise not from these 'vestiges' (*FP*: 102) but from the issue of their relation to representation.

Ricoeur then advances to the *Papers on Metapsychology*, in which he finds a coherent thematisation of the first topography (conscious; preconscious; unconscious); and a new analysis of the two directions of the *Triebvorstellung* (instinct-idea): from consciousness to the vicissitude of instinct, and then the reverse movement into representation. It is proposed that there are two modalities of the unconscious: the first as adjectival, recognised in relation to consciousness, the non-known that can be reconstructed from signs; the second as substantive, with dynamic attributes (posthypnotic suggestion, hysteria, psychopathology), constituted by thoughts barred from consciousness rather than merely latent in relation to it. Thus the first becomes the preconscious, accessible to description; the second the unconscious demanding systematisation (dreams establish it not only as a locality, but also as having its own '*legality*' (*FP*: 119), autonomous laws that must be posited in themselves). Consciousness becomes a 'truncated, lacunary text' to be rendered intelligible through seeing the unconscious as 'a work of interpolation that introduces meaning and connection into the text' (*FP*: 120). In contrast to Husserl's 'reduction *to* consciousness', Freud performs a 'reduction *of* consciousness' (*FP*: 121–22). The consequence of this 'epoche in reverse' is that the subject–object pole is suspended in favour of the aim of instincts which are governed by the constancy principle of pleasure–unpleasure: 'the notion of object is recast in accordance with the economic distribution of libido' (*FP*: 125). Similarly the ego itself may be treated as an object of instincts, subject to the 'same market-place of cathexis' (*FP*: 133).

So once we have been suitably disabused of the 'prejudice of consciousness' (*FP*: 117) how do we achieve knowledge of the unconscious? This hinges on the presupposition of a common structure of psychic representations on both sides of the barrier between conscious and unconscious systems. The instincts are never known in themselves, in their biological reality, but must remain on the level of postulate. Ricoeur draws two conclusions. First, their 'irreducible character' demonstrates that 'the language of force can never be overcome by the language of meaning' (*FP*: 149); secondly, because the pure economics can only be realised in the realm of the sayable, there can be no hypostatised theory of the unnameable of desire. Thus in this detailed and at times laborious analysis, Ricoeur has absorbed the decentring of the conscious, but maintained the link through the continued necessity of representation with the role of conscious interpretation. There can be an autonomy ascribed to the unconscious – various empirical and methodological reasons demand it – but this is still the result of interpretation applied to intermediaries of the two systems.

The second cycle, 'The interpretation of culture', presents Freud's cultural critique as an analogical transposition of the economic explanation, pleasure/unpleasure, and other transposable features such as wish-fulfilment; the disguise of the dreamwork, paradigm of stratagems of desire; the embodiment of infantile wishes, exemplified in the phenomenon of regression; and the symbolic language of desire. There are counter-balancing problems: what provides the analogue in the waking sphere to such concepts as instinctual narcissism, the dream-work, and regression, and if symbols in dreams are culturally derived, how is their original production to be accounted for? Nevertheless, *The Interpretation of Dreams* is acknowledged as providing a technique for revealing the 'nocturnal life', that may be 'generalised to the dimensions of a universal poetics' (*FP*: 162).

In stark contrast to Lacan, this transposition is seen as an 'expansion and deepening' (rather than a 'betrayal') that establishes the sphere of validity of psychoanalysis: it has an unlimited field but sharply demarcated boundaries to its perspective founded on the topographic-economic model. It will deal with ideals and illusions as fundamentally derivative, dependent on the vicissitudes of instincts, figures on an economic balance-sheet of pleasure and unpleasure, with the constituent purpose of wish-fulfilment. This view is seen as 'fragmentary, though extremely penetrating in the narrowness of its attack' (*FP*: 155).

Secondly, the influence is two-way: the analogical transposition has influenced the original model. This is crucial in the transition to the second topography of ego–id–superego. Ricoeur argues that the first topography is sufficient motivation for psychoanalysis: the second represents not merely a reworking but a fundamental revision so as to take account of the nonlibidinal factor of culture. The first deals with instinct, the second with renunciation: the first is fundamentally solipsistic, the second deals with a libido situated within culture in a variety of roles.

Ricoeur approaches Freud's treatment of art not in search of a developed theory of aesthetics, but for the hints it might offer of a more sympathetic treatment of religion as a 'nonobsessional, non-neurotic form of substitute satisfaction' whose 'charm ... does not stem from the return of the repressed' (FP: 163) (though this in turn must be denigrated by the standard of truth set up by scientific rationality). There is no analytic context for the interpretation, no free association or intersubjective relation: therefore no direct transposition of the categories of dream is possible. A relation is established between the pleasure the work gives rise to and the pleasure it employs: it allows us to enjoy fantasies without shame, as a 'detonator of profound discharges' (FP: 167). But specific studies such as 'The Moses of Michelangelo', though suggestive, remain inconclusive: what gives the art-work permanence in contrast to the sterile transience of the dream? How does it serve as not merely a regressive symbol of unresolved conflict, but also a 'sketch of the solution' (FP: 175)? And at what point does its capacity for prospective meaning override the economics of desire?

At this point, Ricoeur is content to bypass the issue of creativity, and regard a Freudian aesthetics as solely concerned with an equilibrium of pleasure. He is more interested in grounding the teleological emphasis of his final section. To this end he turns his attention to the sublime, which he enlarges to include 'the process by which man, with his desires, effects the ideal, the supreme' (FP: 178). This involves a displacement of attention from the repressed to that which represses. This 'makes its appearance as a prior social fact' (FP: 178): the question of authority is inevitably cultural. (Ricoeur insists on the social implications of the Oedipus complex to the extent of seeing an active repression of them in The Interpretation of Dreams.) To assimilate this new material psychoanalysis has to have recourse to the genetic (as opposed to the timelessness of the unconscious): the history of desire. The consideration of ethical phenomena leads to new analytic formulations, and a virtual decomposition of conscience. Now the 'true problematic' of the ego is 'expressed basically in the alternative of dominating or being dominated, of being master or slave' (FP:

181); consciousness on the other hand is a 'being-for-the-outside', perceptual, a surface phenomenon. Man is perpetually 'threatened from within': the ego is primarily that which is 'weak in the face of menace'. This holds not only for the neurotic but also for the moral man. 'Man's relation to obligation is first described in a situation of weakness, of nondomination' (*FP*: 183), and it is in this 'striking affinity' to Nietzsche that psychoanalysis makes its most penetrating analysis of morality: a condition of vulnerability and fear which Freud transcribes in the ego–superego relation. The superego becomes a scornful observer and abuser of the ego, yet also serves as an ideal to emulate. Thus where Kant speaks of a pathology of desire, Freud responds with the 'pathology of duty' deriving from this process of 'observation, condemnation and idealisation' (*FP*: 185). By rejecting the 'primordial givenness of the ethical ego', Freud's account concentrates exclusively on the 'internalisation of the external' (*FP*: 186), and so can be readily linked to Nietzsche and, as Ricoeur's vocabulary suggests, to Hegel.

The theme of prehistory occurs in a multitude of guises: the indestructibility of wishes, the timelessness of the unconscious, the belatedness of consciousness itself. The crux of Ricoeur's argument is that Freud's excursions into ethnology, however empirically ill-founded and populist, become the occasion for major revisions of the original topology. He freely acknowledges that such texts as *Totem and Taboo* and *Moses and Monotheism* pillage a wide range of contemporary anthropology for disparate Oedipal elements: the most severe indictment offered, however, is 'an impressive number of hazardous hypotheses' (*FP*: 245). The value of the text is seen as located in its introduction of the work of the negative in the form of the liberating crime, and the problem of institution (for example, how the taboo against fratricide arose out of an original parricide). The 'change from war to law' shifts the 'whole problematic' from 'the birth of the Oedipus complex' to 'its dissolution in the building-up of the superego' (*FP*: 211). The Oedipus complex deciphered in myth and history must now have its 'corresponding energy distribution' stated in topographic and economic terms.

Freud's explanation of the relation of sublimation, idealisation and identification remains piecemeal; their common linkage to the Oedipus complex is never analysed; and the crucial role of identification, with the lost object in melancholia and with the father in the Oedipal complex, is never addressed. Ricoeur singles out one issue in particular: 'how can the regressive character of narcissistic identification accord with the structuring function of the identification that results in the superego?' (*FP*: 217). A lot hinges on this apparently recondite question: notably the relation of archaeology and teleology, the capacity to create new meaning, and the possibility of a benign transformation of the father. Freud makes a rather inconclusive division of identification into benign emulation, appropriative object choice, and neutral projection (as in hysteria). In *The Ego and the Id* there remains a disjunction between the origin of the superego in parental authority and its tapping of energy sources in the id: the necessary identification of the father with the abandonment of object-cathexes in the lost object is never made. Essentially the discussion reaches an impasse because of the lack of a factor of negativity taken from another instinctual source that will produce a progressive element lacking in the mere internal differentiation of the id. Freud's increasing emphasis on the severity of the parental threat of punishment provides considerable incentive for detachment to occur, but this remains incomplete without the introduction of the death instinct.

Ricoeur now returns to the problematic of religion, repeating his initial premise that though the psychoanalytic critique might provide 'a faith purified of all idolatory' (*FP*: 230), the question of 'whether the destruction of idols is without remainder' falls outside its competence (*FP*: 235). Freud equates religious observance with obsessive behaviour, and Ricoeur concedes 'many clusters of resemblance' (*FP*: 232), such as punctilious regard for esoteric and trivial detail. But he argues that religion only becomes 'neurotic ceremonial' (*FP*: 232) when it loses contact with its own founding symbolism, and that the gap between private obsession and public religion remains unbridged by Freud. Secondly, he argues for illusion as a necessary compensation. In the ethical sphere, ideals represent an internalisation of authority in the impersonal manner of the imperative; in the religious the image of the father is elevated into equally penal status. Illusion is the result of 'complicity between wish-fulfillment and unverifiability', and serves as 'the point of return of fantasies to their primal expression' (*FP*: 234). Freud deals not with the truth of religion, but with its function in balancing renunciation and satisfaction within the harshness of life. But the scale of the analysis is vast compared to individual fantasy: it must be grounded in an 'Oedipus complex of the species' (*FP*: 235).

Though Freud's analogies between psychological phases and cultural stages are weak in the extreme, he acutely singles out 'the first religious problematic' as one of omnipotence (*FP*: 238). Religion deals with the emotional consequence of the murder of the father and attempts reconciliation with him, but also contains a 'disguised remembrance of triumph'. Thus its 'history does not constitute an advance, a discovery, a development, but is the sempiternal repetition of its own origins' (*FP*: 243). Freud refuses to distinguish between (utilitarian) civilisation and (educative) culture: both are assessed on the same cathectic balance-sheet. He dwells on the harshness of life: the subjection of the ego, the primacy of fear, the incompatibility of narcissistic fulfilment with the task of culture. Ricoeur argues that religion may be seen as the 'benevolent visage' of culture (*FP*: 250). It promises alleviation through repeating the prototype of all figures of consolation: 'because he is forever helpless *like a child* that man remains stricken with longing for the father' (*FP*: 251). Through the image of a paternal deity, nature may be appeased and influenced: 'desire is what creates religion, even more than fear' (*FP*: 251). The projection of a personalised relation serves the same function as other aspects of culture, of defence against nature. This detaches religion from moral prescription, and aligns it with consolation: its role is to protect as well as to prohibit.

The third cycle of Ricoeur's detailed exegesis of Freud is based on the 'recasting from top to bottom' (*FP*: 255) compelled by the emergence of the death instinct in *Beyond the Pleasure Principle*. Broadly speaking, this is seized upon as providing a quasi-Hegelian negation that subsists outside the pleasure–unpleasure cathexis and compels it to accommodate a concept of progression. This occurs on the level of psychoanalytic discourse; of interpretation of the semantics of desire; and of the theory of culture. There is a drastic shift from the quantitative mental physics to a quasi-Romantic, even pre-Socratic mythology (*FP*: 256): 'under the coating of a scientific surface there arises the Naturphilosophie' remythicised in the contemporary guise of metabiology (*FP*: 313). The libido is relabelled Eros, coupled with the opposing force of Thanatos; and the reality principle itself is transformed into Ananke. The relative simplification involved has often provoked protest. Might not awareness of, access to, the unconscious be best served by the comparatively fragmentary method of analogy? Must Freud's work be seen as a progressive deepening of insight? Might it not lose the obstinate decentring of its naturalism if it relinquishes a literal-minded grip on cathexis? One may at least suspect Ricoeur of a covert privileging of the 'single and strong idea ... global and sovereign' (*FP*: 258) of the mythological mode.

Ricoeur firstly seeks to establish the relationship between the pleasure and the reality principle, notably the shifting meanings of the latter with its 'rather considerable margin' between the perceptual function and the submission to necessity (*FP*: 256). With the introduction of the death instinct, 'what at first was merely a principle of "mental regulation" now becomes the cypher of a possible wisdom' (*FP*: 262). Reality, taken as a synonym for environmental adaptation, can be seen as 'a roundabout path to satisfaction' (*FP*: 264) and hence the complement or outcome of the pleasure principle. Yet the pleasure principle can equally well be seen as infinitely resourceful in the ruses of its figurative and substitutive mode of satisfaction, hence reality becomes a virtually unattainable object. At its solipsistic extreme, 'hallucinatory satisfaction is a biological impasse' (*FP*: 265).

Secondly, in object choice, reality 'entails renunciation and mourning over archaic objects' (*FP*: 271). The theory of stages attempts to narrate a history of desire in these terms. With regard to sexual libido, it entails recognition of the desire of the other and submission of the individual to the species: thus it is 'difficult and precarious' through 'structural necessity' (*FP*: 273). Object-choice is both 'prospective and nostalgic' (*FP*: 273): the refinding of a lost happiness in another object. The importance of the Oedipal complex lies in desire's wish for the impossible, the fact that it is 'necessarily disappointed and wounded' (*FP*: 274). Hence 'this loss or renunciation, together with all the pruning it involves of the realm of fantasy, turns the theme of reality toward that of necessity' (*FP*: 276). Thus the ego must adopt a 'conciliatory or diplomatic position', and become 'a mediatory creature, more courtier than arbiter, which must make itself beloved by the id to make the id pliable to the world's order' (*FP*: 278–9). Without this 'prudence principle' the ego would fall prey to the excessive demands of the superego. This is the 'culmination of the reality principle' and therefore 'in sum the ethics of psychoanalysis' (*FP*: 278). The psychoanalyst operates a similar mitigation; his 'abstention from all moral preaching' shields the patient through 'the substitution of a neutral regard in place of condemnation' (*FP*: 279–80). The refusal to denigrate the values of utility and prudence ('not the whole of ethics but ... its threshold' (*FP*: 280)) should be compared with Wittgenstein's verdict of ethically squalid. Ricoeur sees a courageous unmasking of the seductions of condemnation in this abstention from judgement, a kind of charity in that prudence, a generosity to the health of the other.

Now Ricoeur switches his attention to the death instinct which, he reminds us, emerged not out of the impulse to destroy but to repeat.

The pleasure principle has a sharply restricted sphere: elsewhere it is 'inefficient and even dangerous' (*FP*: 283). The postponement of pleasure can be seen as a 'roundabout path' to later satisfaction; and even 'neurotic suffering' can serve 'as the mask that the most archaic pleasure adopts in order to assert itself in spite of everything' (*FP*: 284). Thus the 'circumstances that confirm the pleasure principle are also the ones that weaken it'. The clinching argument appears to be the wilful repetition of past suffering as present experience: tolerating the unpleasure of remembering cannot be assimilated to the pleasure principle. But this only leads to the insertion of a prior principle, borrowed from Breuer, of binding free energy: the compulsion to repeat represents a re-enacted opportunity to achieve this mastery. Ricoeur lays the stress in the well-known fort-da episode on the positive creation of symbolism out of absence in play: the nonpathological instinct of repetition as mastery of the negative. The 'decisive breakthrough' comes in the extrapolation of '*an urge inherent in organic life to restore an earlier state of things*' (*FP*: 289); the earliest being, of course, inertia. Ricoeur insists on the relation of Eros to the other – 'in the living substance *by itself* he finds only death' (*FP*: 291) – to the point of regarding it as a principle of social cohesion. There is a further complication in the 'dramatic *overlapping of roles*' (*FP*: 292); everything is death because self-preservation is only a detour in the pursuit of one's death, but everything is life because narcissism, the obstruction of survival and reproduction, is Eros. The instinct is, however, 'mute': Freud cannot establish 'equivalence between what is deciphered and what has been conjectured' (*FP*: 294), and is therefore obliged to extend the sphere of interpretable signs to war to provide a visible manifestation of 'the clamor of death' (*FP*: 306).

This 'replacement of the compulsion to repeat by destructiveness' through 'the switch from a metabiology to a metaculture' (*FP*: 296) compels another revision of the original topography, this time in the sphere of sado-masochism. *The Ego and the Id* develops the concepts of fusion and defusion 'to state in energy language what happens when an instinct places its energy at the service of forces working in different systems' (*FP*: 297): 'the harshness and cruelty' of the superego becomes 'charged with destructive rage thanks to the defusion of the death instinct' (*FP*: 298–9). Ricoeur draws a striking analogy between the ego caught between a murderous id and a punishing conscience forced to self-torment or the torturing of others, and the 'religious extension of this ethical cruelty in the projection of a higher being who punishes inexorably' (*FP*: 299): hence such paradoxical concepts as the unconscious sense of guilt, resistance to recovery, the need for punishment. Ricoeur is quite prepared to countenance the argument of *Civilisation and Its Discontents* that unhappiness exceeds any erotics due to 'the primordial hostility of man toward man' (*FP*: 305). This involves a new interpretation of guilt as restraint: self-violence is employed to curb violence against others and so 'by mortifying the individual, culture places death in the service of love' (*FP*: 308). A fairly horrific paradox, but one whose anti-libertarian implications seem congenial to Ricoeur.

Beyond the Pleasure Principle demonstrates that all direct speculation about the instincts is *per se* 'mythical' (*FP*: 311). Ricoeur posits the death instinct to be an assemblage of disparate elements: 'the inertia of life, the compulsion to repeat, destructiveness'. These possess a 'normal nonpathological expression, the disappearing-reappearing in which the elevation of fantasy to symbol consists' (*FP*: 314). The mastery of negation in play is evidence of a broader 'negativity in consciousness': firstly in the resistance that must be overcome in the process of self-awareness; secondly in reality-testing, going beyond the demands of the pleasure principle. Ricoeur wishes to elicit a work of the negative situated in the place of but not identified with the death instinct: the evidence is nearly as piecemeal as Freud's own, and constantly tempted towards a 'direct Hegelian translation' (*FP*: 317).

Ricoeur notes that the binding of energy already posits something prior to the pleasure principle; and more penetratingly, that the death-instinct itself is the logical extension of the principle of constancy, inertia to inertia. The definition of pleasure itself dissolves: the initial assumption of 'the discharge of tensions within an isolated apparatus' could only apply to autoerotic sexuality and is contradicted by the intersubjective contexts of both analysis and sexual development.

> If man could be satisfied, he would be deprived of something more important than pleasure – symbolization, which is the counterpart of dissatisfaction. Desire, qua insatiable demand, gives rise to speech. The semantics of desire . . . is bound up with this postponement of satisfaction, with this endless mediating of pleasure.
>
> (*FP*: 322)

It is difficult not to see 'symbolisation' as having the inevitable addendum 'of the sacred' (though this emphasis on the substitutive and inherently self-defeating nature of desire is also extremely Lacanian). Ricoeur very justly emphasises the crudity of Freud's pleasure when set against the finely nuanced variety of pain: this 'disparity between the diversity of suffering and the monotony of enjoyment' (*FP*: 323) appears to show an underlying pessimism, that we must all bear 'the excess of suffering with resignation' (*FP*: 324).

Initially reality is identified with the useful, environmental adaptation. The opposition between desire and reality is radically transformed with the new theory of instincts: the meaning of pleasure opens up, and reality is seen as containing death. Not the death instinct, however, but the necessity of personal death. There remains a fundamental tension between Freud's ameliorative post-religious rationality and his own exposure of destructive force against and within the ethical. The consoling father-figure must be replaced by the acceptance of chance and of the absence of relation between nature and human desire. Ricoeur relates this to Spinoza's and Nietzsche's *amor fati* as 'the victory of love of the whole over my narcissism, over my fear of dying, over the resurgence in me of childhood consolation' (*FP*: 328). We expect a payoff: none is forthcoming except a somewhat untrustworthy interposing of aesthetic pleasure as intermediary between religion and scientific reality. 'Nothing indicates that Freud finally harmonized the theme of the reality principle with the the theme of Eros': the ideal of 'lucidity free of illusion' compels acceptance of death as 'one of the necessities of blind nature', but this is balanced by the demand to 'struggle against the human instinct of aggression and self-destruction, hence never to love death, but to love life, in spite of my death' (pp. 337–8). Is this a restrictive judgement: philosophy can make clear the failed reconciliation of psychoanalysis, its lack of self-reflection? Or is this 'fine discordance' between the critical and lyrical 'the essence of the philosophical tone of Freudianism' (*FP*: 325), offered as some kind of fundamental human paradox which must be lived rather than conceptually resolved? When Ricoeur defends Freud is it in spite or because of this crucial aporia? The third book, 'The dialectic', may perhaps be regarded as his own intervention against the seduction of this fine and dignified and unresolvable impasse.

LACAN AND THE EPISTEMOLOGY OF PSYCHOANALYSIS

Ricoeur initially seeks to define the epistemological status of psychoanalysis in relation to both scientific psychology and phenomenology, and thereby establish its legitimacy as an essentially hermeneutic discipline. This may be compared to Lacan's diatribes against ego psychology as not only a retreat from but a perversion of Freud's original insights. Ricoeur's critique of this tradition is, I think, not only more respectful, and more precise, but ultimately more devastating in its exposure of the codification of the metapsychology. The scientific assimilation of Freud, however sympathetic, runs into problems at an early stage; and Ricoeur brings out with exemplary clarity the aporias produced by 'the temptation to blend psychoanalysis into a general psychology along behaviourist lines' (*FP*: 344).

According to positivist criteria, psychoanalysis does not satisfy even the most 'elementary requirements of a scientific theory': the response of the psychoanalytic community has been either 'flight', 'the adduction of additional scientific criteria', or attempts at 'reformulation' (*FP*: 345).

The first charge is that Freudian energy theory, its use of the constancy principle for psychic forces, is incapable of empirical verification: though suggestive, it is so vague and metaphorical that its 'invincible ambiguity' becomes impossible to refute (*FP*: 346). Secondly, there is no clear definition of the conditions on which an interpretation is valid: is it because it is acceptable to the patient, because it improves the condition of the patient, or because it is objectively coherent? To satisfy scientific requirements, independent inquirers must have access to the same data under standardised conditions; there must be a means of adjudicating between rival interpretations; and diagnosis must lead to verifiable predictions. Needless to say, the intersubjective relation of analyst and patient, with all the variables of transference and counter-transference, are wholly insusceptible to such demands for comparative procedures and statistical corroboration.

Ricoeur finds this 'unanswerable' if psychoanalysis is placed alongside the observational sciences. He then examines attempts at 'operational reconversion' of psychoanalysis to meet these demands (*FP*: 347). These claim that its subject-matter of behaviour is not different in kind from psychology; or only in the secondary aspect of its stress on latent motives. It shares the principle of the integration and

wholeness of behaviour; and similar interconnections may be established between all levels of the human psychic system. Freud's metapsychology is then broken up into a series of sub-models: the
topographic is assimilated to the reflex arc; the economic viewpoint to
the entropic context of tension and tension reduction. The theory of
stages and the role of fixation and regression are assimilated to the
evolution of learning systems, with greater emphasis on the formative
impact of early experiences. Finally this is assimilated to a hierarchy
of integrations, with systems of a higher level controlling those of a
lower.

These models can be shown to have substantial common ground
with other contemporary schools of psychology: behaviour is
regarded as part of a genetic series; it involves unconscious determinants; it is controlled by drives; it draws on and is regulated by
psychological energy; it is determined by reality, or an adaptive
function to environment. Thus psychoanalysis can be assimilated
fairly comfortably: its distinctiveness lies in its stress on the entropic
model, in its privileging of instinctual effects over sensory learning
and experience, and refusal of priority to the adaptive function of the
ego.

Ricoeur insists on the complete inappropriateness of demanding a
translation of concepts derived from the situation of language in the
analytic context into observables, perception and response (for
example, the absurdity of seeking to 'distinguish *real* sex, subject to
observation, from sex merely *statable* in the framework of Freud's
translation rules' (*FP*: 357)). 'A psychology of positivist inspiration'
is unable to 'furnish an equivalent of relations of signifier to signified
that place psychoanalysis among the hermeneutic sciences' (*FP*:
358). The subtle delineation of the language of motive in analytic
philosophy (see Toulmin, 1948) – first-person proclamations,
reported reasons, causal (physiological) motivation, and finally psychoanalytic explanation – are enlisted to support his distinction
between psychoanalysis and the observational sciences. An adequate
account must comply with the conditions of being a plausibly stated
motive for the patient, for a third party plausibly reported; for the
analyst, plausibly causal; and receiving a final acceptance from the
patient. Ricoeur sees the strength of this analysis as lying in its respect
for the 'hybrid character of psychoanalysis' (*FP*: 347): its use of
motive in so far as it deals with psychical reality, but its resemblance
to causal explanation in its topographic aspect. Without this recognition, he goes on to suggest, one of three alternatives must be

adopted: to regard Freudian practice, concerned with motives, as contradicting its theory, with its hinterland of unverifiable psychic causes; to assign it completely to the area of motives, and regard Freud's contribution as having extended the region of latent and unacknowledged intentions – hence the unconscious becomes a series of unconscious motives; and finally to reduce analytic discourse to empirical propositions, and to regard the motive/cause distinction as one of kind rather than degree (see Flew, 1949; 1956). So Ricoeur is in the delicate position of wanting to situate psychoanalysis among the human sciences of interpretation while preserving some of its decentring force as a causal and necessitarian explanation. Later he will emphasise the positive structuration achieved by the patient in the narrative of his own life: here he stresses the distinction between scientific data and 'signifiers for the history of desire' (*FP*: 364): 'the analyst does not observe, he interprets' (*FP*: 365).

Ricoeur acknowledges considerable overlap between his position and Lacan's critique of 'behaviourist reformulations of psychoanalysis', but distinguishes his hermeneutic reading by its refusal to 'eliminate the energy concepts in favour of linguistics' (*FP*: 367). For Lacan these represent an obsolete mental hydraulics: more appropriate terminologies can be borrowed from contemporary disciplines such as anthropology, mathematics, and above all linguistics. For Ricoeur they played a crucial role in both overriding the language of motive, and in providing a prospective model from which a kind of quasi-causality may be elicited. 'The search for meaning in a place that is off-center with respect to apparent meaning' still involves a conscious pursuit by an intentionality directed towards self-understanding and positive restructuring. For Lacan, analytic discourse is the sphere in which the false pretensions of the cogito are laid bare: the hermeneutic vantage is rendered impossible by the impersonal operations of the signifier (though these are arbitrarily restricted to a methodological level that precludes the question of the subject). For Ricoeur there is nothing inherently desubjectivised in the relation of signifier and signified comparable to Lacan's autonomous chains of signification. These at times extremely direct transpositions of structural linguistics (another less intertextual age might have called them plagiarisms) are actually employed by Lacan to rescientise the claims made for his own practice of psychoanalysis, but without in any way addressing the epistemological requirements previously listed. And while a Lacanian might argue that the application of such criteria is merely a desperate pre-emptive strike, designed to shield the self from recognising its fragmentation and contingency, the questions still remain to be answered. Whether or not structural linguistics qualifies for the title of science (and the simple fact that its object of study is language itself leads it into some insoluble paradoxes concerning metalanguages (see *RM*: 143–8)), the arbitrary appropriation of its terminology certainly does not have that effect. Lacan, it must be acknowledged, constantly raises the issue of the border-line status of psychoanalysis (e.g. 1977a: 19, 47, 265; and 1977b: 57, 92, 148); but this must be set against his practice of explicitly claiming binding logical and mathematical status for his formulations (e.g. 1977b: 306, 313).

Ricoeur's discussion of overdetermination as a relation of meaning to a lost object is decidedly Lacanian (*FP*: 368–9), as is his insistence that 'absence is not a secondary aspect of behaviour, but the very place where psychoanalysis dwells' (*FP*: 369). He protests equally vigorously against reifying 'instinctual representatives' as factual determinants rather than the product of a 'signifying dimension'. There is a forceful rejection of any mitigation of the 'scandal of psychoanalysis'. The 'question of adaptation' is necessarily posed on the basis of 'reified ideals', that refuse to acknowledge the possibility of disjunction with the practical dealings of any given society (*FP*: 373). The specific strength of psychoanalysis is its painful recognition of 'frustrated demands': hence its sombreness and overall mood of pessimism. There is a similarly absolute divide between the reality principle as primarily adaptive and regarded as a 'struggle for self-recognition' (*FP*: 371). 'The abandoned object' has brought 'absence into the very makeup of the ego' (*FP*: 372). Lacan uses the same pieces, notably 'Mourning and melancholia', to establish a similar incompletion and instability in the ego: what is absent, however, is Ricoeur's (and Freud's) stress on coping-with. Mourning is not simply the acknowledgement of the object as lost: it is the coming to terms with and going beyond this 'internalised absence' (*FP*: 372).

This leads on to the most specific and damaging criticism of Lacan. The problem with the famous dictum, 'the unconscious is structured like a language', is, as Ricoeur notes, 'to assign an appropriate meaning to the word "like"' (*FP*: 400). Although analysis moves 'entirely within the element of language', it brings to light another discourse governed by rules of symbolisation and substitution: 'properly speaking, are the laws of that other discourse linguistic laws'? (*FP*: 397). Lacan, as is well known, offers an 'interpretation of condensation as metaphor and displacement as metonymy' (Lacan,

1977b: 158). This, it should be noted, substantially alters Jakobson's work on aphasia, from which it is often assumed to derive its authority: here it is suggested that contiguity should be equated with 'Freud's metonymic "displacement" and synecdochic "condensation"' and similarity with 'Freud's identification and symbolism' (1987: 113). Broadly speaking, however, the detailed criticism to which Ricoeur submits Jakobson's argument in *The Rule of Metaphor* (1975a: 175–80) is still applicable. The argumentative convenience of the schema is achieved only at the cost of restricting the entire linguistic field to two tropes. It is posited, according to the fallacious principle of a hierarchical organisation, that these are equally dominant at every level; though contiguity, for example, is a markedly different phenomenon on the level of predication from that of the concatenation of morphemes. Rather than attempt to remedy the fundamental shortcomings of his model, Lacan accentuates its extreme restrictiveness; and consequently his transposition of tropic structures onto psychic processes invites dismissal as both crude and misleading.

Ricoeur proceeds to enumerate the features that distinguish the dream text from ordinary language. The first is its 'absence of logic, their ignorance of No' (which must be distinguished from repression, 'the prior refusal of admission' (*FP*: 397)). The representations in a dream are 'signifying' but 'not yet linguistic' (*FP*: 398); a presentation of things rather than of words, which themselves frequently dissolve into pictorial images. Freud's own explanations are related to fantasy and images rather than speech, focusing on 'a signifying power that is operative prior to language' (*FP*: 398). In addition they operate on both the supra-linguistic level of fable, legend, and myth, and the infra-linguistic one of condensation and displacement, and so are best regarded as 'paralinguistic distortions of ordinary language' (*FP*: 404). It is also pointed out that the original signifier (S) comes to occupy the position of both signifier and signified, 'a situation for which there is no linguistic parallel' (*FP*: 404), once it has been replaced by a substitute signified and reduced to a latent signifier. Ricoeur preserves a healthy scepticism about the value of such 'jumbling', and remains equally unconvinced by claims for the creative power of the unconscious.

It is against the algebraic inscription of relations of the signifier that Ricoeur scores his most resounding success. He does not reject the legitimacy of

$$S'/S \times S/s \text{ or } S'/S/s$$

as a 'useful schema' for 'stimulating reflection about the *bar*' (*FP*: 402). This is not only a 'linguistic phenomenon' but also that which 'expresses repression which impedes transition to a higher system' (*FP*: 402). The Lacanian formulation depends on a 'force of exclusion' to sustain its own extended parallelisms: striking testimony, as Ricoeur says, to the 'irreducibility of the energy aspect' (*FP*: 404). Thus Lacan's attempt to equate the role of the dynamics in Freud's thought, its force, life energy, to the ancillary effects of the functioning of an autonomous linguistic system ('desire is only that which I have called the metonymy of signification' (Lacan, 1970: 194) 'in the drive there is no question of kinetic energy . . . . The discharge in question is of quite a different nature and is on quite a different plane' (Lacan, 1977a: 165)) is refuted by his own formula. The attempt to equate metaphor and repression within a single schema fails because the 'barrier' preserves a 'double nature': as both 'a relation between signifying or signified factors and as a force for exclusion between dynamic systems' (*FP*: 404). (The formula is borrowed from Laplanche and Pontalis rather than taken directly from Lacan; but the subsequent fiercely contested polemics hinge on a single relatively minor point, the scholastic intricacies of the double inscription theory (when an idea is repressed, is it literally moved or is a duplicate taken?), and Ricoeur's observations about the unacknowledged presence of an energy factor in a linguistic equation are equally relevant. (For fuller discussion see Lacan's preface to Lemaire, 1977: xii–xiii; and also Gallop, 1985: 114–32.)

This concludes one of the most beautifully sustained pieces of argumentation in the book. It coordinates a series of arguments from a positivist tradition of psychology, acknowledges their local coherence, but then directs them towards a radically different conclusion. The specifically hermeneutic response called for by the 'mixed constitution' of psychoanalytic thought comes across far more powerfully here than in the introduction. There it was announced in the context of a putative 'unification': here it is allowed to emerge gradually from the accumulation of aporias that emerge from the attempt to redefine analysis according to behaviourist principles. So we get a linguistic Freud, but not one whose insights involve the total subversion of all principles of coherence: instead an unlikely alliance is formed whereby transcendental deduction is employed to 'order and systematise analytic experience' and so establish '*the conditions of possibility of a semantics of desire*' (*FP*: 375). The criterion of adaptability is forcefully rebutted in the name of a reality principle equated with reflective self-consciousness, but the idea of the self-that-is-to-come has undergone considerable modification in the light of Freud's tutelage.

ARCHAEOLOGY AND TELEOLOGY

Ricoeur now goes on to address the archaeology of the subject. He initially points out that 'Freud very clearly ignores and rejects any problematic of the primal and fundamental subject' (*FP*: 420). Within the topography there is no privileged element: each presupposes and leads onto the others. Freud's naturalism becomes a strategy of dispossession, a making 'completely homeless' (*FP*: 422). The three stages of this ascesis are: the acceptance of the unconscious; the abandonment of the object, now recognised as 'the mere variable of the aim of an instinct'; and the acknowledgement of narcissism, which reduces the ego to the object of desire. Combined they represent 'the necessary discipline of an anti-phenomenology', whose 'first task – the displacement – cannot be separated from the second task – the recapture of meaning in interpretation' (*FP*: 423–4). Because an instinct is a biological unknowable, it can only enter the mind through ideational representation: and this preserves an 'affinity of meaning' across the barrier between conscious and unconscious (*FP*: 429). This both gives evidence that the psychical exceeds apperception; and conversely implies it 'cannot be defined apart from the possibility, however distant or difficult it may be, of becoming conscious' (*FP*: 430).

Ricoeur then proceeds to develop a Kantian critique of the concepts of psychoanalysis: to justify them by 'their power of regulating a new domain of objectivity and intelligibility'. Within this context, the 'realism of the unconscious' can be made not only legitimate, but even respectable. The metapsychology determines the field of investigation; analysis is not interminable; there is a grammar of psychic configurations, a finite number of combinations; and these require an endorsement of the mechanistic laws governing the unconscious. The following premises are offered as sufficient conditions for avoiding any 'naïve realism of giving the unconscious a consciousness, of reduplicating consciousness in consciousness' (*FP*: 439). The reality of the topography constitutes itself within hermeneutics, but in a purely epistemological sense, existing relative to the rules of deciphering; the necessary interposition of the intersubjective relation with the analyst; and the singularity of the relation of transference with the analyst.

Ricoeur then goes on to characterise Freudianism as 'a revelation of the archaic, a manifestation of the ever prior' (*FP*: 440). There is a constant tension between the temporal nature of consciousness and the timelessness of the unconscious. Freud distinguishes three forms of regression: formal, from logic to pictorial form; temporal, to childhood; and topographical, the movement of an idea back from the perceptual pole, ending in hallucination. There is comparatively little attention to the potentially progressive aspects of secondary revision. It remains belated, relatively ineffectual compared to the indestructibility of the primary to which the dreamwork is ineluctably drawn. It must be supplemented by repression; this in turn leaves the self an ever-vulnerable prey to the infantile, the indestructible. The climax of the archaeology lies in the revelation of the omnipresence of primary narcissism, over which lie the sedimentations of its secondary forms.

The second topology employs an additional archaic agency – the superego – to that of the id: as the father-complex it has both progressive (educative, renouncing infancy) and regressive (punitive, encouraging dependence) aspects. The ambivalence of desire and fear extends into a psychopathology of taboo including the Kantian imperative: 'a precipitate of identification, hence of abandoned objects, but it is a precipitate that has the remarkable power of turning back against its own instinctual base' (*FP*: 450). Cumulatively, the 'modalities of archaism' form a complex figure of a destiny in reverse, a destiny that draws one backward' (*FP*: 452).

Ricoeur now insists on the archaeology having 'a relationship of dialectical opposition to the complementary concept of teleology' (*FP*: 459); there must be a new 'decentering that is prospective, directed towards the figure of the spirit for which Hegel's Phenomenology provides a model'. Dispossession is actual: reaffirmation, strangely hypothetical, with the perspective of absolute spirit discreetly elided. 'What is essential' occurs in the middle, the 'movement of the figures': 'master and slave, the stoic exile of thought, skeptical indifference, the unhappy consciousness' and so on (*FP*: 463). What matters is the encounter with meaning as both ahead of oneself and in a social realm. The true is disclosed only in the light of later figures: it is constituted by their advance. Thus the self is produced through a 'progressive synthesis' (*FP*: 463).

Ricoeur then points out some 'one-to-one' correspondences: the birth of culture in the movement of desire; the abandonment of the object as putting one's life at stake or the process of mourning; Freudian identification and Hegelian constitution of the self. The most important correlation is that of the resistance of the object of desire which can only be overcome by the transference onto another person who can respond, give recognition. So the problem of recognition by the other is an extension rather than sublation of the original desire. Ricoeur emphasises the element of savagery in this struggle: its presence in the realm of spirit in the form of violence: 'the positing of desire is mediated and eradicated: it is not a sphere that we could lay aside, annul, annihilate' (*FP*: 472). The truth of desire is known only retrospectively: all presents will contain their unknown that will similarly only be comprehended in the future; the *Unruhigkeit*, the restlessness of life, therefore ensures a movement of infinite openness. The opposition may be summed up in the following terms. Spirit has its meaning in later forms or figures; it is a movement that always destroys its starting point and is secured only in the end. The intelligibility of the unconscious, on the other hand, always proceeds from earlier figures, whether this anteriority is understood in a strictly temporal or in a metaphorical sense. 'Man is the sole being at the mercy of his childhood: he is a creature continually dragged back' (*FP*: 468).

'To put the antithesis most concisely . . . the spirit is history and the unconscious is fate' (*FP*: 468). Ricoeur appears to have reneged on the labour of the negative, the capacity of spirit to destroy the past rather than awaken as yet uncomprehended meanings within it; and also to have conveniently disregarded the strongly determinist elements of the dialectic that prevent it from being unproblematically identified with freedom. The continued presence of life and desire as 'initial positing, primal affirmation, immediate expansion' seem relatively easy to demonstrate: there appears nothing inimical to Hegel in preserving them as a motive force at higher stages. With Freud the question is more complex, particularly as Ricoeur has explicitly aligned his thought with regression, archaeology. It demands the exposition of 'an implicit and unthematized teleology within Freudianism', that would constitute 'an inverted image of Hegel' (*FP*: 461).

First an analogy is made between the analytic situation and the Hegelian struggle for recognition, somewhat overstated as a 'remarkable structural homology' (*FP*: 474). Secondly, the latent dialectical structure in Freud's use of opposition in concepts is stressed: ego–id, ego–superego, ego–world are all dependent relations demanding to be surpassed as in Hegel's master–slave dialectic. Thirdly the concept of identification is said to exceed its role in the meta-psychology: Ricoeur stresses the role of negativity as a means to educate and humanise desire, and the move from a solipsistic model to an inter-subjective realm involving a recognition of the desire of the other, or in the Hegelian phrase, a reduplication of consciousness. The 'educative' function of 'the loss of the object' places negation right at the heart of desire rather than as an external censorship; and Ricoeur goes on to correlate this with 'the death instinct, the mourning of desire, and the transition to symbols' (*FP*: 482). The problem is that this kind of posited 'emergence of self-consciousness' relegates the economic schema to a merely ancillary function on various stages of the ascending dialectic. Ricoeur nevertheless insists that the reduplication is essential to rescue the economic model from its implicit solipsism, the struggle between beings reduced to no more than a vicissitude of instincts.

With sublimation, Ricoeur is more or less interpolating a concept of his own invention onto an area where Freud's treatment is sketchy, to say the least. He distinguishes two primary aspects: as involved in the sublime or highest aspects of man, and as the symbolic instrument of the construction of this sublime. The first remains irreconcilable with the economic model. The superego both draws off the energy-reservoir of the id while at the same time being externally acquired, the image of paternal authority. The concept of sublimation thus contains an 'unbridgeable hiatus' (*FP*: 489) between the externality of law (because of the refusal of any inherent ethics in the ego) and the solipsism of desire, according to the economic model. The consequence of the absence of any adequate dialectical concept is that it cannot bring itself to acknowledge even a precipitate of ethical progression. Thus a relationship must be posited between 'desire and a source of valuation external to the field of energy', and also a 'pairing of subjectivities' to allow the ego to identify with its other (*FP*: 492). Both are required by the lacuna in Freud's cultural theory which has been previously demonstrated to be a direct transposition of the economic model. Two other demands are more complex: an original self-regard must be posited to allow identification to be included in the process of idealisation; and the loss of the object must be seen as an educative process rather than a compensatory illusion, with identification positing an outward-directed movement. Both of these suggest an 'aptitude for progression' unthematised on the level of the meta-psychology, and rendering the 'empty concept' of sublimation structurally necessary (*FP*: 488).

'Authentic symbols' are 'regressive-progressive; remembrance gives rise to anticipation; archaism gives rise to prophecy' (*FP*: 497). For reflection to become 'concrete' both aspects have to be fused into each other: symbols must 'conceal the aims of our instinct' through the same expression that 'discloses the process of self-consciousness'. Through their over-determination, they 'realize the concrete identity between the progression of the figures of the spirit or mind and the regression to the key signifiers of the unconscious' (*FP*: 497). This, as Ricoeur acknowledges, flies in the face of Freud's own treatment of the symbol as possessing a 'permanently fixed meaning in dreams, like the grammalogues in shorthand' (*FP*: 499). It is 'not the dream-work that constructs the symbolic relation but the work of culture' (*FP*: 500): hence the monotonous repetition of basic sexual motifs within a limitless variety of contexts. Ricoeur has to go in hard here to clear room for his own theory of overdetermination; and Freud's ingenuous borrowings of anthropological speculation on the sexual origin of language are almost cuttingly dismissed as 'certain supplementary but disastrous hypotheses' (*FP*: 501). (Though his own hierarchy is not exempt from challenge: an extended footnote discussing the work of Ernest Jones on symbol draws a rather haughty contrast between the 'immense symbolic domain explored by Western thought' and the 'pale metaphors of ordinary language and its rhetoric' (*FP*: 505).)

To substantiate this claim, Ricoeur offers one of his rare detailed readings of a literary text, and a concluding discussion of the paternal symbol central to Judaic and Christian theology. *The Symbolism of Evil* had offered a reading of *Oedipus Rex* as an exploration of the archaic determinants of guilt, and so 'wholly a tragedy of retrospection' (*SE*: 221); *Freud and Philosophy*, in contrast, stresses the prospective dimension of self-knowledge. The claim of the sphinx-archaic to be the source of ultimate meaning is challenged by the insight of the Tiresias-seer. Oedipus's presumption of his own innocence as an adult and a king is an issue of greater importance than either his childhood wishes or actions as a young man. 'His guilt is no longer in the sphere of the libido, but in that of self-consciousness: it is man's anger as the power of untruth' (*FP*: 516). There is an alliance between the drama of truth and the question of the father, of birth, of origin: both involve curiosity, resistance, pride, distress, wisdom. But Ricoeur insists that the second-order tragedy of truth exceeds and subsumes the drama of sex rather than providing what Freud called, almost as an aside, 'a misconceived secondary revision of the material'. 'Art calls forth archaic energies but in activating these figures, comparable to oneiric and neurotic symptoms, the creator reveals man's most open and fundamental possibilities, and erects them into new symbols of the suffering of self-consciousness (*FP*: 522).

The book concludes with an attempt to transpose this structure onto the 'new dimension' of the sacred. Freud's treatment of the instinctual substrate of religion attaches it to neurosis through fear, and to desire through its provision of substitute satisfaction. Ricoeur nevertheless contends that the primal-scene fantasy may be detached from the function of 'an infantile and quasi-neurotic repetition', and that the 'affective dynamism of religious belief' is sufficiently powerful 'to *overcome* its own archaism' (*FP*: 534). He stresses the creative aspect of the projection of the father in the Old Testament as name-giver and law-proclaimer. Instead of the paternal symbol serving as the occasion for the return of the repressed, 'from the start' it is 'not an object of desire but a source of institution', both as a 'being of language' and figure of the God who is to come (*FP*: 542). Thus religious consolation may be regarded as performing a 'non-narcissistic reconciliation'; and guilt itself may be transformed into the 'non-infantile, non-archaic, non-neurotic' fear of not loving enough (*FP*: 547).

Thus Ricoeur accepts the Freudian critique of religion as a projection of the father, which converges with Nietzsche's proclamation of the necessity of nihilism. The parallel is more fully developed in 'Religion, atheism, and faith' (*CI*: 440–67). Condemnation descends from an ideal realm, the projection of slave morality, the non-existent source of actual prohibition. Thus the task of philosophy in our time is the destruction of metaphysics regarded as synonymous with scorn for life, hatred of vitality, and resentment of the strong. The archaic structures of accusation and consolation, taboo and refuge, invested in the father figure must be unhesitatingly designated corrupt. Yet there is sufficient resource within the genuine symbol to transform the tyrant of the Oedipal complex, the interdiction of the *nom-du-père*: not into a benign authority (which would be mere inversion), but into a progressive-archaic structure that permits opposing directions of interpretation. It is important to grasp that the value of the paternal symbol lies not in any essential meaning that it may possess, but in the activity of interpretation transferred onto the exegete. At certain points, Ricoeur adopts an explicitly dialectical structure where atheism goes beyond 'the mere negation and destruction of religion' and serves as a mediation that opens the possibility of a 'postreligious faith'. But against this must be set the repeated insistence that 'the process of nihilism has not achieved its end, perhaps not even its culminating point' and the philosopher must think in 'this intermediate time' of indefinitely postponed synthesis (*CI*: 440).

The closing pages of the book, it must be admitted, fail to acknowledge the extent to which the interpretative procedures have been transformed by the shift away from the symbol to text, a concept whose potential domain now includes all the signs of human culture, raising suspicions that the psychoanalytic critique has been utilised to add a certain piquancy to a prescribed plenitude of the symbol. So Paul de Man's verdict on 'Ricoeur's Freud' – 'at the moment when all seems lost, all is regained' – possesses at least a preliminary plausibility.

> The originator of this discourse . . . remains a center of authority to the extent that the very destructiveness of this ascetic reading testifies to the validity of his interpretation. The dialectical reversal that transfers the authority from experience to interpretation and transforms, by a hermeneutic process, the total insignificance, the nothingness of the self, into a new center of meaning is a very familiar gesture in contemporary thought.
>
> (de Man, 1979: 174–5)

To engage fully with this comment would require extended analysis of de Man's own relation to Hegelian dialectic, in particular his insistence on the self-constitution of the subject through 'the rigor of its negativity' within a purely linguistic space (1979: 172). The phrasing of Ricoeur's initial question, 'what self is it which thus comes to self-understanding?' (*FP*: xii), may appear to predetermine the reply: the kind of self that can consciously pose questions and retain trust in these terms, and that is therefore incapable of addressing the true radicalness of psychoanalysis. There is, I would concede, some force in the Lacanian objection; but there is surely more complacency in the satisfied acceptance of disintegration. Too often the giving up of the illusion of mastery merely serves as the prelude for a lurch into the solipsism of a libidinal anarchy. For Ricoeur, a desire always remains a desire for; it can be revealed as the hidden motive within conscious intention, but nevertheless remains projective, outward directed.

'The subject' in Ricoeur may, as de Man claims, be 'reborn in the guise of the interpreter' (de Man, 1979: 175; compare Derrida, 1981: 45). There need, however, be nothing surreptitious about this. Thus it is not the attempt to 'incorporate' psychoanalysis within the philosophical tradition that will be crucial for Ricoeur's later work (*FP*: 455); but the ethic of interpretation that if offers. 'One cannot overestimate the amazing audacity of ... treating the intersubjective relationship as *technique*' (*FP*: 406), a composite involving the interpretation of the analyst, the gaining of insight of the patient, and the revelation of the mechanisms of the neurosis. 'To interpret and to work coincide': thus psychoanalysis becomes a collaborative hermeneutic exercise and a 'unique and irreducible form of praxis' (*FP*: 408). Ricoeur repeatedly insists on dispossession of subjectivity as the prelude to a restoration of the problematic of existence as force, effort-to-be; and the centrality given to the issue of instinct and representation offers powerful continuities with his previous accounts of affirmation. What will become crucial in his subsequent hermeneutic philosophy, which we shall now go on to address, is the intersection of this as yet transcendental principle with more technical issues of exegesis in relation to 'a manner of existing which would be from the very beginning a *being-interpreted*' (*CI*: 11).

5

The hermeneutic turn

STRUCTURE

If psychoanalysis sharpened Ricoeur's sense of the 'conflictual structure of the hermeneutic task' (*RM*: 309), structuralism reinforced his rationalism. There are deep continuities between his early insistence that phenomenology must be 'structural' and his later incorporation of a moment of objective explanation within the hermeneutic arc. The aspiration to univocal meaning, belief in the intelligibility of essential structures, and pretension to an ahistorical vantage are common to both. There may be commerce between them. For Ricoeur, Saussure's assault on the natural attitude places him amongst the masters of suspicion; the moment of objective understanding is superimposed onto the necessary impulse of demystification, and, as we shall see, comes to represent a key moment of reconnection of a broadly Heideggerian ontology with the interpretative practice of the human sciences. Despite its grandiose proclamations of the death of man, anthropocentrism, humanism, the chief ambition of the structuralist project appears in retrospect strikingly traditional: a unified theory of knowledge in the human sciences supported by objective procedures of explanation. The continued, perhaps excessive, prominence of structuralist thought in Ricoeur's work should therefore come as no surprise: he may, indeed, be seen as one of its most vigorous upholders in the face of the post-structuralist critique.

Following Benveniste, Ricoeur comments that 'the distinction between semantics and semiotics is the key to the whole problem of language' (*IT*: 8); and the great strength of his exposition is the dialogue that this demarcation permits between previously estranged traditions of linguistics. In this chapter, I shall begin with his account of structural analysis, and move progressively upwards through his

90

composite theory of discourse, his analysis of the transformation incurred by the phenomenon of fixation, and the dialectic of understanding and explanation at the level of text. I shall then try to situate Ricoeur's contribution in the context of the German hermeneutic tradition, examine his attempted arbitration of the dispute between Gadamer and Habermas, and conclude by linking the positions there enunciated to his own work on ideology and utopia.

It is worth running through Ricoeur's account of the basic elements of structuralism in some detail: much of this may be almost wearisomely familiar, but there are nevertheless some important internal clarifications to be made. Firstly, the work of Saussure provides merely the 'beginnings of structuralism': it receives its 'properly phonemic orientation' in the reformulations of later linguists such as Trubetskoy, Jakobson and Martinet. Even this simple admission moves us beyond the all-too-frequent lip-service paid to the *Course in General Linguistics*, and specifies a particular area of legitimacy: 'the consciousness of the validity of a method is never separable from the consciousness of its limits' (*CI*: 30–1). The achievements of structuralism in its own sphere cannot be dislodged by the post-structuralist critique; we are not beyond structuralism in the sense that its capacity to organise a field of inquiry is now obsolete and its conclusions invalid. Whereas historicism was concerned with 'the genesis, the previous form, the sources, and the sense of evolution', structuralism is preoccupied with 'the arrangements, the systematic organisations of a given state' resulting in a 'reversal of the relation between system and history' (*CI*: 31). Thus the conventions presupposed in the use of language at a given point (*langue*) are privileged above the speech-acts of individual subjects within that system (*parole*). For any investigation concerned with the operation of the code, 'what counts are not the terms, considered individually, but the differential variations' (*CI*: 31). Thus each sign is 'arbitrary, insofar as it represents an isolated relation of a meaning and a sound' (*CI*: 32): in so far and no further. This way of regarding the signifier is an abstraction of an abstraction: an artificial isolation of the unit from the system of which it is a part and within which it is *not* arbitrary. The system in turn has only been constructed as a methodological convenience to organise a domain of intelligibility: the code, unlike the message, has no actual existence.

The term 'arbitrary' has exercised a fatal seduction over the literary theory of the last twenty years. There has been little discernible recognition that the arbitrariness of the sign has been a commonplace of linguistics at least as far back as Locke (see Aarsleff, 1982). All too often the Saussurian postulate has been employed to debunk as insufferably naïve 'the illusion that the signifier answers to the function of representing the signified' and so refers to the world (Lacan, 1977a: 150). De Man, for example, never ceases to warn against the 'archetypal error' of 'the recurrent confusion of sign and substance' (1983: 136) and to berate 'the myth of semantic correspondence between sign and referent' (1979: 6). Ricoeur speaks with rare acerbity of the 'intimidation, the veritable terrorism which some nonlinguists impose, on the basis of a model naïvely extrapolated from the conditions of its functioning' (*CI*: 85).

Saussure's work does not demonstrate the arbitrariness of the sign, as is commonly assumed: it seeks to demonstrate its intelligibility when regarded as part of a synchronic structure. Thus semiotics renders various fields of investigation susceptible to rational analysis as a series of differential variations: Barthes's *The Fashion System* seeks to demonstrate that fashion possesses an internal coherence beyond the taste or purchasing power of the individual consumer. This does not however reveal the mystification of the commodity: it renders apparent the system within which individual decisions take on meaning. So Ricoeur's preliminary limitation serves to deflect some of the wilder accusations hurled against structural analysis; but also undercuts a good deal of its popular dissemination. Saussure's work does not entitle us to break with a supposedly naïve idea of reference: it provides the means for establishing an alternative problem-set which may or may not prove appropriate to different fields of study.

In Saussurian linguistics, the sentence is divided into two planes: the 'axis of coexistence', the class from which an individual term is selected, and the 'axis of succession', the combination of terms in linear sequence. This separation permits the development of 'a science of states in their systemic aspects', from whose perspective 'history is secondary' (*CI*: 32). But this does not mean the death of historical study as a 'science of evolutions', only that to achieve this kind of intelligibility, a suspension of diachronic inquiry is necessary. In Saussure, the motivation for transitions between stages of the system is never satisfactorily established: thus 'diachrony itself is intelligible only as a comparison of states of anterior and posterior systems; diachrony is comparative, and in this depends on synchrony' (*CI*: 32). This, famously, is the procedure of Foucault's *The Order of Things*. It is crucial, however, to realise that because the question, 'why did this change?' is invalid, other models of intelligibility are not thereby precluded. The insights obtained by regarding the depth structure of knowledge of a specific period as a unified episteme do not allow the extrapolation that all causal inference is henceforth invalid, only that at some point a further synthesis of the causal model and the synchronic will be necessary. For example Lucien Goldmann's thesis in *The Hidden God*, that Pascal, Racine, and Port-Royal Jansenism may be regarded as a single thought-constellation, does not mean that the break-up of that elite cannot be accounted for by empirical historical circumstance, only that within the structuralist perspective events are only apprehended as functions of the system rather than changes to it.

The analogues between Saussure and neo-Kantian thought are fairly obvious: most notably, the *a priori* constitution of a field of thought as a 'categorial, combinative unconscious'. Structuralism however dispenses with even a transcendental subject: 'it is a finite order or the finitude of order, but such that it is unaware of itself' (*CI*: 33). Thus it will necesarily be 'anti-reflective, anti-idealist and anti-phenomenological'. The relation to the system is 'objective, independent of the observer' rather than a relationship of understanding that is historically situated: 'that is why structural anthropology is science and not philosophy' (*CI*: 34).

Derrida exploits the paradoxes generated by the model without seeking either modification of its premises or its total replacement. Individual subjects can never claim to be outside the field of language: therefore there is no 'outside of the text'. Their language must be perpetually subject to the system of differential variations that constitutes meaning; any conceptual network that claims exemption from this movement must establish its authority through 'a centre which arrests and grounds the play of substitutions' (Derrida, 1978a: 278). Hence the paradoxes of the 'structurality of structure' (1978a: 278): structure demands a point outside its object of study which is unattainable when that object is language. That is why the centre is simultaneously '*within* the structure and *outside it*' (1978a: 279). This may be disputed on simple empirical grounds. There is no single monolithic linguistic system: in *The Rule of Metaphor*, Ricoeur discusses the 'legacy of perplexities' left by the 'simplifying and purifying action' of this aspect of Saussurian linguistics: 'perhaps one should go further and refuse to call a "code" a system about which so little is systematic' (*RM*: 121). But it is more effective to expose the central fallacy of this apparently irrefutable position. Derrida talks of 'the moment when language invaded the universal problematic, when, in the absence of a centre or an origin, everything became discourse' (1978b: 280). What exactly can be meant by 'discourse' here: speech-acts, texts, metaphysics? There is an implicit and wholly unsubstantiated endorsement of the principle of structural homology: the assumption that phenomena detected on an infra-linguistic plane will repeat themselves on each successive level. Derrida in fact has virtually nothing to say about discourse: his argument depends on a refraction of phonemes onto metaphysics. Though it is legitimate to regard meaning as constituted by differential variation within a given semantic field, this requires a preliminary decision to apply a synchronic mode of analysis, and also an eventual recuperation of the results obtained. As Derrida himself acknowledges, 'the centre also closes off the play that it opens up and makes possible' (1978b: 279). Furthermore, no justification is given for the importation of a temporal element into the purely formal disjunction between signifier and signified: 'the use of language ... presupposes a retention and protention of differences, a spacing and a temporalizing, a play of traces' (1973: 146). But the definition of meaning in terms of differential variations itself depends upon a preliminary decision to regard language in purely synchronic terms: as Ricoeur says in another context, the deconstructive trace is 'always relative to some abstract system and itself as detemporalised as possible' (*TN* 3: 151).

Lacan repeats the argument about 'the status of the problem of the structure' (1970: 187), though in less elegant and sophisticated fashion: 'there is no meta-language because "structured" and "as a language" are for me exactly the same thing' (1970: 197). The mechanisms detected by structural linguistics become determinants of language at every level: 'there is only one sort of language' (1970: 188). The argument collapses unless one is prepared to grant without qualification the claim that 'the automatism of the laws anchored in the signifying chain' (1977a: 258) necessarily conditions the operations of all other levels of linguistic phenomena.

Ricoeur himself observes that an 'order posited as unconscious can never be more than a stage abstractly separated from an understanding of the self by itself: order in itself is thought located outside of itself' (*CI*: 51). Structural explanation may be more or less appropriate for different cultural traditions, and Ricoeur is willing to extend a generous subordinate role to its findings. ('I do not at present see any more rigorous or fruitful approach than the structuralist method at the level of comprehension which is its own' (*CI*: 30).) But the inherent contradiction in an autonomous order of thought posited outside itself condemns structuralism 'to oscillate between several rough outlines of philosophies': 'a Kantianism without a transcendental subject', dependent on a fundamental confusion between the laws of language as 'instrumental mediation' of the individual speech-act and as an abstracted and hypostatised model of consciousness itself; an attempted, though scarcely convincing, *rapprochement* with Marxism through redefining 'the structures as the superstructures of praxis'; and finally, on the premise of a strict parallelism between the laws of language and those of nature, a quasi-Platonist revelation of the geometrical structure of binary differentiation underlying the contingency of individual phenomena.

Lévi-Strauss, in the *The Savage Mind*, announces the ambition of articulating an 'entire level of thought, considered globally'. Ricoeur points out that savage thought 'orders but does not think itself' (*CI*: 40), and is thus ideally suited to structural analysis. In no way does this justify the assumption of priority over more sophisticated historically oriented traditions. The initial limitation of ethnographic material has 'stacked the deck': 'the insignificance of the contents and the luxuriance of the arrangement seem to me to constitute an extreme example more than a canonical form' (*CI*: 41). The 'diachronic fragility' of these traditions facilitates the attitude of bricolage, working with a 'repertory made up of the remains of previous constructions and destructions' that 'represent the contingent state of instrumentality at a given moment' (*CI*: 43). It is the very instability of the myth which becomes a 'sign of the primacy of synchrony'. Lévi-Strauss offers the pragmatic open-endedness of bricolage as both a more fundamental psychic mechanism and a more unillusioned realisation of how reality is. For Ricoeur, it 'works with debris': 'the structure saves the event; the debris plays the role of a preconstraint, of a message already transmitted. It has the inertia of something presignified' (*CI*: 47–8).

An extended contrast is then drawn between societies which can only be threatened by event, change, with Gerhard von Rad's *Theology of the Historical Traditions of Israel*: 'a historical interpretation of the historical' that constitutes a genuine 'interpreting tradition'. Successive reinterpretation of founding events produces a developing unity irreducible to system. The 'temporal import' of the symbol, however, makes it a reusable reservoir: any interpreter within the same semantic field is capable of drawing on the resources of this overdetermined substratum. The status of the Old Testament tradition is not altogether clear – whether it serves as an alternative primitive culture or as the paradigm of living tradition – but the relegation of totemism to a relatively restricted special case appears eminently justified.

Lévi-Strauss's initial justification for the application of structuralist principles to the study of kinship is that the network of family bonds constitutes 'a system of communication'. A fairly mild demurral at the principle of 'structural homology' (*CI*: 37) does startling damage: this decouples the theory of meaning from the theory of relations, which must now be preceded and enveloped by a more broadly defined hermeneutic comprehension. Ricoeur proceeds to distinguish a number of levels within this domain – signs of exchange, without linguistic articulation; language itself; and more complex systems such as art and religion where language serves a constituent though by no means dominant role – and stresses the wholly unproven status of the assertion that 'the relation between synchrony and diachrony, valid in general linguistics, rules the structure of particular discourses in equally dominant fashion' (*CI*: 38). The interesting question is not how to extend structuralism over the whole human sciences; but how to relate its findings to a philosophy operating on an alternative and implicitly more adequate theory of language, what Ricoeur calls 'collaboration with other modes of understanding' (*CI*: 39).

Hermeneutics thus encounters structuralism as 'a support and not as a contrast' (*CI*: 30); and Ricoeur remains committed to a modified variant of structural analysis long after it had ceased to be where the 'real action' was perceived to be (Miller, 1987: 1104). Structural analysis is acknowledged to have overthrown 'the primacy of subjectivity so strongly emphasised by existentialism': it offers a perspective from which semiotic structures may replace intention, and the hermeneutic circle may be regarded as an intertextual rather than an intersubjective relation, not a meeting of minds but a superimposition of texts. De Man's assimilation of structuralism provides an illuminating contrast. The 'structural moment of concentration on the code for its own sake' is valuable for the 'preventative semiological hygiene' (1979: 4, 6) that it performs. The methodological abstention from organising a field of knowledge around a constituting subject involves a 'disincarnation and reduction of meaning' (1983: 158), and a consequent exploration of the issue of the 'existential status of the focal point' (1983: 11). For Ricoeur too, structuralism represents a moment of dispossession, of humility, of submission to the text: it may play the role of 'leading hermeneutics through the discipline of objectivity, from a naïve to a mature comprehension' (*CI*: 30). But the question of the residue, re-entry, appropriation by the interpreter remains. It must be stressed that the function of structural analysis is not to provide an objective knowledge of the text through application of a scientific methodology, but to disclose a diachronic kernel by means of achronic structures. Therefore the most immediately visible impact of structuralism on Ricoeur's work – the replacement of symbol with written language, text, as the immediate object of investigation – is perhaps more apparent than real. 'Structural analysis, far from getting rid of this radical questioning, restores it at a higher level of radicality' so producing a 'depth semantics' of 'boundary situations' (*IT*: 87). Ricoeur's arguments are in my opinion clearly decisive with regard to the necessity of a further stage of interpretation subsequent to formalist analysis (though structuralism need not be the sole privileged occupant of this phase, and in Ricoeur's theological hermeneutics other modes of analysis serve equally well). The question that remains, and which will be returned to later, is what kind of hermeneutic is appropriate to this final stage of meaning.

DISCOURSE

On an infra-linguistic level such as phonology, language may be treated without hesitation as an object of empirical science, defined as a synchronic system, a finite inventory with no absolute terms, only relations of mutual dependence. 'The new unit of discourse represented by the sentence', however, represents 'a break, a mutation' requiring 'quite another sort of intelligibility'. Though it may be 'decomposed into words, these are something other than short sentences. A sentence is a whole irreducible to the sum of its parts' (*IT*: 7). Thus any extension of the structural model onto larger textual units and beyond that onto non-linguistic entities can be no more than 'tentative' (*IT*: 4), justified by heuristic fecundity rather than logical necessity. An entirely separate and autonomous characterisation of discourse is required.

The linguistic event is a more perplexing phenomenon than it may at first appear. Its 'temporal dimension' is a source of 'epistemological weakness': 'events vanish while systems remain' (*IT*: 9). Derrida's preface to Husserl's *Origin of Geometry* seizes upon this point: even geometrical formulae can only be preserved through recourse to a system of material inscription existing outside of individual consciousness (hence the priority of writing over voice and speech). Ricoeur robustly insists upon 'the ontological priority of discourse'

97

over 'the mere virtuality of the system' (*IT*: 9). Yet though discourse may be 'actualised as an event', as such it remains transient, eva-nescent; analysis must deal with the meaning 'insofar as it endures' (*IT*: 12). An act of discourse possesses a reidentifiable propositional content, semantically defined through possession of a predicate (rather than the semiotic differential variation) which cannot be integrated at a higher level. 'The genuinely logical subject is always the bearer of a singular identification' and so opposed to the uni-versals of predication that refer to 'a quality, a class of things, a type of relation, or a type of action' (*IT*: 10–11). The structure of discourse lies in the 'intertwining and interplay' of these two functions (*IT*: 10–11). Following Frege, Ricoeur makes a further distinction be-tween the sense and reference of discourse, that which it says and that about which it speaks. An initially contextual definition of reference – 'to refer is what a sentence does in a certain situation and according to a certain use' (*IT*: 20) – is rapidly expanded to include the postulate of 'a previous and more originary move starting from the experience of being in the world' (*IT*: 21). This will be a persistent and dis-concerting procedure: establishing a working framework derived from philosophical semantics, then abruptly inserting it within a hierarchy in which it is made ultimately dependent on a sphere of pre-linguistic experience at no point subjected to the same degree of stringent criticism.

The typology of speech-acts developed by J.L Austin is also ad-duced. The formal truth-claim, or constative, is omitted: all events of discourse become performatives ('a specific commitment by the speaker who *does* what he says in saying it'). This may be further divided into 'the locutionary act ... which has a meaning; the illocu-tionary act which has a certain force in saying something; the perlocu-tionary act which is the achieving of certain effects by saying something' (Austin, 1975: 121). Ricoeur attaches to these an 'interlo-cutionary act': only in a phenomenological tradition would it be necessary to insist that 'dialogue is an essential structure of dis-course'. 'For an existential investigation, communication is an enigma, even a wonder ... a way of trespassing or overcoming the fundamental solitude of the human being' (*IT*: 15). In a kind of doubling-back, the intention of the speaker implies the intention of being recognised, hence the intention of the other's intention: a structure which appears more Hegelian than 'the noetic in the poetic' (*IT*: 18). Ricoeur's continued affiliation to a Husserlian model of language results in the awkward interpolation of several concepts, most notably the distinction between 'speaker's meaning' and 'what the sentence means'. Its superfluity is indicated by the subsequent admission that 'mental meaning can be found nowhere else than in discourse itself' (*IT*: 13). Following Paul Grice, the self-reference of discourse is said to reside in 'shifters': pronouns, adverbs of time and space, and demonstratives. 'No mental entity need be hypothesized or hypostatized' (*IT*: 13): the subject becomes a function of language to an extent surely unacceptable to even a modified phenomenology, though it should be pointed out that Husserl is as aware as Lacan of the purely formal notation of the I: 'every expression, in fact, that includes a *personal pronoun* lacks an objective sense' (1970a: 1:3:26 315–16). Intentionality appears to have been reduced to a purely private and presumably unrecoverable dimension. 'Language itself is the process by which private experience is made public' (*IT*: 19); the redundancy of epithet in the equation suggests a potential tautology – language is language made language.

So meaning, far from being the 'most obvious fact' becomes a 'miracle'; but one which also implies the converse of the 'radical noncommunicability of the lived experience as lived' (*IT*: 16). (Ricoeur writes eloquently of the 'magic' of the 'short-circuit' performed by omniscient narration which allows unimpeded access to other minds (*TN* 2: 89–90).) It is this sense of sheer tenuousness and fragility of access that lies behind de Man's denunciation of 'the duplicity, the confusions, the untruths, that we take for granted in the everyday use of language', with its 'distinctive curse' (and 'privilege') of being 'able to hide meaning behind a misleading sign' (1983: 12). This somewhat bizarrely overstated account of the 'Sisyphean task' of polite conversation may be refuted by a simple empirical appeal to the effectiveness of the screening context of dialogue in overcoming most potential misunderstandings. But a more fundamental ethical decision is also involved in the elevation of swerve, deviation, betrayal to the founding principle of language, which may be contrasted with Ricoeur's enthusiastic endorsement of Austin's paradigm of discourse: the promise, a bond of good faith underlying all human communication (*TN* 3: 232–3).

There are immediate problems with this syncretic amalgamation, notably the unexamined juxtaposition of the idioms of existentialism and linguistic analysis, and the apparent dispensability of the Husserlian perspective. Nevertheless it is adequate for a preliminary characterisation of discourse, language functioning at and above the level of the sentence, a category which, Ricoeur holds against Derrida, stands prior to both speech and writing. Where Derrida intensifies Husserl's opposition between physical sign and animating intention, Ricoeur regards the 'exteriority of discourse to itself' as the very condition of meaningful communication: that which '*opens* discourse to the other' (*IT*: 16). Although 'the human fact disappears' in writing, the 'detachment of meaning from the event' overcomes the transience of the instance of discourse (*IT*: 25–6). The propositional content of the locutionary act is preserved in its entirety, whereas the immediate force of the illocutionary only remains in the form of additional punctuation marks, and the emotional, even physical, impact of the perlocutionary virtually disappears. Nevertheless all three 'are susceptible, in decreasing degrees, to the intentional exteriorisation which renders inscription by writing possible' (*HHS*: 135).

These may seem rather laborious and unwieldy distinctions. But Ricoeur's careful demarcations bring out the vulnerability of de Man's utilisation of speech-act theory to demonstrate his thesis that 'the discrepancy between meaning and assertion is a constitutive part of their logic' (1983: 110). In 'Rhetoric of Persuasion' (1979b: 119–31), de Man appears to believe that it is somehow improper for a proposition about the world (a constative) to be simultaneously an active intervention (hence a performative). The 'speech-fact' must at all costs be segregated from the 'speech-act' in order to repress 'the possibility that all being, as the ground for entities, may be linguistically "gesetzt", a correlative of speech-acts' (1979: 122–3). This overlooks the elementary observation that any descriptive proposition can be prefixed by 'I affirm that'; there can be no sentence wholly divorced from some context of utterance. Furthermore de Man retains an intentional framework (not merely Nietzsche not knowing what he knows but the reader duplicating this failed pursuit of knowledge) that refuses to distinguish between verbal and textual utterance. His painstaking analysis becomes almost entirely redundant if, following Ricoeur, one accepts that the proposition has an illocutionary or performative force when spoken; but that this persuasive element is reduced to comparative irrelevance in written form, where the noema or propositional content predominates. The same distinctions offer the possibility of some kind of *rapprochement* between Derrida and Searle (Derrida, 1977b, 1977c; Searle, 1977). Derrida's travestying of Searle's text presumably indicates a refusal to accept the possession of language by the intention of any individual subject. This is obviously hyperbolic to the point of absurdity in the case of spoken utterance, but possesses considerable plausibility as a hermeneutic principle for textual interpretation where, even Searle would be obliged to admit, the conditions for a 'felicitous' act of communication must be substantially modified.

Thus the 'material support' of discourse represented by writing implies not a 'fall into exteriority' that debases the pure self-present meaning of mental soliloquy (Derrida, 1978b: 12–13), but the 'full manifestation' of its 'spiritual' potential (*IT*: 31). Derrida's protracted analyses of the origin of writing do not deign to expend even the most cursory attention to its function as social praxis. Certain pervasive assumptions concerning speech, antecedent meaning and identity are exposed: a prejudice against writing is impressively demonstrated in the denunciations of writing by Plato (as a substitution of dependence on written marks for internal wisdom), Socrates (as a relapse from dialogue to an object promiscuously meandering through the world), Rousseau (as the point of transition from a period of independence to one of alienation and tyranny) and Bergson (as a material deposit separated from living thought). But very little is actually said for writing. Ricoeur, in contrast, firstly adduces some simple but telling examples of its status as a 'tremendous human achievement' (*IT*: 26). In politics, it enables orders to be carried to imperial boundaries; in law, it allows the preservation of codes of jurisprudence; in economics, it permits the precise stipulation of rules of reckoning, and in history it inaugurates the preservation of documents in archives. (Thus to the extent that history could not have emerged as a discipline without the phenomenon of fixation, de Man is correct to say 'the bases for historical knowledge are not empirical facts, but written texts, even if these texts masquerade in the guise of wars and revolutions' (1983: 44).) Drawing on the work of François Dagognet, Ricoeur goes on to argue that writing, like painting, offers a form of renewal through an (optic) alphabet: its iconicity is the means of an intensification and restructuring of reality. It permits an 'upheaval' in the referential relation of language, one that will be explored throughout Ricoeur's later work, through which the disclosure of a 'world' is made possible (*HHS*: 147). I shall defer fuller discussion of the issue, but here it is worth stressing that 'world' is a notoriously tricky term in Ricoeur, that slides between an intertextual concept of the total 'ensemble of references' (in the sense that we talk of the classical world) and the concepts of *Lebenswelt* in late Husserl and *Umwelt* in Heidegger (in the sense of the primordial experience of the subject).

Text, that much bandied about but curiously elusive term, is defined, simply enough, as 'any discourse fixed by writing' (*HHS*: 145). When these terms are reversed, however, a distinctive sense emerges: 'fixation by writing is constitutive of the text itself' – not structure or intention or intelligibility, but fixation. The secondariness of writing, far from merely ensuring the 'persistence of speech', provokes 'a radical change in our relation to the very statements of our discourse'. The inscription of spoken language represents 'human thought brought directly to writing without the intermediary stage of spoken language'; through this 'short-cut', it is 'capable of taking the place of speaking' (*IT*: 28). One or two distinctively Derridean themes can be glimpsed: the estrangement of written language from voice; the irrelevance of the conditions of intersubjective truth to textual meaning; and polysemy as the endemic and inescapable condition of language. Writing is linked to reading rather than speaking:

> It is not a relation of interlocution, an instance of dialogue. It does not suffice to say that reading is a dialogue with an author through his work, for the relation of the reader to his book is of a completely different nature... The writer does not respond to the reader. Rather, the book divides the act of writing and the act of reading into two sides, between which there is no communication. The reader is absent from the act of writing; the writer is absent from the act of reading. The text thus produces a double eclipse of the reader and of the writer.
>
> (*HHS*: 146–7)

In contrast to the customary privileging of the vocabulary of living interchange, of dialogue with the dead, Ricoeur insists 'it is when the author is dead that the relation to the book becomes complete, and, as it were, intact. The author can no longer respond; it only remains to read his work' (*HHS*: 147). There is no symmetry whatsoever between the relation of speaker, message, and auditor, and of writer, text, and reader. The 'dialogic situation has been exploded', 'the author's intention and the meaning of the text cease to coincide', and 'the text now matters more' (*IT*: 29–30).

Somewhat surprisingly given Ricoeur's phenomenological background, there is little or no interest in the question of literary intentionality. Priority is unhesitatingly accorded to the present act of interpretation over the recovery of authorial meaning ('often unknown to us, sometimes redundant, sometimes useless, and sometimes even harmful' (*IT*: 76)). Ricoeur prefers to speak in terms of

categories of 'practice and work', and the 'rules of a kind of crafts-
manship': the speaker becomes 'the maker of the work' (*IT*: 33). This
is defined as longer than a sentence, codified within a literary genre,
and possessing a unique configuration of style. Language is regarded
as a material to be worked on and formed, and therefore the object of
praxis and techne (thus resolving the 'dialectic of work and the
spoken word' debated throughout *History and Truth* (*HT*: 4)). The
literary work is not infused with intention so much as wrought. Thus
it becomes 'a practical mediation between the irrationality of the
event and the rationality of meaning' (*HHS*: 157). The somewhat
opaque account of stylisation is designed to bridge the gap between
the individual, strictly speaking irrational, singular, without meaning
beyond itself, and the universal, concerned with the genus, the permanently intelligible. 'Style is labour which individuates' (*HHS*: 138)
not in the sense of making distinctive but in literally bringing into
existence a unique individual. The author is also coextensive with the
meaning of the work: it is that which he has made. There seems to be a
fair degree of circularity involved: he or she has produced structuration which allows the work to subsist as a thing, yet also provides the
ideality of meaning that may be identified with intention, noesis.
(The same duplication is central to 'The intentional fallacy' of the
New Criticism: the work is presumed to possess a unified structure
which in effect differs little from the concept of 'design or plan in the
author's mind' that is so vehemently rejected elsewhere (Wimsatt,
1954: 4).)

The emancipation from 'the narrowness of the face-to-face situation' allows a written text to be 'addressed to an unknown reader and
potentially to whoever knows how to read' (*IT*: 31). While this
'universality' is only hypothetical, it still remains prior to any contingent circumstance of 'social exclusion and admission' (*IT*: 31). A
work creates its public and is capable of initiating new modes of
communication. Though it may be occluded by the reception of its
immediate audience, an appeal always lies open to future generations. Its importance lies not so much in the readings that have
accrued, but in the potential infinity of interpretations that are to
come. (There are obvious parallels with the theology of the promise:
the perpetual reconfirmation of a pledge of future abundance.) A
continuous tension is established between the objective structure to
be disclosed, and the prospective trajectory of presumably changing
readings. For Hirsch, authorial meaning must be preserved as a
stable and recoverable standard against which to measure the

historical variations of significance: for Ricoeur, no such point of-stability can be detached. It is necessary to acknowledge that 'all textual meaning has to be constructed, that all construction involves choice, and that all choice involves ethical values' (1977c).

'To understand is to generate a new event beginning from the text in which the initial event has been objectified' (*IT*: 75). The 'new event', however, is better understood as already bifurcated, both prior and subsequent to the moment of dispossession by the text (the term is less overtly theological than in the hermeneutics of suspicion, but capable of bearing much the same force). Ricoeur's later work will more sharply differentiate this double sense of understanding – as correctable foreknowledge, the initial orientation through the guess, and as the ultimate assimilation of the residue of formal analysis. Although the logic of the hermeneutic circle demands that any con-clusion merely opens a new phase of understanding, Ricoeur chafes at a formal endlessness, preferring a culmination in praxis. Here what should be stressed is the linkage with his later account of narrative: the act of emplotment, the semantics of action, the priority accorded to practical reason. The text is the consequence of an act, the embodi-ment of action, and an incitement to act: a structuring, a structure, and an imperative to restructure. I shall postpone further discussion of the final stage of assimilation or, to use Gadamer's term, appropri-ation, till the final chapter, where the key phase of transition from structure to reader will be more fully addressed.

Because made, an artefact, the text is no longer dependent upon author or reader. Its very externality and materiality enables it to stand free of both. And to comprehend this moment of self-sufficiency fully requires an appropriate objectivity on the part of the interpreter: only through explanation of structure will understanding be possible. This is the point at which the theory of the text intersects with a more general hermeneutic problematic: 'one appropriates only what has first been held at a distance and examined' (*CI*: 30). Ricoeur's attitude is distinguished by its insistence that 'interpretation, philosophically understood, is nothing else than an attempt to make estrangement and distanciation productive' (*IT*: 44). Critical rationality must be incorporated into the hermeneutic process rather than repudiated as a violation of primordial belonging. For the full force of this formulation to become clear, it will be necessary to set it in the context of the classical problematic of the hermeneutic tradi-tion.

TEXT

Ricoeur identifies two preoccupations in the history of hermeneutics. The first is a 'movement of *deregionalisation*' (*HHS*: 45), a progressive enlargement that seeks to incorporate all varieties of hermeneutics within a general framework. But this can only be achieved through the delimitation of the 'properly epistemological concern of hermeneutics in relation to ontology' that will allow a '*radicalisation*' of the problematic so that hermeneutics becomes 'not only *general* but *fundamental*' (*HHS*: 44). The 'operations of understanding' may be theorised, and this in turn leads to Ricoeur's conviction that the 'disastrous' opposition between explanation, the attitude of methodological detachment necessary for scientific knowledge (*erklären*), and understanding, the empathetic access to another subjectivity demanded by the human sciences (*verstehen*), may be overcome (*HHS*: 45).

Schleiermacher was the first to try to synthesise the traditions of Biblical exegesis and tradition of classical philology, so as to establish fundamental principles of interpretation, to classify and organise its operations within a general problematic of understanding: a thoroughly Kantian enterprise. His work attempts to make concrete the anonymous epistemological subject by adducing the Romantic concept of the creative unconscious. The inevitable tension between the critical organon and the commitment to individualism is reflected in the oppositions between grammatical and psychological interpretation; between words as common cultural discourse and as infused by the singular genius of a specific author; and between objective and subjective moments of interpretation. In his later work, the second line predominates: the '*divinatory*' character of interpretation is stressed as the means of access to the unique individuality of the author. But this in turn can only be grasped through contrast and comparison: 'we never directly grasp an individuality, but grasp only its difference from others and from ourselves' (*HHS*: 47). (Thus the premise of necessary misreading, or blindness to achieve insight, far from originating with de Man, is one of the founding axioms of the hermeneutic tradition.)

With Dilthey the question of historical interconnection precedes hermeneutics: 'before the coherence of the text comes the coherence of history', and behind both lies 'the *expression of life*' (*HHS*: 48). He forges the alliance of hermeneutics and history, now somewhat unfairly disparaged as historicism, the victim of obstacles of its own making and the shift to structural models. His work reflects the rise of positivism and the discrediting of the Hegelian ambition; the human sciences must be endowed with an epistemology as respectable as the Kantian foundation of the natural sciences. To this end he severs the understanding of history from the explanation of nature, and makes it still more dependent on psychological intuition. It presupposes a primordial capacity of sympathy, the ability to enter. into other human individualities, as opposed to thingness, brute and obdurate. The neo-Kantian heritage is clearly visible in the emphasis on the individual above culture, institutions, the sphere of objective spirit; social relations are regarded as 'fundamentally singular' (*HHS*: 49). The intelligibility of history lies in its interconnection: knowledge of others is possible because life externalises itself in stable configurations which offer themselves for deciphering within structured totalities. This sense of structure was reinforced by a Husserlian idea of intentionality as the objective correlative in which mental life transcends itself.

This poses a double problem. Hermeneutics constitutes the 'objectified layer of understanding' directed towards the inscription of culture in which life has expressed itself, but its ultimate justification remains psychological, the lived experience posited behind it: 'not what a text says but who says it'. To prevent relapsing into a 'philosophy of life with its profound irrationalism', it becomes necessary to resort to a teleology of life as a 'dynamism that structures itself' (*HHS*: 52). Hence the structure of interconnection must be grounded in a speculative idealism with the 'same pretensions as the Hegelian philosophy of objective spirit' (*HHS*: 52). Ricoeur credits Dilthey, however, with perceiving the 'crux of the problem' – 'namely that life grasps life only by the mediation of units of meaning which rise above the historical flux' (*HHS*: 53) – which allows 'a mode of transcending finitude without absolute knowledge' at the cost of renouncing any allegiance to psychological origin (*HHS*: 53).

The enterprise of twentieth-century hermeneutics breaks with the attempt to establish an epistemology of understanding and instead strives to 'uncover its properly ontological conditions' (*HHS*: 53). Thus in Heidegger, 'the question of the *world* takes the place of the question of the *other*', and so understanding becomes 'de-psychologised' (*HHS*: 56). Ricoeur stresses the inappropriateness of the idea of existential psychology to such analysis. The 'anticipatory structure of understanding' is projective, concerned with opening up a world. The founding question of philosophy ceases to be the relation of a knowing subject to an object, and instead becomes 'what kind of being is it whose being consists in understanding?' (*CI*: 6). It is necessary to understand the conditions of understanding, now raised to a constituent of and virtual synonym for Dasein.

The problem can be developed in two directions. The first response, roughly that of Rorty and Cavell, regards this preliminary displacement of epistemology as the opportunity for examining an alternative value-hierarchy of terminologies – care, anxiety, to-handness – and so eminently compatible with a secular pragmatism. The second demands that these categories be treated as signs for a further interpretation of Being; roughly the procedure of Ricoeur's *Fallible Man*. Even in Heidegger's later work, it should be noted, where so much appears to be accorded to the power of the word, it is opposed to speaking, and linked with hearing and keeping silent. There is a saying of which we are not the subjects, and on a different level from that of speech. But in both cases, the aporia of explanation and understanding is 'displaced elsewhere and thereby aggravated': 'we are always engaged in going back to the foundations, but we are left incapable of beginning the movement of return' (*HHS*: 59).

The scepticism towards Heidegger within the Anglo-American tradition centres on whether numinous ruminations of this kind deserve the title of an 'Analytic' of Dasein after their haughty dismissal of all questions of method. There could not be a conflict of understandings in the Heideggerian sense. What is required is a kind of leap of faith into a vague and diffusive awareness: the mysterious, if not the miasmic. The historian, for example, understands his object because both are historical: 'life's ability to stand at a distance from itself' is enshrined as a 'structure of finite being' (*CI*: 9). Redubbing a problem an ontological trait elegantly 'short-circuits' the whole problem of historical knowledge ('extraordinarily seductive'), but Ricoeur resists: 'this hermeneutic is designed not to resolve' the problems of textual exegesis, 'but to dissolve them' (*CI*: 10). Without establishing a 'backward relatedness' to questions of technical exegesis in the human sciences, the very claim to uncover foundations must be suspect.

This in turn leads to Ricoeur's most original contribution to this debate: the positing of a 'productive notion of distanciation' as that which permits 'communication in and through distance' and so constitutes the very historicity of human experience. Understanding and explanation, far from designating opposed fields of inquiry, presuppose and enrich each other (compare *HT*: 24). There can be no imperious separation of truth from method: the legitimacy, indeed necessity, of methodological rigour must be respected, and its results made a further point of departure. Language must be not be privileged as a saying of our being, but examined as the manifestation of a structure. As with the physical nature of the sign and the material inscription of the text, this objectification is seen as both necessary and beneficial: 'distanciation is not the product of methodology and hence something superfluous and parasitical; rather it is constitutive of the phenomenon of the text as writing' (*HHS*: 139). Ricoeur's earlier analyses of feeling as a kind of primordial bond with the world somewhat begged the question of how it could be analysed: indeed, at times the appropriate discursive mode appeared to be rhapsodic invocation. Now it is posited that 'the very experience of belonging to ... requires something like externalisation in order to apprehend, articulate and understand itself' (Ricoeur, 1976e: 691). Distanciation, far from representing rupture or exile, is the very condition of understanding. It is no longer a question of seeking an objectivity outside of the hermeneutic circle: instead the full rigour of logical analysis must be installed within it.

So distanciation becomes the condition of the liberation of the text, not only from its conditions of production, but also from its material substratum. The concept of text becomes available as analogy: if determinate procedures of interpretation can be established, the possibility arises of transposing them onto other cultural spheres. 'The model of the text: meaningful action considered as a text' (*HHS*: 197–221) begins by offering two premises; firstly, an action as object of study displays a sufficient number of common features with a text to be treated as such, and secondly, that similar interpretative procedures may therefore be applied to both. This hypothesis requires a preliminary objectification equivalent to fixation, which allows the whole question of intersubjective relations to be suspended, and the criteria of practical knowledge, knowing how, to be firmly subordinated to interpretation. Action becomes a 'delineated pattern which has to be interpreted according to its inner connection' (*HHS*: 204); its meaning, like that of a speech-event, is detached from the occasion of its performance (for a fuller account of the propositional content of action-sentences, see Kenny, 1963). As de Man puts it, 'the empirical situation which is open and hypothetical' requires 'a consistency that can exist only in a text' (1979: 151).

The social dimension of action lies in its unintended consequences ('our deeds escape us'): 'the doer is present to his doing in the same way that the speaker is present to his speech (*HHS*: 206) – as much and no more. There should be no privileging of the intentions of the agent: the meaning resides in the work itself, leaving a concrete manifestation in documents, signs. 'History is this quasi-"thing" *on* which human action leave its mark'; a remark which will be later expanded into a full-blown problematic of the historical trace. The importance of an action 'exceeds, overcomes, transcends, the social conditions of its production, and so may be re-enacted in new social contexts' (*HHS*: 208). Thus 'social structures', no less than literary texts, can be read as attempts to deal with existential perplexities: institutions may be renewed through reinterpretation. The potential horizon is unlimited: human action is an open work, the meaning of which is held in suspense, addressed 'to anyone who *can read*' and over which contemporaries hold 'no particular privilege' (*HHS*: 208–9).

The argument should be seen as more speculative than dogmatic, though one may point to the influence of a similar textualisation of social processes in the New Historicism, notably in the work of Stephen Greenblatt. The analogy with action is a grossly over-extended transposition from the linguistic sphere, an example of the imposition of homology for which Ricoeur had criticised structuralism (for a partial retraction, see *TN* 1: 56–57). There is no fixed noematic content to an action; any attempt to establish one could only lead to a damaging hypostasis of meaning. The demotion of the perspective of present participants in relation to that of future interpreter is unsustainable: the example of Napoleon may have inspired a whole generation of romantic thinkers – Coleridge, Carlyle, Hegel – but this is hardly equivalent to their fighting at Waterloo. There is no adequate engagement with the problematic of power: though institutions may perhaps be regarded as texts, texts are seldom mistaken for political institutions. In addition, the singularity of the text as a unique individual appears impossible to apply to a network of social relations without obvious parameters.

Finally, there is little or no indication as to what might defeat a specific claim in particular cases. While Ricoeur seeks to preserve a scientific objectivity for depth analysis of the text, there is no detailed consideration of problems of verification and adjudication of the residue thereby revealed. In the sphere of theology, and to a lesser extent literary criticism, the methodological deficiency of this 'hasty and unhappy alliance of Hirschian validity and Heideggerian truth' (Thompson, 1981: 194) can be elided by an insistence on the ultimately personal nature of appropriation; in the context of the social sciences, it is severely damaging. Ricoeur is consistently over-sanguine about the existence of 'criteria of relative superiority which can easily be derived from the logic of subjective probability' (*IT*: 79): even qualified acceptance of the axiom that theories construct their own criteria of relevance fatally undermines such an appeal to fair-minded arbitration. Validation is conceived in so benignly inclusive a fashion as to renege on the '*risk* of interpretation', its participation in the 'internal warfare that the various hermeneutics indulge in among themselves' (*CI*: 23). I shall now go on to consider Ricoeur's attempted arbitration in one of the most prominent of these contemporary contests.

GADAMER AND HABERMAS

The debate between Gadamer and Habermas is arguably the most important post-war exchange in the human sciences: its breadth and seriousness raise the possibility that Anglo-American literary theory has been seduced into engagement with a lesser problem-set through its encounter with the French intellectual debate centred on structuralism and post-structuralism. I have suggested that Ricoeur provides a viable *modus vivendi* with structuralism, shorn of some of its headier proclamations perhaps, but thoroughly mastered and respected. That particular issue if not altogether closed is at least secondary; if anything there seems to to be a strong case for seeking to revive some of its objectivist ambitions. And in so far as post-structuralism or deconstruction is seen as developing out of the paradoxes engendered by structuralism operating outside its limits of validity, or at least, more sympathetically, its more venturesome forays, this too must be a known quantity by now. The kind of rarified linguistic problematics dwelt upon by Derrida undeniably have their fascination, and the brilliance of individual readings is surely beyond dispute. But the great strength of early structuralism, its claim to provide a unified theory of knowledge based on linguistics that could provide the basis for a coordinated objectivity in the human sciences, must now be withdrawn. This ambition is still vigorous within the German hermeneutic tradition; the protest here might be directed against its complicity, its cultural acquiescence, its unlimited supply of deference to the political institutions of late monopoly capitalism.

Ricoeur initially situates the debate as yet another conflict of interpretations, this time over the issue of tradition; Habermas's Freudio-Marxist critique of systematically distorted expression certainly invites this kind of alignment. But here the issues have been enlarged from the insight to be gained from the symbol to the responsibility of the contemporary intellectual in the broadest sense. 'Hermeneutics and the critique of ideology' opens by declaring that what is at stake is a 'fundamental gesture of philosophy' as either 'an avowal of the historical conditions to which all human understanding is subsumed under the reign of finitude' or 'an act of defiance, a critical gesture, relentlessly repeated and indefinitely turned against "false consciousness", against the distortions of human communication which conceal the permanent exercise of domination and violence' (*HHS*: 63). Ricoeur posits that the alternative itself must be overcome. But first the extremity of the divide must be fully acknowledged. (For a fuller chronological account of the debate, see Warnke, 1987: 107–38.)

The critical point in Gadamer's work is seen as his 'provocative rehabilitation of the three connected concepts of prejudice, authority, and tradition' (*HHS*: 64) against the objectivity sought by the human sciences. There is a paradox of simultaneous universality of claims and acknowledgement of historical finitude, characteristic of a post-Heideggerian hermeneutic. The conflict with the critique of ideology is seen as dating back to the tension between Enlightenment and Romanticism: struggle against prejudice set against nostalgia for the past. Neatly enough, the unexamined prejudice of a critique of prejudice is that prejudice is an inherently negative category compared to judgement, equated with deracinated reason, the Cartesian ideal of methodical consciousness. In the wake of Heidegger's break with the enthronement of self-consciousness in the subject–object polarity, Gadamer may proclaim 'the prejudices of the individual, far more than his judgements, constitute the historical reality of his being'. This represents the death of man conceived as subjectivity, individuality: 'history precedes me and my reflection: I belong to history before I belong to myself' (*HHS*: 68). Ricoeur points out that Gadamer is linked to Dilthey by the priority given to understanding history, historicality *per se*, over questions of text and exegesis. The question remains as to the extent of his vulnerability to the critique previously directed against Heidegger, of providing no route back from ontology to epistemology. Gadamer's prejudice obviously takes substance from Heidegger's account of the structure of anticipation; and there is a similar hostility to the 'alienating distanciation' of critique that ruptures the primordial relation of belonging.

The idea of authority is rehabilitated, desynonymised from

domination and violence, as that which elicits recognition. This is linked to tradition, defined almost tautologously as 'that which has authority'. The past is distant, other, yet still operative, suffusing. Thus the idea of a history without presupposition is chimerical: 'man's link to the past precedes and envelops the purely objective treatment of historical facts' (*HHS*: 76). Hermeneutics lays claim to universality in three respects. First, it seeks to found the knowledge provided by science in an experience of the world that precedes it. Secondly, it proposes a kind of level of depth consensus; Gadamer posits that every misunderstanding presupposes a 'deep common accord'. Thirdly, language is itself conceived as a kind of sedimentation of prior questions, ongoing dialogue. Cumulatively, this amounts to a meta-critique of critique, which seeks to prove there is no 'zero point' from which an objective analysis might be launched. The critical theory of the Frankfurt School is, from this perspective, essentially parochial, merely reflecting the unacknowledged prejudices of a specific interest group. Equally, they are open to the charge of avoiding the question of a potential conflict of emancipations, offering no form of verification other than a proclaimed self-evidence. How, for example, are we to arbitrate between Benjamin's messianic Judaism, Marcuse's libidinal emancipation, and Adorno's negative aesthetics?

Ricoeur then considers the response of Habermas in four key areas: prejudice is met with a concept of interest; cultural tradition by the critical social sciences; mis-understanding by the systematic distortion by ideology; the 'dialogue which we are' set against the regulative ideal of unconstrained communication.

The concept of interest seeks to divest the subject of its pretensions to situate itself outside desire, and to unmask its concealed motives: the hostility to allegedly disinterested knowledge is unexpectedly comparable to Gadamer's participation. There is a 'pluralism of basic interests' of which Habermas singles out three. The first is the technical or instrumental interest, for which the facts of empirical science are valued according to their technical exploitability, a quasi-pragmatist thesis. The second is the practical interest, the domain of the 'historico-hermeneutic sciences', constituted by understanding meaning, whether in the exchange of ordinary language messages, interpreting the texts of the tradition, or the internalisation of norms governing social roles. As Ricoeur points out, this comes surprisingly close to Gadamer's condition of preunderstanding, which also has a practical dimension, the 'application' of laws. The third is an 'interest in emancipation', the prerogative of the critical social sciences. These must resist the authority of tradition, the ready-made being that supports and confines us, and instead espouse the Enlightenment ideals of autonomy, independence, and self-transformation.

There is hermeneutics because there is misunderstanding, but also because there is confidence that misunderstanding can be corrected by a critique on the same level. Habermas opposes this with a concept of ideology that borrows heavily from psychoanalysis. Distortion is seen as always related to repressive authority and therefore violence; censorship returns to the political sphere enlightened by Freud. Because distortion is always related to labour and power, it is unrecognisable by members of the community. To analyse it demands the importation of the concepts of illusion (or error), of projection (or constitution of false transcendence) and rationalisation (or a subsequent reshuffling of motives). Misrecognition must be combated with procedures of explanation. Habermas uses a loose and unsatisfactory analogy with psychoanalytic scenes – symptomatic, transference, primitive – that is gently but firmly dismissed by Ricoeur: there is no equivalent to the relationship of patient and analyst, no experience of transference, and above all no ultimate purpose of therapeutic cure in critical theory (*IU*: 217–31). But the principle of a metahermeneutics to correct misrecognition remains plausible.

For Gadamer, the consensus that supports us in the form of the prior meanings sedimented in a linguistic heritage is an ontologically constitutive experience; for Habermas, it is a special case incommensurate with the omnipresence of ideology. Anticipation must replace a passively assumed and politically complicit tradition: 'self-reflection cannot be founded on *a priori* consensus, for what is prior is precisely a broken communication' (*HHS*: 86–7). Therefore a regulative idea of unlimited communication is necessary, an anticipation of that which ought to be. This has obvious parallels with the eschatological structures in Ricoeur's own work, which avoid Habermas's awkward duplication, of polemic for a limit idea beyond polemic, debating a position that is beyond debate: 'it's finally the argument that is the aim and the criterion' (Ricoeur, 1979b: 208; for further discussion, see McCarthy, 1982; and Benhabib, 1985).

The critical impulse is not entirely absent from the hermeneutic tradition, but remains little more than a 'vague desire constantly reiterated but constantly aborted' (*HHS*: 88). At a key moment in *Being and Time* (1962: 195), Heidegger demands that genuine foreknowledge be distinguished from 'fancies and popular conceptions', but immediately subsumes this under a higher level of transcendence.

Hermeneutics becomes synonymous with the question of being, and the area of illusion expands to include the whole history of metaphysics: hence 'all critical effort is spent on the work of *deconstructing metaphysics*' (*HHS*: 89), a task which replaces the previously hinted-at critique of prejudices. 'The obsessive concern with radicality thus blocks the return route from general hermeneutics to regional hermeneutics' (*HHS*: 89); an objection which, if rephrased in terms of the Transcendental and the empirical, has particular application to Derrida. Gadamer's attention to the 'moment of derivation' largely exempts him from this charge; but the hermeneutic experience, even in his formulation, effects a similar discouragement of critique. Ricoeur argues that distanciation must be recognised as a 'positive component of being for the text' (*HHS*: 92): formal modes of analysis must be recognised as a necessary check on any blind acquiescence in the authority of tradition. Though there may be no position of overview, finitude is not an absolute restriction but rather a flexible horizon. The concept of fusion of horizons emerges from the rejection of objectivism (the forgetting of self to allow the other to be viewed objectively) and absolute knowledge (the encompassing within a single horizon by a single subject). There must always remain 'the play of differences in the process of convergence': 'a paradox of otherness, a tension between proximity and distance . . . is essential to historical consciousness' (*HHS*: 62).

The critique of ideology cannot be detached from hermeneutical presuppositions: the two universes are 'interpenetrating'. The theory of interests, for example, cannot be empirically verified as a field of explanatory hypotheses: Habermas's trilogy of labour–power–language appeals to 'a philosophical anthropology similar to Heidegger's Analytic of Dasein' (*HHS*: 95). This could claim to be meta-hermeneutics in relation to an idealism of lingual life, but operates on the same level in so far as it provides a hermeneutics of existential finitude. Ricoeur insists that emancipation cannot be separated off from creative recovery of the past. Otherwise it would become 'empty and abstract', with no reference to the empirical conditions of communciation: 'he who is unable to reinterpret his past may also be incapable of projecting concretely his interest in emancipation' (*HHS*: 97). 'Critique is also a tradition' grounded in the Enlightenment, and behind that in Exodus and Resurrection. The antithesis between hermeneutics and critique puts us in the position of having to 'choose between reminiscence and hope!' (*HHS*: 100).

The issue seems somewhat less clear-cut than Ricoeur's closing adjudication might suggest. Obviously there are moments of ethical and political crisis where the past is overridden through commitment to the future, the future forsaken through allegiance to the past. There is little sense here, however, of the possible brutality of the choice involved. I shall now go on to examine some of the problems raised when Ricoeur restates this debate in his own preferred terms.

IDEOLOGY AND UTOPIA

Both ideology and utopia are seen as deriving from a common origin in a 'social or cultural imagination' (*IU*: 1; see also Ricoeur, 1978b). Ideology is redefined as the necessary adhesive symbolism of a community, and utopia given a perhaps untenable complementary role as the vantage of the possible. Their 'non-congruence', however, does not prevent them from being 'constitutive of social reality' (*IU*: 3).

Ideology has become almost automatically equated with 'a problematic of interested and unconscious distortion' that can only be regarded as a negative phenomenon: it is always 'the thought of my adversary, the thought of the *other*' denounced from one's own position of supposed disinterestedness (*HHS*: 223–24). (The term 'ideologues' originated as Napoleon's favourite term of abuse for the *philosophes*.) Following Weber, Ricoeur insists on the perennial gap between power and legitimation in political institutions – 'there is always more in the claim which comes from the authority than in the belief that is returned to it' – and insists that ideology serves as a kind of 'transmitter of surplus value' that bridges this divide. As such it necessarily possesses a 'dissimulating quality': 'we do not desire it but desire *within* it' (*IU*: 229).

This may be justified on a simple pragmatic level: without this 'essential opacity', the state would necessarily resort to the direct coercion of violence. Ricoeur, however, insists on the integrative function of ideology as a means of endowing action with intelligibility and value. Thus its justification of authority through symbolic concepts is merely one aspect of its dynamising, propulsive character, that represents on a social level what a motive is to an individual project: a means 'to prolong the shock wave of the founding act' (*HHS*: 227). It serves as 'a function of the distance that separates the social memory from an inaugural event' which can be 'revived and reactualised only in an interpretation which models it retroactively, through a representation of itself' (*HHS*: 225). Although this involves an inevitable simplification and 'loss of rigor', this 'schematization, idealization, and rhetoric' is a necessary price to pay for the social efficacy of ideas. Ideology is 'operative and not thematic'. The impossibility of total reflection, the necessary dependence of thought on unstated propositions, is used to insist upon the inescapability of this element of 'non-transparence': 'we think from it rather than about it' (*HHS*: 227). Ricoeur does acknowledge an 'attrition', a potential 'inertia', that cannot tolerate novelty or innovation. But though this 'closure', indeed 'blindness', at times 'veers towards the pathological', it never entirely loses its initial function as a cultural bonding. Moreover, it is not something that may be voluntarily adopted or dismissed – 'it is impossible for consciousness to develop other than through an ideological code' (*HHS*: 228).

The most vigorous challenge to such an identification emerges from the Marxist denunciation of ideology as an instrument of class domination. Marx's favoured model of the *camera lucida*, however, may itself be challenged for its dependence on a trope of inversion, an imaginary reflection of the material base, and thus its 'failure to think of the production of illusion in non-metaphorical terms' (*IU*: 78; for a more detailed deconstructive reading of Marx, see Koffman, 1973). The declared aim of a reversal of projection to re-establish the primacy of the concrete invites the rejoinder that 'an inverted image is always the same' (*IU*: 79); furthermore the basic optical analogy of 'an image on the retina' (the etymological meaning of ideology) is unsustainable 'since there are images only for consciousness' (*IU*: 78).

Though 'ideology' as a specific term appears in neither the *Critique of the Philosophy of Right* nor *Economic and Philosophical Manuscripts*, the concept of a shadow-world of false consciousness is already present. The reality to which it is opposed undergoes considerable modification. Though Marx criticises the residual idealism of Feuerbach, his early work remains indebted to the model of a collective subject of humanity that is ultimately no less theological. Ricoeur insists that the crucial development (the infamous 'coupure' or epistemological break) comes not with 'the abolition of the individual' but 'the emergence of the individual from the idealistic concept of consciousness' (*IU*: 97). Priority is accorded to the 'working and suffering individual' as the centre of production, whose creativity resists any 'flattening' to merely economic relations. This stress on self-realisation through individual action, which may be traced back to Fichte rather than Hegel, comes close to Habermas's reading of Marx, though Ricoeur feels no need to authenticate the concept by insisting on a parallel between labour and the Kantian synthesis of the categories of consciousness.

In common with the majority of humanist readings of Marx, Ricoeur emphasises the concept of alienation, the fulfilment of the individual, and the utopian dimension of the end of history: 'the idea that transparence is not behind us, at the origin, but in front of us, at the end of a historical process which is perhaps interminable' (*IU*: 238). Such an anthropological emphasis almost inevitably concedes *Capital* to an Althusserian reading, in which ideology is no longer opposed to concrete praxis but to a supposedly scientific knowledge of the material basis of anonymous entities (city and country, modes of production, above all the class struggle) that have been elevated to the motivating force of history.

The claim of Althusserian Marxism to oppose ideology with science is countered with the question: 'does there exist a non-ideological place, from which it is possible to speak scientifically about ideology?' (*HHS*: 231). The social sciences demonstrably fail to meet the criteria of positive science: explanatory coherence and resistance to falsifiability. As with Lacan, Ricoeur insists that one cannot buck these positivist criteria and simultaneously claim the status they allow. In particular, he condemns the 'epistemological naïveté' of believing that explanation in terms of unconscious factors must itself be necessarily objective (shared partially by the Frankfurt School): 'this elimination of subjectivity on the side of historical agents in no way guarantees that the practising sociologist has himself risen to a subjectless discourse' (*HHS*: 233). The increasing formalism of explanatory apparatus violates the density and empirical fidelity of Marx's thought: the much-vaunted borrowings from the alternative domain of psychoanalysis are a sign of weakness rather than strength (a charge equally pertinent to Habermas): 'what is alleged but poorly verified in one discipline' cannot be 'better verified in another' (*IU*: 234).

The more elegant argument concerns Mannheim's paradox of the auto-implication of ideology. There can be no absolutely value-free social science: any methodology that possesses sufficient self-consciousness about its own ideological status is destined 'to be absorbed, to be swallowed by its own referent'. Althusser himself ends up by offering a kind of 'apology for ideology' (*IU*: 7): the 'extension of the concept ... acts as a progressive legitimation and justification of the concept itself'. It expands to include not only praxis but all aspects of lived experience: illusion, therefore, has an empirical actuality wholly lacking in the theory. There is a paradoxical collapse back into Nietzschean consolation, the vital lie, and a kind of inverted testimony to the necessity of ideology: 'it becomes so completely constitutive of what we are that what we might be when we are separated from it is completely unknown. We are what we are precisely because of ideology, the burden of ideology is to make subjects of us' (*IU*: 148). Thus the previous opposition of praxis to ideology is replaced by a mutual constitution 'where human beings exist, a non-symbolic mode of existence, and even less a non-symbolic kind of action, can no longer obtain' (*IU*: 12). Thus the very failure of the ambition of scientific knowledge of ideology points to 'the necessity of another type of discourse, that of the hermeneutics of historical understanding' (*HHS*: 243).

So we arrive back to 'under Gadamer's guidance, a reflection of the Heideggerian type' (*HHS*: 243). The question must be raised whether Ricoeur avoids the charge of a certain stagnancy in his adoption of this vocabulary. 'Ideology is the unsurpassable phenomenon of social existence, insofar as social reality always has a symbolic constitution, and incorporates an interpretation, in images and representations, of the social bond itself' (*HHS*: 231). This cuts both ways: instead of an ontological trait, a textual heritage; and while 'social bond' sounds ominously Burkean, one should note the possibility of alternative modes of 'interpretation'. The integrative role of ideology, however, seems endowed with a formal priority, with comparatively little emphasis on the negative force of demystification. Distanciation appears to remain, ultimately, a contained moment: the force of rupture in critical disengagement, the destructive scepticism towards an inhibiting tradition, and the necessary forgetting of the past, have diminished to the point of virtual extinction. Ricoeur's response is to attempt to provide a counter-balancing pole in the form of utopian thought.

In contrast to the anonymity of ideology, utopia is a 'declared genre' (*IU*: 269), personalised and idiosyncratic. Though there are recurrent themes of transformed family structure, sexual relations, forms of worship, there is no internal consistency: utopias can, for example, equally well be ascetic or orgiastic in sexual outlook; anarchic or geometrically hierarchical in politics; and atheistic or fundamentalist in religion. They must be defined in terms of function rather than 'dispersion' of their empirical content (*IU*: 270). Utopian thought is the product of our 'ability to conceive of an empty place from which to look at ourselves'. Thus it represents 'one of the most formidable contestations of what is', and possesses 'a constitutive role in helping us to understand our social life'. It should be seen not as a retreat into a realm of wish-fulfilment, but as an 'exterior glance' (*IU*: 16) necessary for any radical re-appraisal. Utopia is no less concerned than ideology with the problematic of power: its 'eccentricity' will invariably be denounced from an interested vantage. 'For the representatives of a given order, the utopian means the unrealizable' but nevertheless it is 'defined formally precisely by its capacity for change' (*IU*: 176). It is connected with the discourse of an emergent group, expressing their 'dominant wish' (*IU*: 274). Hence it is not a theoretical but a practical concept, that 'shatters a given order by offering alternative ways to deal with authority and power' (*IU*: 179). The 'criterion of realizability' will necessarily be biased towards the past and unwilling to acknowledge the capacity of the future to be different: utopia should be defined by the formal criteria of creating 'a distance between what is and what ought to be' (*IU*: 179). Thus its decisive trait becomes the 'preservation of *opposition*' (*IU*: 180).

'Imagination has the function of a social dream' (*IU*: 288). This invites the simple rejoinder of what guarantees this against the leverage of the actual, the sedimentation of shared beliefs, and the brute mechanisms of power? Who controls the social bond, and possesses the capacity to enforce their interpretation? The 'new vantage on the given, and new possibilities within it' provided by utopia seem closer to a purely aesthetic mode of consolation than 'one of the most formidable contestations of what is' (*IU*: 16), abstention rather than critique, and certainly an inadequate substitute for the principles of universal morality to which Habermas aspires. When safely contained within a literary realm, it must risk the charge of harmless fantasy. (Ricoeur concedes the necessity for 'a kind of complicity or connivance on the part of the well-disposed reader' (*IU*: 270).) The socialist visionaries, particularly Fourier, come close to being amiable eccentrics; and little or no attention is directed towards the possibility of dystopia.

In the context of the political imagination, far too much is accorded to the mere fact of otherness, equated with 'Husserl's imaginative variations concerning an essence' (*IU*: 16). The argument will be more effective when cast in the indirect form of metaphor and narrative, to which we shall now turn, where Ricoeur's affiliation to the somewhat acquiescent retrospection of the German hermeneutic tradition may be set against his stress on the new event of our making, the actualisation of the past through active interpretation in the present moment.

6

The rule of metaphor

STRUCTURAL AND SEMANTIC APPROACHES

The Rule of Metaphor is more wide-ranging than its title might suggest. It is concerned with aligning three levels of discourse: the word, the sentence, and the text. The distinction between semiotics and semantics is again crucial. There is a sympathetic and admiring exposition of the semic analysis undertaken by structural linguistics; a detailed examination of the interaction theory of metaphor developed in philosophical semantics; and, most problematically, an extension of this into an ontological tension within the second-order reference of metaphorical language. On one level, the elaborate detour undertaken through the history of conceptions of metaphor represents a renewed attempt to induce this ultimately Heideggerian vocabulary into a productive engagement with more empirically based traditions rather than resort to an imperious transcendence of their concerns. The book needs re-reading to appreciate its calm and large-scale tempo of argumentation. The prose is unashamedly academic, at times laboriously precise and reiterative, with no charismatic aspirations. Nevertheless it possesses wit and elegance in many of its argumentative manoeuvres; an unerring capacity to hold the whole tradition of debate in a single stable focus; and also a final audacity, a willingness to risk opening new territory rather than simply establishing itself in a position of authority over previous terrain. It is a bold, admirable, and somewhat daunting text.

Ricoeur states his 'double allegiance' to French and English-language philosophy, and promises a separate study of the German hermeneutic tradition (though its influence is more prominent than this might suggest). It is yet another open-ended project that he has got himself into. Even as a historical survey of disparate theories, a coordination of traditions between which there is usually little or no dialogue, the book is already a major achievement. The refusal of polemic, of 'blistering refutations' (*RM*: 6), seems clear-cut; but the very fashion in which Ricoeur stakes out his terrain suggests considerable vigour of rebuttal. The characteristic deference and generous acknowledgement are here, but this should not lead one to underestimate the severity of rebuke to doctrines that 'proclaim themselves to be exclusive' (*RM*: 8). From the viewpoint of criticism influenced by deconstruction, this book must be felt as a rebuke, even a threat. Ricoeur refrains from drawing any more general conclusion from his concluding analysis of Derrida's *White Mythology*: it is no more than 'one episode in a much vaster strategy of deconstruction that always consists in destroying metaphysical discourse by a reduction to aporias' (*RM*: 287). But it is not difficult to find examples of Derrida insisting upon 'the "literal" meaning of meaning as metaphoricity itself' (1977a: 15), or opposing the 'nonspatial signified' to the 'metaphorical signifier' that implicitly includes all language (1982: 228; see also 221). Certainly extensive damage is inflicted on this single issue.

The very title of the English version of *La métaphore vive* raises an immediate problem. Why *The Rule of Metaphor* rather than *The Life of Metaphor*, *Living Metaphor*, *The Vitality of Metaphor*? 'Vive' catches the plasmic sense of language underlying Ricoeur's scrupulously conducted arguments; something in language allows, perhaps compels, the disclosure of new meaning. This underlying dynamism conforms to the structure of Ricoeur's other underpinnings of faith: the limit-idea of hope, the prospective transformation of the symbol of the father, the renewal of a promise of future abundance, here becomes a kind of forward-directed confidence in the human capacity for creativity. But the programme outlined in 'Existence and hermeneutics' (and indeed the long-awaited third volume of the *Poetics of the Will*) could be said to have been fulfilled, in suitably indirect fashion, in Ricoeur's work on metaphor and narrative. What was previously intimated appeared to be something like the techniques of *Finitude and Guilt* applied to the paradisal (though we should not forget the dialectical stress on the unfallen in the first volume, and the implied teleology of self-knowledge in the second). The question seemed to be, could this kind of study be conducted without reduplicating the shortcomings of a phenomenology of the sacred? Ricoeur's assimilation of the Anglo-American tradition of linguistic analysis allows him to focus specifically on metaphor as the point of emergence of meaning, and so engage in a tacit celebration of the human power to create and order new worlds, or new forms of worlds. But this may only emerge out of a contrapuntal narrative that recounts the death of metaphor on the 'entropic slope of language' (*RM*: 309), its dwindling to the comparative inertia of polysemy. It is with this tradition that Ricoeur begins.

The initial grand, even majestic, gesture is the characterisation of traditional rhetoric as an 'ironic tale of diminishing returns' (*RM*: 9). Aristotle's original categorisation of metaphor 'on the basis of a semantics that takes the word or the name as the basic unit' (*RM*: 3) is seen as dominating its subsequent history in Western thought. This sounds technical, perhaps rather dull. Part of the skill of the exposition is to centre on this single point so that the conception of language and thought itself is seen to hinge on this preliminary choice of definition. Within this tradition, the individual word, usually the noun, is assumed to have a proper or original meaning. Metaphor deviates from this literal sense in order to bring about an extension of meaning. The primary motivation for this deviation is resemblance, which justifies the substitution of figurative meaning. The original term, however, could have been used in the same place. Hence metaphor is essentially translatable: substitution plus restitution equals zero. It does not represent any genuine semantic innovation: no new information about reality is conveyed. Therefore it may fairly be relegated to the merely emotive function of 'making the probable more attractive'. (Although all these premises can be derived from Aristotle, the thrust of Ricoeur's reading of the *Poetics* is to detach lexis from a single word-trope, usually the noun, and connect metaphor with muthos and mimesis; ultimately providing a grounding for the revised concept of reference that will dominate *Time and Narrative*.)

The consequences of this 'excessive and damaging emphasis put on the word' (*RM*: 44) are examined in a late development of the rhetorical tradition: Pierre Fontanier's *Les figures du discours* (1830). Ricoeur demonstrates the necessary termination of such a methodology in 'classification and taxonomy, to the extent that it focuses on deviation'; and that this essentially static view of figuration as 'deviant denomination' cannot account for the production of new meaning. The reduction of tropology to metaphor and metonymy, resemblance and contiguity, prefigures structural linguistics, notably Jakobson; though in Fontanier, it should be noted, synecdoche is still preserved as a separate category. The primary delineation of kinds of metaphor is on a sliding scale of physical and spiritual, a point upon which Derrida will later seize. The degree of visibility is, however, implicitly circumscribed: '*to figure* is always *to see as* but', Ricoeur insists, 'not always *to see* or *to make visible*' (*RM*: 61). The trope of catachresis, the extension of meaning in response to semantic deficiency, is opposed to the figurative invention that takes place in the 'living event of actual speech' (*RM*: 62). The dichotomy between these two rival concepts will run throughout the entire book: a pessimism of linguistic entropy set against the renovation of new meaning.

Proper meaning is lexical, catalogued: emergent meaning, because wholly contextual, the product of 'semantic collision', can occur only in the present. 'The dictionary contains no metaphors: they exist only in discourse' (*RM*: 97). But the converse must also be recognised. Metaphor, far from being 'at once meaning and event' (*RM*: 99), has something of the transitoriness of an ignition, a flaring. Although paraphrase must be 'infinite and incapable of exhausting the innovative meaning', temporality can reduce metaphor to the comparative impotence of polysemy. It may tell us something new about reality, but this could be seen as the inevitability of its own demise, a kind of emblematic warning of attrition and decline.

Ricoeur now opposes the word-metaphor to the statement-metaphor ('impertinent predication'), and argues for the advantages of the tension theory developed in the work of I.A. Richards, Max Black and Monroe Beardsley over the substitution theory. Tropology leads to a taxonomy preoccupied with nominal definition: a theory of metaphor must consider 'discourse and not just the word' (*RM*: 65). There are no metaphorical words, only metaphorical utterances, and no deviation from a literal meaning, only an operation of predication.

The major innovation of Richards's *The Philosophy of Rhetoric* (1936) is to break with the 'proper meaning superstition' in favour of an 'undisguisedly fully contextual theory of meaning' (*RM*: 77). It restores the earlier amplitude that the discipline of rhetoric possessed, embracing 'thought as discourse' (*RM*: 76). Meaning does not belong to individual words, only to the event of discourse at the level of the sentence, which itself is always constituted as a part of a larger context: 'constancy of meaning is never anything but the constancy of contexts' (*RM*: 78). The polysemic potential of words allows opposing semantic fields to be simultaneously invoked. This 'interanimation of words in the living utterance' (*RM*: 79) is not an subsidiary facet of language but constitutive of it: Ricoeur's later addendum will be, and of being. Richards consciously avoids any opposition between literal and figurative, original and borrowed; instead he adopts the terminology of tenor and vehicle, the initial context of meaning and the new set of associations introjected into it. A literal meaning can be determined by the absence of division between the two fields. This is a matter of usage and degree: in fact a wholly literal sentence is a rarity outside scientific discourse. The relation cannot be reduced to comparison because of the degree of tension retained within the utterance, the continued friction of resistance and dissimilarity. There is an implied but at this point unspecified ontological bearing: 'the process of interpretation takes place at the level of modes of existing' (*RM*: 83).

Max Black offers an epistemological clarification of the 'pioneering work' of Richards in terms of logical grammar. Unlike such forms as proverb and allegory, not all words in metaphor are used metaphorically. Black's terminology of focus and frame allows an emphasis on the metaphorical word while retaining a grasp on its necessary context of the sentence, preserving its status as what Ricoeur elsewhere calls a 'trader' between structure and event (*CI*: 79–96). The interaction theory is decisively opposed to any reduction to comparison: metaphor creates similarity rather than appealing to a pre-given order, operates on a semantic level without involving mental imagery, and cannot be translated without loss of its cognitive content. Where Richards relies on either an act of mental juxtaposition or a somewhat indeterminate idea of simultaneity of thought to link tenor and vehicle, Black defines the relation of focus and frame in terms of a reorganisation of associated commonplaces. In his own example, 'man is a wolf', the lupine connotations of fierceness, predatoriness, and strength must be brought into relation with a similar range of human qualities. But no account is offered of how metaphor might construct new implications: for example, the maternal love evoked by 'sleep under the harbouring fur' in the 'wolf's lair' (Hill, 1985: 18). The denial of genuine redescriptive power results in a reliance on pre-established connotation: 'the enigma of novel meaning beyond the bounds of all previously established rules' remains (*RM*: 90).

The tension theory is further developed in the work of Monroe Beardsley. By disrupting any unitary primary signification, the metaphorical utterance compels recourse to secondary 'self-contradictory attribution', a 'twist' that generates a multiplicity of meanings which may be whittled down according to principles of plenitude and relevance (*RM*: 95). Thus logical absurdity accentuates the 'inventive and innovative character of the metaphorical statement' (*RM*: 96). Such an account, however, leaves the question of where the secondary meanings in metaphorical attribution come from unresolved, and in general there is inadequate recognition of semantic innovation. The invocation of language as a repository of potential meaning merely displaces the problem, by substituting a system of apparently invariant commonplaces for proper meaning.

To take Ricoeur's own example from Shakespeare: 'Time hath, my lord, a wallet on his back/ Wherein he puts alms for oblivion,/ A great-sized monster of ingratitude' (*Troilus and Cressida* III: iii ll.145–50). Taken literally, the tenor, frame, primary attribution of 'Time is . . .' cannot be reconciled with the vehicle, focus, secondary attribution of beggar: hence the attributes of beggarliness – dishevelment, wandering, despisedness – have to be brought into relation with those of time – its flowing, its relentlessness, its power of ageing. The advantage of such an account is that it remains on a strictly semantic level: the lines may perhaps conjure an image of Father Time, sickle in hand, as a down-at-heel tramp, but any such iconic evocativeness remains a random impressionism compared to the stable public associations of frugality, vagrancy, and impoverishment. As yet, however, little or nothing has been said about the specific quality of Shakespeare's metaphor: 'wallet', for example, becomes an image of memory, that which is stored and preserved, supported by the multiple meanings of 'oblivion', which evokes the forgetfulness of the elderly, the 'ingratitude' of the vagrant, the disdain of the alms-giver. While the interaction theory provides an excellent framework for comprehending such effects, it cannot account for the transformation of the original connotation achieved by the passage. Time which possesses the power of ageing is itself presented as decrepit: put crudely, the new information conveyed is the self-delusion of those who presume to master time and a certain inexorable ruthlessness in its response. It is this transformation of the original connotation that the interaction theory as such has difficulty in accounting for.

Structural semantics approaches the problem of multiple meaning by attempting to match variants of meaning to specific classes of contexts. These variants may then be analysed in terms of a fixed nucleus common to all contexts, and contextual variables. By reducing lexemes to a collection of semes, it seeks to account for the possible meanings of any given word as derivatives of these sub-lexical particles, arising out of the interplay of semic nucleus and its varying contexts. Structuralist analysis remains rooted in the same fundamental hypothesis as classical rhetoric: 'the metaphor is a figure of one word only' (*RM*: 101). It is the issue of polysemy which stimulates the most impressive work from the semiotic tradition: though unable to account for the birth of meaning, it may offer a scientific analysis of its constitution through decomposition into sub-lexical particles. 'Polysemy is just an already more ordered and a more determinate characteristic of the more general phenomenon of lexical imprecision' (*RM*: 114). This is a 'healthy feature' of language, even conforming to the principle of economy (*RM*: 115). Change of meaning is always a sudden innovation, but one made possible by the indeterminacy of semantic boundaries and 'cumulative capability' proper to words, their 'quality of openness' (*RM*: 116–17). Metaphor, therefore, possesses a dual status: as part of the code (as the 'accepted deviation' of polysemy) and of the message (as innovation of the level of discourse). A Saussurian linguistics is obliged to have recourse to a psychological element to account for meaning change. This has the advantages of enabling it to bridge the individual character of speech and the social activity of language, introduce an operative principle within an otherwise static taxonomy, and provide in the concept of association a common foundation for metaphor and metonymy. But the consequences for its account of metaphor are 'ruinous' (*RM*: 132). It is placed in a false symmetry with metonymy, and deprived of its properly predicative status: the figure remains within the domain of denomination and is thus reduced to a substitution of names motivated by private mental association.

Recent developments in linguistics represent 'a revolution within the revolution, that confers a sort of crystalline purity on the postulates of Saussurianism' (*RM*: 134). The relation of signifier and signified becomes wholly detached from consciousness, decomposed down to the level of the seme. This does not result in an alternative theory, however, merely 'an even tighter pact between metaphor and the word' (*RM*: 135). The new rhetoric, for all its ambitious reclamation of cultural spheres previously ceded to philosophy, remains essentially traditional in its characterisation of metaphor: the opposition of the proper to the figurative; the motivation of semantic lacunae; the borrowing of an alien term; the postulate of deviation; the axiom of substitution, usually through resemblance; the possibility of restitutive substitution and exhaustive paraphrase; the absence of new information; and an ultimately decorative function.

Ricoeur sees the achievement of this tradition as lying in a 'highly clarifying explanation resulting from the integration of the trope into a general theory of deviations' (*RM*: 137); but if deviations, deviations from what? Language wholly devoid of rhetoric 'cannot be found' (*RM*: 138). One possibility is to take as the standard of measurement a virtual language, defined as equivalent to the intention of the speaker, but this reduces metaphor to a mere translation of a non-verbal act of consciousness. A second option is to assume a relative degree zero in the language use of scientific discourse. This at least breaks with the problematic of intention and appeals to an actual semantic form, but loses all idea of the internal tension of the statement. A third direction is to construct a model of deviation entirely from semes, a purely methodological construct of the linguist that completely ignores the plane of manifestation.

In all three cases, the status of the implied spatial model is itself fraught with paradoxes. 'Rhetoric battles valiantly with this meta-phoricity of the metaphor, which leads it to remarkable discoveries about the status of the literal in discourse, and thus about "literature" as such' (*RM*: 143). As Fontanier pointed out, figure itself is beset by figurality, torn between 'a quasi-corporeal exteriority, and contour, feature, form'; similar problems arise with the movement implied in meta-phora. The status of any metalanguage dealing with deviation may thus be called into question: as Ricoeur later concedes, there is 'no principle for delimiting metaphor in which the defining does not contain the defined' (*RM*: 287). And the 'space of discourse' may be equated with a theory of denotation: 'what is untranslatable is its power to evoke an affective tone, a literary dignity' (*RM*: 146).

Ricoeur's response is to posit a double movement of a deviation from an impossible literal interpretation of a given sentence, followed by a movement of restructuring. 'The change of meaning is the answer of discourse to the threat represented by semantic impertinence. Metaphor is not deviation itself, it is reduction of deviation' (*RM*: 152). Structural linguistics may offer 'a *semiotic* equivalent of the semantic process' (*RM*: 157) in its description in terms of substitution of lexemes. But it has no adequate vocabulary to address the new semantic pertinence on the syntagmatic level. The immediate consequence of defining metaphor as a collection of nuclear semenes is to make it impossible to distinguish figure and polysemy. While synecdoche may conform perfectly to the system, metaphor demands a separate level of predication.

The final arbitration of semiotics and semantics suggests the approaches are 'equal in force and differ only in choice of a different system of fundamental axioms' (*RM*: 168). Analysis at the level of predication, however, allows an account of 'augmentation' of polysemy rather than remaining confined within an already constituted semantic field. Semic analysis separates out metasemenes (sub-lexical particles within the metaphor) and metalogisms (deviation between word and reality); predication holds them together. The reduction to merely lexical mutation keeps the process within a connotative and emotionalist theory of poetry, with no innovation on the referential level. In addition, it is by no means clear how meaning at the level of discourse can be related to infra-linguistic units. For all Ricoeur's deference, it is difficult to escape the conclusion that semiotics merely provides more cumbersome and ultimately dispensable equivalents to results attained 'directly and with greater elegance' within the tradition of English-language philosophical semantics (*RM*: 67).

THE WORK OF RESEMBLANCE

Ricoeur now takes up the problem of the creation of a new semantic pertinence by concentrating on the notion of resemblance, a commonsense notion fallen on hard times. Nothing may seem more obvious than that a metaphor involves comparison, presenting something in terms of something else on the grounds of its common features. The increasing sophistication of predicative analysis, however, leads to a reduction of role for resemblance, primarily on the grounds of its logical laxity (everything resembles everything else apart from a certain difference) and its tendency to introduce unverifiable and extraneous factors of individual psychology: Max Black, for example, omits it from his discussions altogether.

In classical rhetoric, metaphor is little more than an abridged simile ('Time is like a beggar who hath . . .'). The initial motivation of the epiphora is resemblance: the positive converse of deviation, which serves as an internal link within substitution; and a directing of the restitution of proper meaning. These postulates are taken up by structural linguistics, whose 'binarist zeal' reduces the entire domain of tropology to metonymy and metaphor, contiguity and resemblance. In Jakobson, the pairing is elevated to the governing principle of language itself. The Saussurian axis of combination (signifiers present in message) and selection (between alternatives in the same group) becomes transposable to any level in the linguistic hierarchy. No distinction is made from semantics, which simply forms an additional polarity with syntax. The empirical grounding for this ambitious schema is aphasia. Jakobson famously identifies two kinds of disorder: contiguity (agrammaticality) or similarity (metonymy overriding metaphor; expanded to include definition, naming, synonymy, circumlocution, and paraphrase).

'The strength of the bipolar scheme lies in its extreme generality and its extreme simplicity' which enables metaphor to be generalised 'beyond the sphere of the word, and even beyond tropology' (*RM*: 178). But this necessitates a restriction of the tropological field to two figures (synecdoche is mentioned, but on both sides of the equation). The failure to acknowledge a separate level of semantics means basic distinctions are 'obliterated in vague resemblances and in equivocations' (*RM*: 179). There is no justification whatsoever, for example, for treating contiguity of morphemes within phonemes as homogeneous with the syntax of predication. The definition is too wide, in its equation of resemblance with metalinguistic operations; and too narrow, in that it omits any account of the predicative nature of metaphor. Metaphor collapses back into a form of substitution, though this ought to apply more convincingly to metonymy as a movement from name to name. Metaphor, in bringing two ideas together, has obvious affinities with the axis of combination. The schema is incapable of distinguishing new metaphor from polysemy, the freedom of innovation from merely remedying a semantic deficiency. For Jakobson, selection takes place within preformed combinations of the code: he offers no account of 'unusual syntagmatic liaisons' (*RM*: 181).

The question of resemblance is better posed in terms of the 'associated image' rather than 'semic abstraction' (*RM*: 185). Ricoeur feels it is necessary to preserve a '*non-verbal* kernel of imagination' (*RM*: 199) that will provide a necessary element of disruption in 'obliterating the logical and established frontiers of language' (*RM*: 197). The account of imagination is disconcertingly devoid of positive content: a moment of grasping together, a change of distance in logical space, which may be equated with an act of predication. The transposition of pure imagination is one of Ricoeur's most unsatisfactory borrowings from Kant (see Schaldebrand, 1979). In the extended discussion in *Fallible Man*, for example, where the faculty bears the weight of mediating the poles of finite and infinite, we are told 'this mediating term has no intelligibility of its own' (*FM*: 42), and is 'not susceptible of being captured in itself' (*FM*: 37); it can only be retrospectively inferred from the syntheses that it performs.

In Ricoeur's most concise discussion of the faculty, 'Imagination in discourse and in action', 'ambiguities and contradictions' are said to be 'constitutive of the phenomenon of the imagination as such'

(1978b: 3–4). The suspicion has grown, most powerfully voiced in the work of Gilbert Ryle, that the linchpin of romantic aesthetics is no more than a loose conglomerate of unrelated mental capacities (see Ricoeur, 1981b: 3–11). At the very least the term encompasses such disparate phenomena as the arbitrary evocation of things absent but existent elsewhere; the controlled projection of an image that replaces an absent thing; an evocation of non-existent things (such as dreams); and the succumbing to a domain of total illusion. These conflicting possibilities may be assessed on the axis of presence and absence – the retained but weakened sense-impression (Hume) versus an act of negation of the perceptual image (Sartre) – and by the degree of belief involved – from the conscious fabrication of pastoral poetry (Empson) and scientific models (Hesse) to insidious seduction by the beguiling image (Pascal). Ricoeur prefers to regard it as 'acts of distanciation ... by which consciousness posits something at a distance from the real, thereby preserving otherness at the very heart of its experience' (1981b: 6); a formulation that obviously invites comparison with de Man's insistence that allegory lies 'on the far side of the existential project' because of its 'already demystified awareness of this temporal lag' and thus of 'the distance constitutive of all acts of reflection' (1982: 35, 213).

At this point the concept of 'iconic function' is somewhat problematically introduced; not in any quasi-sensorial sense, but as 'seeing as', the properly semantic operation of seeing the similar in the dissimilar (*RM*: 6). The basic etymological trope of metaphor – displacement, the sudden proximity of things previously set apart – is now glossed as an apperception that may legitimately be described in terms of a metaphor of visibility. The iconic moment of metaphor may be rehabilitated provided that the imagination is restricted 'prudently' to a Kantian definition. 'Nothing is displayed in sensible , images, therefore; everything, whether associations in the writer's mind or in that of the reader, takes place within language' (*RM*: 189).

Little seems gained by such a detour, which provokes unease at the final destination of this phase of Ricoeur's argument: a Bachelardian account of the 'reverberation' of the poetic verb in an 'aura surrounding speech' (*RM*: 214). The concept of resemblance has the unfortunate tendency to set off a chain reaction in Ricoeur: correspondence, analogy, divine order. (Compare, for example, his somewhat ingenuous citation of Baudelaire's sonnet, 'Correspondance' (*IT*: 68), with de Man's exemplary reading in *The Rhetoric of Romanticism* (1984: 243–52).) Two powerful arguments against resemblance – its laxity of logical definition and its apparent appeal to pre-established affinities – are utilised as points in its favour, indicating a point for possible re-insertion of the numinal symbol. The issue is not broached directly in *The Rule of Metaphor*, but the preferential value-judgement is explicitly stated in the third essay of *Interpretation Theory* (*IT*: 45–69; see also Adams, 1984: 372–89). Instead of tension between literal and figurative, there is an assimilation (perhaps ascension would be a better term) of a secondary meaning through the literal. 'A symbol always refers its linguistic elements to something else' (*IT*: 54) whereas the 'individual windfalls' of metaphor remain merely semantic: 'language only captures the foam on the surface of life' (*IT*: 63). It becomes a positive benefit that things appear 'so fascinating, so deceiving – all the boundaries are blurred' (*IT*: 56). 'Metaphor occurs in the already purified universe of the *logos*, while the symbol hesitates on the dividing line between *bios* and *logos*. It testifies to the primordial rootedness of Discourse in Life' (*IT*: 59).

The merits of Ricoeur's account of the symbol deserve separate consideration: at the very least, it is refreshingly uncovert about its sacramental dimension. Metaphor, however, remains within language. The importance of resemblance here lies in the 'tension between identity and difference in the predicative operation set in motion by semantic innovation' (*RM*: 6). Time both is and is not a beggar: the simultaneous apprehension of both possibilities is made possible by the split nature of the copula that allows seeing-as to contain within itself the power of being-as. This somewhat gnomic assertion will be more fully developed in the discussion of metaphorical reference, to which we shall now turn.

METAPHORICAL REFERENCE

The problem of the status of metaphorical description in relation to sense, constituted by internal organisation, and reference, directed towards reality outside language, involves a crucial transposition of level. Ricoeur's exposition of reference is consistent with his general characterisation of discourse. Firstly, it is situated at the level of the sentence and above, that is, semantics, and involves the 'essentially synthetic character of predication' opposed to the differential play of signifiers. The intended of discourse is irreducible to the signified of semiotics: 'sign differs from sign, discourse refers to the world'. It is necessary to 'clearly subordinate' the semiotic to the semantic, from which the closed world of signs is an 'abstraction'. The reidentifiable sense that preserves the transient speech-event demands a subsequent outward movement of application that 'carries us across the threshold from the *sense* towards the *reference* of discourse' (*RM*: 216–17).

The corollary, however, that the distinction between sense and reference originating with Frege 'holds in principle for all discourse' (*RM*: 217) remains to be demonstrated. Ricoeur sees no incompatibility between 'analytic dissociation' down from the sentence to the word (in which case the referent of the name is a specific object) and 'synthetic composition' from the proper name upwards (in which case the referent is a state of affairs). The Wittgensteinian pairing of fact and thing is contrasted with Strawson's return to the 'strict Fregean position', where reference is linked to singular identification 'carried by the logically proper name', and opposed to predication which merely 'characterizes' and so does not raise the issue of existence (*RM*: 218). What initially appears to be a contextual definition of truth, according to use and situation, suddenly acquires the 'postulate' of a world existing beyond language – 'something must be in order that it may be identified' – but this merely displaces the question onto what counts as a valid postulation. The subsequent problems are sidestepped by positing a 'striving for truth' which 'suffuses' the entire proposition (*RM*: 218): Ricoeur presupposes that if a metaphor occurs on the level of the sentence, it can be regarded as making a statement about reality equivalent to a logical proposition, or at least in some way comparable. But this in turn raises the question of how this might be verified: by what criteria is it true? On strict positivist grounds, the very concept of a 'metaphorical statement' would be meaningless. Frege himself would certainly have deplored such a dilution of the stringent demands of verification. Not to have a reference is to fall outside the category of true propositions. Ricoeur coolly opts for a somewhat broader question – 'do we actually know what "reality", "world", and "truth" signify?' (*RM*: 221).

Ricoeur insists that 'displayed reference' appears only 'amidst the ruins of the literal sense' which allows it to be 'set free' (*RM*: 221). Frege's exclusion of the name Ulysses from any claim to reference (1970: 63) which ought to be extremely troublesome is readily enlisted as evidence that such a divorce is a necessary condition of achieving second-order reference. The basic analogy invites scrutiny: it is at least possible that, in the transformation of sentences into the work, a shift takes place comparable to that on the level of the sentence from lexical units. And the wholesale suspension of primary reference is to be regretted. One would like to have ways of discussing *King Lear* as in some way about the Elizabethan ideal of kingship without resorting to mere reflectionism or empirical correlative: on Ricoeur's model, it would be the remaking of the ideal of kingship, the disclosure of new possibilities within it, which its contemporary audience would be obliged to appropriate in the same manner as ourselves. This utopian dimension is attractive in certain ways, but surely overtly hostile to any form of interpretation that stresses the intersection of historical discourses in a given text. Any attempt, for example, to relate the double (and visually self-contradictory) sense of impotence and power in the comparison of time as beggar to 'a giant-sized monster of ingratitude' to the Elizabethan fear of wild men, and savage proscription of vagrants, would be regarded as illegitimate.

Ricoeur locates the chief argument against second-order reference in the presumed self-referentiality of the poetic text that 'intercepts reference and, in the limiting situation, abolishes reality' (*RM*: 222). The 'poetic', however, in Jakobson's terms, is not synonymous with poems, but with the predominance of the highlighting of the message for its own sake, and so in direct opposition to the communicative function. The presence of this one function does not mean the absence of all others: Jakobson himself links epic to reference; lyric to emotiveness; apostrophic poetry to either supplication or exhortation. It may seem that Ricoeur accepts the postulate of message for its own sake too easily: the point of 'I like Ike', a frequently quoted example of the poetic function, is after all not to provide 'a paronomastic image of a feeling that totally envelops its object' (Jakobson, 1987: 70), but to elect a US President.

Ricoeur sees the dominant preoccupation of contemporary literary criticism as the 'destruction of reference' and the conversion of the message into an 'enduring thing' (*RM*: 224). Langer, Wimsatt, Hester and, most prominently, Frye are all cited as exponents of an aesthetic celebrating a centripetal movement of words. What will be taken up in Frye, however, is the suggestion that 'the unity of a poem is a unity of mood' (1957: 80), phrasing that invites a Heideggerian recuperation. (The misquotation of Sidney's dictum as 'the poet (nothing) affirmeth', occurs in the English edition only, but nevertheless has a certain appropriateness (*RM*: 226).) There is an explicit repudiation of the internalisation of emotion, its confinement within the subject: it is demanded that the whole opposition of denotation and connotation, fact and feeling, be abandoned. All the patient exposition of Ricoeur's early work is brought to bear on this one point. His position certainly manages to bypass the insuperable problems raised in 'The affective fallacy' by accepting Richards's distinction between referential and emotive usages of language: the affective responses of individual readers are continually denounced as a distraction from a proper attention to the object of study, which, however, is itself constituted as an 'emotional universal' (Wimsatt, 1954: 34–9).

In a different linguistic tradition, however, moods sound fairly insubstantial things to build worlds out of: 'can there be a virtual life without a virtual world capable of being inhabited?' (*RM*: 229). One is tempted to add to the list, virtual clothes and virtual televisions and virtual houses to put them in. The 'break-up' of descriptive discourse allows a somewhat ominous recourse to the 'more fundamental modes of reference' and a revelation of the 'sadness' at the heart of things (*RM*: 227). The whole timbre becomes almost lugubrious, as if the moment reality and truth come into play, all other human perspectives and experiences must be ignored. For a theory of literature, Ricoeur is perhaps inclined to overlook the simple and at times trivial pleasure of variety; there's a sense that in asking the question of being, we predetermine the kind of answer we shall receive – sonorous, portentous, and at times even bombastic (see Flew, 1979 for a particularly aggrieved protest). When 'the affirmative vehemence of the poetic experience' is invoked (*RM*: 249), it is difficult not to resent the hijacking of the word 'poetic' at such moments: all those human experiences which subsist pleasantly and unconcernedly without 'vehemence' are implicitly devalued in favour of the 'ecstatic moment of language' (*RM*: 249). What about everything that isn't ecstasy, one wants to retort; is that devoid of rationale, of dignity? But as decon-struction has landed us in this Heideggerian idiom (ek-stasis), albeit from a rather triumphalist perspective, we must come to terms with the formidable sophistication of its hermeneutic vocabulary and its frankly superior resources in many of the standard critical debates – intentionality, historicism, and the like.

Ricoeur then goes on to claim that this 'blockage' produces 'a new semantic pertinence . . . on the level of both metaphor and text' (*RM*: 230), and turns for support to Nelson Goodman's *Languages of Art*. This provides an enlarged notion of denotation that can contain representation in art and description by language. Sounds, images, feelings, exemplify rather than denote: these qualities of transferred possession, however, have no less validity than scientific traits. They are true in so far as they are appropriate, and therefore possess a referential capacity no less than descriptive discourse. To represent ceases to be imitation through resemblance but instead becomes a remaking of symbolic systems. The force of this displacement is devalued, however, by seeing the only resistance to such transference in habitual usage. A nominalist perspective regards both denotation and reference as the applying of labels. Metaphorical application is essentially no different from literal, though subject to rather different criteria of appropriateness through not being sanctioned by previous usage. It simply becomes a function of transference common to a diverse range of tropes. As such it remains a relatively ornamental concept. Nominalism cannot clarify why certain transferred predicates are appropriate and others are not: its impoverished account of linguistic invention cannot fully acknowledge the redescriptive power of poetic fictions.

Ricoeur now turns to Max Black's article, 'Models and metaphor', in order to connect second-order reference with the theory of models in science. Here fiction and redescription are reunited in a common logic of discovery which 'involves a cognitive process, a rational method with its own canons and principles' (*RM*: 240). Three levels are distinguished: scale models (e.g. toy boat), faithful in relevant detail, with only proportions altered; analogue models (e.g. electronic diagram), whose resemblance lies in the presumed isomorphism of their structural identity rather than sensible features; and theoretical models, which alter a domain of reality through changing the language of investigation. It is mistaken to try and make the use of models conform to general criteria of falsifiability and predictability. The procedure involved is not in essence deductive. The poetic analogue is not the individual statement but a 'metaphoric network' which covers an 'area' of experience rather than being restricted to a local 'pin-point' existence (*RM*: 244). Somewhat ominously, the cumulative force of this linguistic field is credited with a revelatory power of discovery: 'only a feeling transformed into myth can open and discover the world' (*RM*: 245); elsewhere the accumulation of 'root-metaphors' will acquire a specifically theological dimension (see, for example, *IT*: 66–8). Ricoeur seizes upon Frye's phrase, 'hypothetical verbal structure' (1957: 79), and pushes it hard in order to emphasise the heuristic function of poetic language. In a rhapsodising outburst sharply at odds with the terseness of the preceding analytic arguments, we now have 'lyric *mimesis*', through which we feel 'participation in things', a 'reciprocity of the inner and the outer', an 'intropathic fusion' (*RM*: 246).

This redescriptive power is designated 'metaphoric truth'. This involves a tensional theory at three levels: within the statement; between a literal interpretation destroyed by semantic impertinence and a metaphoric one arising from its ruins; and in the copula, between identity and difference in the interplay of resemblance. This 'tensive sense of the word truth' permits Ricoeur to establish an antimony between 'ontological naïveté', with its fervent belief in the power of 'it is', and reductive scepticism that reduces the 'is' to a mere 'is as if'. The first is represented by the Coleridgean 'mélange of non-philosophy and Schellingian philosophy' (*RM*: 249); Ricoeur is prepared to accept its reintroduction of philosophy of nature, organicism, as a necessary price of romantic ecstasy. In effect, there is little to say except that a tensionist theory is 'dissipated by the intuitionist and vitalist tendency' (*RM*: 251). This is opposed to Colin Turbayne's *The Myth of Metaphor*, an attempt to expose the abuse of metaphor as a pretence, a make-believe. This concentration on the 'dissimulative trait' – one might almost say the bad faith – of metaphor comes very close to de Man, and raises the intriguing possibility of a convergence between the deconstructive imperative to 'unmask' the dream of coincidence and the 'critical vigilance' (*RM*: 253) of a positivist critique directed against the invalidity of statements overreaching legitimate boundaries. Positivism, however, would disdain to apply the degree of attentiveness necessary to uncover aporias within this mode of thought: it has simpler and more pugnacious arguments at its disposal. Ricoeur objects to Turbayne's pre-selection of reified conceptual world views 'where the border between model and scientific myth tends to be erased', and displays an implicit distaste for the kind of technocratic mastery implied by the restriction of models solely to the realm of the manipulable: the critique of 'mythicised metaphor' is 'precisely that which is least transposable' (*RM*: 253). Furthermore, 'critical consciousness of the distinction between use and abuse leads not to disuse but re-use of metaphors, in the endless search for other metaphors, namely a metaphor which would be the best possible' (*RM*: 253).

Such antimonies suggest at least a potential reconciliation. In a truly drastic enlargement of scope, it is posited that 'in order to elucidate the tension deep within the logical force of the verb *to be*, we must expose an "is not", itself implied in the impossibility of the literal interpretation, yet present as a filigree in the metaphorical '"is"' (*RM*: 247–8). This looks back to the split ontology of Ricoeur's earlier theological work, but possesses a far greater vibrancy in its primordial and ultimately Hegelian dialectic of becoming through the experience of negation. This vision of a propulsive force within language must first, however, withstand the encounter with deconstruction.

DECONSTRUCTION AND METAPHOR

It is a remarkable paradox that a book so committed to demonstrating the fundamental importance of metaphor in human creativity should devote so much of its final chapter to trying to fend off the success of its preceding argument. Here some very delicate negotiation takes place in this 'plea for the plurality of modes of discourse and for the independence of philosophical discourse in relation to the propositions of sense and reference of poetic discourse' (*RM*: 7). We have seen these problems repeatedly in Ricoeur: philosophy must sustain itself from metaphor, but not 'proceed directly' from it. This is shown in a teasing and labyrinthine discussion of the medieval appropriation of Aristotelian analogy; and more important for the purposes of this discussion a refusal of the deconstructive claim, in both Heidegger and Derrida, of its indirect 'collusion': 'to *ground* what was called metaphorical truth is also to *limit* poetic discourse' (*RM*: 7). A whole series of challenges are laid down (the use of 'ground' cannot but be provocative in the context of a discussion of *White Mythology*); essentially what is at stake is the claim of reflective philosophy to retain its traditional prerogative as governing metadiscourse. It is important to be clear about the implications of this. Its authority is to be preserved by a self-conscious renunciation of the resources of poetic language that have been Ricoeur's subject: it must recognise its own secondariness and refuse to succumb to the temptation of 'binding metaphorical and speculative discourse' (*RM*: 258). This denial is, however, only partial, or perhaps apparent, for this is what enables it to situate metaphor and through that revise the concepts of truth, reality and being: sprats to catch whales. The proper understanding of metaphor involves something like a complete overhaul of philosophy; but one that philosophy itself must carry out.

The premise to be refuted is that conceptual thought reproduces the semantic functioning of poetic discourse; essentially the claim that new meaning even in the guise of a logical category must remain in some way metaphoric. 'Philosophical discourse sets itself up as the vigilant watchman overseeing the ordered extensions of meaning: against this background, the unfettered extensions of meaning in poetic discourse spring free' (*RM*: 261). It is difficult not to see this as a classic illustration of the policing of boundaries: 'vigilance' inevitably appears a repressive and repressed quality: in its demand for 'regulated polysemy' and 'ordered process'. Aristotle's charge against Plato's theory of ideas as merely 'poetical ideas' is implicitly endorsed: 'philosophy must neither use metaphors nor speak poetically' (*RM*: 261). Aporia, it should be stressed, can be enlisted comfortably on behalf of the 'discontinuity that assures the autonomy of speculative discourse' (*RM*: 258): Ricoeur attempts to demonstrate that philosophy can acknowledge and even draw sustenance from it.

Aristotle's *Categories* are invoked as providing a 'non-poetic model of equivocalness', and thus an exemplary 'act of ordering' (though it should be noted that the 'concentric structure' extending progressively from a 'substantial centre' is itself a figural edifice (*RM*: 261)). 'Extension from a radically nonpoetic pole', however, can only occur 'through the weakening of criteria'; the further analogy is pushed, the more vulnerable it becomes to modern logical analysis which exposes a persistent slippage from proportional analogy (A is to B as C is to D) to analogy of attribution (progressively extended derivation). Nevertheless the 'segment of equivocalness' that has been 'wrested' from poetry (*RM*: 272) resists the Platonic demand for unequivocal truth and provides the resources for moving beyond metaphor towards a 'non-generic bond of being'. It is subsequently conceded that the results of this inquiry are 'admittedly disappointing' (*RM*: 270). Nevertheless Aristotle's project 'attests, by its very failure, to the search that animated it' (*RM*: 272), and in so doing opens an endless labour of conceptualisation: the value of this interminable enterprise remains to be demonstrated.

In Aquinas's discussion of *analogia entis*, there is an explicit 'composite of ontology and theology' which seeks to establish theological discourse at the level of science and thereby 'to free it completely from the poetical forms of religious discourse, even at the price of severing the science of God from biblical hermeneutics' (*RM*: 273). The problem to be faced is that to impute a discourse common to God and his creatures would destroy divine transcendence; total incommunicability would condemn them to involuntary agnosticism. Analogous attribution serves to bridge the gap between a generic unity of being and a simple dispersion of its meanings. The problem arises that this necessarily presumes partial possession of common attributes and thus an 'ontology of participation': this can be seized upon as evidence that 'metaphysics has turned to poetry through its lamentable recourse to metaphor, as Aristotle argued against Platonism' (*RM*: 274). The charge comes closer to home than that: it is directly applicable to Ricoeur's own Heideggerian affiliation in such terms as world, reality, and being. A distinction is made between two modes of analogy: symbolic attribution (God is a lion, sun) where the term implies matter extraneous to the comparison, and transcendental attribution (the good, true) where there is no such excess. The first is the level of metaphor; the second analogy proper. The two levels intersect, however, in a 'criss-crossing' of 'composite modalities': 'the speculative verticalises metaphor, while the poetic dresses speculative analogy in iconic garb' (*RM*: 279). God is wise, for example, could be a proportional analogy with the wisdom of man or a transcendental analogy with wisdom *per se*. Thus it is possible to have 'metaphorical meaning within analogy', which allows extension of meaning without compromising the distinctness of God. 'Being itself revives Saying by means of underlying continuities that provide an analogical extension of its meanings to Saying' (*RM*: 277); but this grace is circular. Analogy is obliged to presume the very thing it sets out to prove. So why does Ricoeur back another loser? Its chief merit is seen as 'the refusal to compromise in any way with poetic discourse': 'it is precisely at the point of greatest proximity that the line between analogy and metaphor is most firmly drawn' (*RM*: 278) – that is, the heliotrope.

A rare joke – 'Ah, the sun! Oh the fire! The heliotrope cannot be far away' (*RM*: 278) – signals an imminent confrontation with deconstruction for which this detour through ancient and medieval philosophy has been mere preparation. It has also been an exemplary reappropriation of a cultural heritage in contrast to 'the convenience, which has become a laziness of thinking, of lumping the whole of Western thought together under a single word, metaphysics' (*RM*: 311). If nothing else, the sheer tedium of a version of intellectual history that presents it as always in thrall to the same structure of error should provoke protest. Such an 'inclosure', a Heideggerian tactic made depressingly familiar by Derrida, is seen as expressing 'a sort of vengefulness – which this thinking nevertheless calls us to renounce – along with a will to power that seems inseparable from it' (*RM*: 311). This is the point that de Man made against Derrida on Rousseau, that he presented himself as merely the latest in a 'massive tradition' of corrective commentaries, 'always accompanied by an

139

overtone of intellectual and moral superiority' (1983: 112, 122). There is an implicit self-righteousness, an absence of the requisite 'solicitude' (1983: 101). (Derrida's subsequent vigorous denial that his work presents the metaphysical as 'l'unité homogène d'un ensemble' (1978b: 110) underestimates the specific strengths of his own argument; the persuasiveness of *White Mythology* must ultimately depend on its construction of a plausible generic definition of philosophical writing. Ricoeur would, after all, readily concede the legitimacy of such a procedure as a methodological convenience).

The challenge of deconstruction is seen as initially and perhaps most powerfully directed against phenomenology, a discipline that itself claimed to break decisively from past error. As with the 'genealogical' aim of Nietzschean questioning, it seeks the motives and self-interests behind declared intentions. Through the disclosure of hidden presuppositions, 'it is not only the order of the terms that is inverted, philosophy preceding metaphor, but the mode of implication is itself reversed, the "un-thought" of philosophy anticipating the "un-said" of metaphor' (*RM*: 280). Note the paradoxical status of such a project within a hermeneutic context. The refusal to allow unthematised presuppositions reveals a highly idealistic orientation; yet one whose exposures, far from being governed by an interest in emancipation, celebrate and implicitly endorse entrapment – 'one always inhabits and the more so when one does not suspect it' (Derrida, 1977: 24).

Ricoeur now glosses Heidegger's maxim, 'the metaphorical exists only within the metaphysical', as suggesting

> that the trans-gression of meta-phor and that of meta-physics are but one and the same transfer. Several things are implied here: first, that the ontology implicit in the entire rhetorical tradition is that of Western 'metaphysics' of the Platonic or neo-Platonic type, where the soul is transported from the visible world to the invisible world; second that meta-phorical means transfer from the proper sense to the figurative sense; finally, that both transfers constitute one and the same Über-tragung.
>
> (*RM*: 280)

Despite the importance attached to metaphor, Heidegger's account of its actual working is cursory in the extreme; an enormous amount hangs on little more than the etymology of a prefix, meta. In his own writing, this polemic is delimited by context, so that his 'constant use' of metaphor can be regarded as 'finally more important than what he says in passing' against it (*RM*: 280). Thus Ricoeur defends metaphor against an attack from the very source of the idiom employed to defend second-order reference. He is acutely aware that the importation of this vocabulary may short-circuit his argument into a 'plea for the irrational': 'when so many firmly recognised distinctions are erased, does not the notion of speculative discourse itself evaporate?' (*RM*: 306). Hence the necessity of the final severance from 'the intermingled and inescapable attempt and temptation' represented by Heidegger's thought (*RM*: 309).

Two contexts are identified for Heidegger's argument. The first is formed by the network of the terms seeing, hearing, thinking, and harmony: an attempt to enlarge the metaphor of reason as clear sight to include other possible modes of apprehension: 'thinking is a hearing and a seeing' that 'are never a simple reception by the senses' (*RM*: 281). The charge is broadened to include the entire transfer from the sensible to the non-sensible in Western thought. Ricoeur rather neatly enlists this in his own argument: the polemic is directed against 'a manner of casting metaphors as particular philosophical statements' (*RM*: 282), and thus serves as a purging of reflective thought rather than a repudiation of metaphor itself. This 'wholehearted denunciation' aims itself therefore at the interpreter 'under the aegis of Platonism' determined to impose the movement from sensible to nonsensible. But, as Ricoeur insists, there is no need for the 'obsolete semantic notion' of 'the distinction between proper and figurative' to be 'tacked onto metaphysics to be taken to pieces. An improved semantics is sufficient to unseat it as a "determinative" conception of metaphor' (*RM*: 282).

The temporality of metaphor, its capacity to grow stale and dwindle to polysemy, provides the point of transition 'from Heidegger's restrained criticism to Jacques Derrida's unbounded "deconstruction"' (*RM*: 284). Here the 'entropy of language' motivates an investigation, or a 'more heightened suspicion' of metaphor itself (*RM*: 285). The crucial linkage is the inverse movement between the wearing-away of metaphor and 'the ascending movement that constitutes the formation of the concept': 'to revive metaphor is to unmask the concept' (*RM*: 286). Derrida quotes the relevant passages from Hegel's *Philosophy of Fine Arts* in full (1982: 225); deferentially, one might say derivatively. Certainly it appears to be offered in order to ground and justify his more adventurous textual forays: as Ricoeur says, he 'bases his work on' it (*RM*: 286). (Derrida takes particular exception to this term (*appuyer*), to the point of angrily inserting a

141

rebuttal in the middle of a quotation (1978b: 112).) Where Hegel saw an innovation of meaning, Derrida sees only a spurious idealisation resulting from the dissimulation of metaphorical origin. This transposition of the material into the spiritual realm brings into play all the familiar oppositions that supposedly characterise metaphysics: nature/spirit, nature/history, nature/freedom, sensible/spiritual, sensible/intelligible, sensible/meaning. This system, according to Derrida, 'describes the space of the possibility of metaphysics and the concept of metaphor so defined belongs to it' (1982: 226).

Ricoeur pays generous (and perhaps pre-emptive) tribute to 'the tight fabric of Derrida's demonstration' that enters 'the domain of metaphor not by way of its birth, but if we may say so, by way of its death' (*RM*: 285), and proceeds to give an admirably lucid summary of an extremely elusive text.

> The concept of wearing away (*usure*) implies something completely different from the concept of abuse that English-language authors oppose (as we have seen) to use. This concept carries its own sort of metaphoricity with it, which is not surprising in a conception that aims precisely at demonstrating the limitless metaphoricity of metaphor. In its overdetermination the concept carries first the geological metaphor of sedimentation, of erosion, of wearing away by friction. To this is added the numismatic metaphor of wearing down the features of a medal or a coin. This metaphor in turn evokes the tie, perceived by de Saussure among others, between linguistic value and monetary value: a comparison that invites the suspicion that the using up or wearing away (*usure*) of things used and worn out is also the usury of usurers. At the same time the instructive parallelism between linguistic value and economic value can be pushed to the point where the *proper* sense and *property* are suddenly revealed as next of kin within the same semantic network. Following this assonance further, one may suspect that metaphor is a sort of 'linguistic surplus value' functioning unknown to speakers, in the manner in which in the economic field the product of human labour is made at once unrecognizable and transcendent in economic surplus value and the fetishism of merchandise.
>
> (*RM*: 285)

The very act of paraphrase is crucial. Once pinned down and pegged out, Derrida can be argued with, and refuted. Two points should be made. The argument might be made that such a reduction travesties a text that claims all the licence of poetic metaphor. Derrida later defends himself by insisting that to talk of metaphor requires a metaphorical idiom: 'elle (la métaphore) continuerait à se passer de moi pour me faire parler, me ventriloquer ... je ne peux en traiter sans traiter avec elle' (1979: 105). His argument is not an 'affirmation' but 'un mode ... déconstructif' of working out the implication of this tradition; certainly not a 'perversité manipulatrice' (1978b: 109; compare 1982: 215: 'not in order to reject them but to reinscribe them otherwise'). Later Ricoeur will concede the separation of poet's from 'philosopher's metaphor' to be a precarious distinction liable to unravel at any moment: the difference can be 'infinitesimal' in a thinking poetry or a 'thinking that poeticizes' (*RM*: 310). But Derrida's own emphasis, in so far as it can be ascertained, precludes the influx of new meaning which would be the justification of his procedure. If it is seen as inhabiting the system of worn-out metaphor, then it can be paraphrased without loss, with the proviso that the text that comments on it can be similarly exposed. From Ricoeur's viewpoint, no philosophical discourse would be possible, not even a discourse of deconstruction, if we ceased to assume what Derrida justly holds to be the 'sole thesis of philosophy', namely 'that the meaning aimed at through these figures is an essence rigorously independent of that which it carries over' (1982: 229; *RM*: 293). In so far as Derrida seeks to retain the status of 'a philosophical rhetoric in the service of an autonomous theory constituted before and outside its own language' (1982: 224). In this I wholly concur. The semi-mystical justifications of *écriture*, the most notorious example probably being Spivak's preface to *Of Grammatology*, themselves derive from the most obfuscating traditions of Romantic aesthetics. The famous style, far from being some kind of liberating breakthrough, derives from the most decadent and obscurantist aspects of the late Heidegger – if one wanted a terse summation, 'hermeticism and affectedness' would do excellently (*RM*: 312) – without the counterbalancing attempt to re-establish an authentic language in the space thus opened. Ricoeur holds fire on the proper/property equation that has already been denounced in Heidegger; and is prepared to allow such linkages as 'evokes the tie', 'the suspicion that', 'can be pushed to the point of', 'following this assonance further'. He refuses to be drawn or provoked by Derrida's ostentatious textuality, and even concedes its appositeness for a position that aims at demonstrating 'the limitless metaphoricity of metaphor': 'there is no discourse on metaphor that is not stated metaphorically within a metaphorically engendered conceptual network' (*RM*: 287). I would suggest that Derrida could not (and does not) put his case more strongly; and there is surely something more genuinely exposed, self-risking, in Ricoeur's willingness to entertain the final proposition that 'metaphoricity is absolutely uncontrollable' (*RM*: 287).

Ricoeur then relates this critique back to Heidegger: the elevation that conceals metaphor within the concept is the 'pre-eminent philosophical gesture' that 'sights the invisible beyond the visible, the intelligible beyond the sensible, after having first separated them' (*RM*: 287). Thus it establishes a binary opposition between the two realms, and then privileges the nonsensible; Derrida seeks to reactivate the sensible in order to provoke a revision of the original polarity. Thus every use of analogy is grounded on this metaphysical concept, a transposition from the empirical to the intelligible; hence the pervasiveness of examples of movement from the animate to the inanimate, the visible to the invisible: 'what must be grasped is the single movement that carries words and things beyond, *meta*' (*RM*: 288). Derrida vigorously protests against this 'geste d'assimilation ou au moins de dérivation', claiming to have demonstrated 'une réserve nette et sans équivoque' towards his predecessor (1979: 109). The sole evidence offered for this, however, is 'la place et la portée' of a single footnote (n. 29: 1982: 226) quoting the key passage on the sensible and invisible from Heidegger's *Der Satz vom Grund*. No serious argument is offered about the overall tradition in which Ricoeur situates his work.

Here we get the heliotrope (brilliantly picked out by the absence of a fourth term for the sun's power to engender in Aristotle's *Poetics*). 'The orbit of the sun is the trajectory of metaphor': it is the 'paradigm of what is sensible and what is metaphorical'. A moving away towards light, the eye, looking, is followed by a return to ground-foundation and home. These twin poles of sun and home seem to have an archetypal status that enables them to govern the whole field of metaphysics: 'by being images for idealization and appropriation, light and sojourn are a figure for the very process of metaphorizing and thereby ground the return of metaphor upon itself' (*RM*: 289). Even this 'fantastic extrapolation' is quite comfortably assimilated to the 'paradox of metaphor's self-implication' (*RM*: 289).

How fair is it to take *White Mythology* as a representative Derridean text, if its conclusion is 'more seductive than earth-shaking' (*RM*: 291)? It ranges from the minutely scholarly (Aristotelian etymology) to the boldly and provocatively fantastic (the rise of the heliotrope); it rings the changes on familiar vocabularies of coins, words, circulation, correlating disparate fields of discourse with elegance and perverse wit; flipping between the literary and the philosophical (Anatole France to Saussure); a bizarre array of tones, from the aphoristic to baroque apostrophe; a variety of different stances towards the reader, complicit, exhortatory, wheedling, resonant; a disconcerting admixture of parody in the homecoming, the philosophic quest turned into a grandiose solar gesticulation; the capacity to extrapolate from virtual asides in dazzling fashion; and its mastery of a whole variety of levels of proof, evidence. The text shows Derrida's raffish bravado at its most impressive.

Yet ultimately I concur with Ricoeur. This is what must be renounced – which may seem harshly ascetic. But this is refutable. It is misleading. It represents a dead-end of ostentatious self-reflexivity, and in this way 'gives new life in this way to the seductions of the unarticulated and the unexpressed, even to a kind of despair of language' (*RM*: 312). Is it possible to read it without entertaining some discursive claim? It would lose much of its point: it is the adoption of the simulacrum of argument that gives it its unsettling, needling quality. Reading Derrida as light entertainment still seems a long way off, and anathema to the devotees. It needs the truth-claim to give it its edge, and those who live by the truth-claim may also die by it.

Ricoeur is typically apologetic before going in for the kill: the attempted exposure of the collusion of metaphor and metaphysics in *White Mythology* represents only 'one tactic' in a 'much vaster strategy' (*RM*: 287); furthermore its account of the repression of metaphor in the concept serves as a valuable preliminary to 'positive clarification of the concept of analogy'.

The initial point of contention is 'the thesis of an unstated effectiveness of worn-out metaphor' (*RM*: 290). This is a 'false enigma' to be 'dispelled'. Far from representing a vast untapped reservoir of meaning, 'dead metaphors are no longer metaphors, but instead are associated with literal meaning, extending its polysemy' (*RM*: 290). There is no longer deviation from a customary sense when metaphor has become that customary sense: 'the expression now brings its lexicalized value into discourse, with neither deviation nor reduction of deviation'. Etymology has little impact against usage: Ricoeur cites the derivation of *tête*, head, from *testa*, little pot. (Derrida himself concedes that the 'critique of etymologism' easily degenerates into a 'kind of nonscientific meandering' (1982: 216); but this does not prevent him claiming that the 'traditional metaphorical burden' of the term 'Idea' 'continues Plato's system into Hegel's' (*RM*: 293), conveniently omitting the antithetical usage of the term in the British empiricist tradition.) Derrida relies on 'semiotic conceptions that impose the primacy of denomination, and hence of substitution of meaning' (see the comments on resemblance and the equivalence to metonymy (1982: 215, 227)). The charge of collusion results from treating metaphor at the level of word rather than of sentence. He attaches 'to the opposition between the figurative and the proper a meaning that is itself metaphysical, one that a more precise semantics dispels' (*RM*: 290). Derrida later denies that he has paid insufficient attention to this distinction ('ni davantage propre, littéral ou usuel, notions que je ne confonds pas' (1978b: 104)), but there is no acknowledgement of the semantic level of metaphor anywhere in the essay. (The charge evidently stung: the same protest is repeated on pp. 105, 107, 111, 117.) His own argument compels him to attribute 'prestige ... to the primitive or original', and so promote 'the mystique of the proper (*RM*: 291). 'White mythology – metaphysics has erased within itself the fabulous scene that has produced it, the scene that nevertheless remains active and stirring' (1982: 213). But no such 'disturbing fecundity' exists (*RM*: 291). It is part of the resources of ordinary language to create meaning from polysemous words: 'delexicalization is in no way symmetrical to the earlier lexicalization' (*RM*: 292). Even in the recourse to etymology, 'the philosopher creates meaning and in this way produces something like a living metaphor'.

Ricoeur acknowledges the concentration of lexicalised metaphor in philosophical discourse, but sees this as a necessary and legitimate response to 'the advent of a new manner of questioning'. The case of 'deficiency' is 'relatively banal' compared to that of controlled innovation (*RM*: 291). Crucially the 'full genesis of the concept does not inhere in the process by which metaphor is lexicalized' (*RM*: 292). He distinguishes two stages: the first purely metaphorical, the transfer of a proper meaning into the spiritual order; and the second, suppression-formation, *Aufhebung* proper, which creates a 'proper abstract meaning' (an unfortunate use of 'proper'). Wearing away is a 'prior condition' but does not itself constitute the concept, which can be 'active as thought in a metaphor that is dead' (*RM*: 293).

Thus 'speaking metaphorically of metaphor' is not at all circular because the 'positing of the concept' signifies a removal to another realm, where epiphora, for example, undergoes a 'conceptual conversion' into a meaning in its own right, rather than the 'the ideal-ization of its own worn-out metaphor' (*RM*: 293). A laborious way of saying metaphor can provide the means of understanding metaphor through such terms as screen, filter, and so on. But this seems to involve an instant arrestedness, a loss of freedom and the reimposition of a 'proper hierarchy' (*RM*: 294). 'Metaphysics instead seizes the metaphorical process to make it work for the benefit of metaphysics' (*RM*: 294–5). This surely approaches the 'instrumental mastery' of language that had been vociferously denounced elsewhere (*RM*: 282): why 'seizes' instead of draws sustenance from, benefits? The first part of Ricoeur's argument endows metaphor with all the potency that has been described and implicitly celebrated through the book. But the second movement of turning a transposed term into a proper concept seems one of virtual petrification. The relation of active concept to active metaphor is never investigated; at certain points it seems to be one of hostility and required subordination. The relatively unprob-lematic account of rhetoric as 'philosophy's oldest enemy and oldest ally' offered in the opening chapter has now become overt confron-tation. The 'claim to truth' of philosophic discourse excludes it from the 'sphere of power', where eloquence holds sway: 'before becoming futile, rhetoric was dangerous' (*RM*: 10). Philosophy is one discourse amongst others, yet claims the authority to arbitrate and situate: its most effective tactic, confirmed by Ricoeur's whole argumentative strategy, is to confine its opponent through characterisation of its governing suppositions. 'Reflective mastery and clarification are closely related' (*RM*: 84).

BEING AND ACT

In the final pages of the book, Ricoeur proposes to 'erect a general theory of the intersections between spheres of discourse', and to attempt to elicit an appropriate ontology from the 'postulates of metaphorical reference' (*RM*: 295). It remains to be seen how discon-tinuity on one plane will be linked to unification on the other. The 'naïve thesis' that metaphor would provide a 'ready-made' ontology is contrasted with the 'liberalism and irenicism' of Wittgenstein's argument that 'language games are radically heterogeneous' (*RM*: 295). Ricoeur argues for 'ordered manifolds', but the air of adjudi-cation is misleading: all the emphasis falls on the 'break', 'cost', the 'irreducible difference' that 'cannot be eliminated' (*RM*: 296). Although the 'semantic shock' of metaphor offers philosophy its 'condition of possibility', it does not in itself produce any 'conceptual gain' (*RM*: 296). It 'remains caught in the conflict of same and different' and so can constitute no more than a 'rough outline' and a 'demand for instruction' (*RM*: 297). (How was the first concept formed if metaphor requires concepts to consolidate and transfer it?)

Ricoeur now wishes to demonstrate that the move from reference to ontology and from metaphor to the concept are 'inseparable'. This is slippery: a fairly broad linkage of the 'semantic dynamism' of both concept and reference is used to justify a wholesale extension of reference beyond 'what we are able to show' onto the 'conceptual traits of reality', that is, the level of metaphysical discourse.

> Unable to fall back upon the interplay between reference and predication, the semantic aim has recourse to a network of predicates that already function in a familiar field of reference. This already constituted meaning is raised from its anchorage in an initial field of reference and cast into a new referential field which it will then work to delineate. But this transfer from one referential field to the other supposes that the latter field is already in some way present in a still unarticulated manner and that exerts an attraction on the already constituted sense in order to tear it away from its initial haven. It is therefore in the semantic scope of the other field that the energy capable of achieving this uprooting and this transfer resides. But this would not be possible if meaning were a stable form. Its dynamic, directional, vectoral character combines with the semantic aim seeking to fulfil its intention.
>
> (*RM*: 299)

This is a long way from Frege, and equally difficult to reconcile with a phenomenological concept of intention. The tension theory has become a force field motivated by the 'ontological vehemence of a semantic aim', which though 'still unarticulated' is sufficiently powerful not merely to 'exert an attraction' but to 'tear away' and to 'uproot'. Both the status of this 'dynamism' – metaphor or concept – and its location – within a self-conscious subject or within language itself – remain uncertain. (The 'universe of discourse' is subsequently described as 'an interplay of attractions and repulsions that ceaselessly promote the interaction and intersection of domains whose organising nuclei are off-centred in relation to one another' (*RM*: 302).) It is difficult not to see a theological dimension in the 'energy' of a call that overrides the 'anchorage' and 'initial haven'. There is a very Heideggerian insistence on language or being through language 'declaring itself', but this is brought sharply to heel by the insistence on being 'reconciled with the requirement of the concept' (*RM*: 300).

Now in another shift, speculative discourse is equated with the process of interpretation, described as 'a struggle for univocity'. Can such a demand tolerate density, ambivalence? It seems eminently ill-suited to dealing with 'mere hints of meaning'. Note that the metaphorical process is here credited as allowing 'experience to come to language' in a manner elsewhere allocated exclusively to the symbol, whose power derives not from a new event of meaning but from tapping a nebulous prelinguistic origin. At this point, interpretation appears to be 'reductive' *per se*, a 'rationalization' and 'elimination' that 'culminates in clearing away the symbolic base' (*RM*: 302–3). The terms are hard, extreme: the 'destruction of the metaphoric' in order to relocate within a horizon that can be 'mastered conceptually'. Ricoeur somewhat plaintively suggests that this need not be the 'only outcome': 'one can imagine a hermeneutic style' (hardly the most felicitous phrasing in this context) drawn equally powerfully towards clarification of the concept and preserving the dynamism of meaning. This appears to weaken the previous conflict of interpretations drastically. For a start, it puts all the rigour of speculative thought on the side of reduction, demystification; and to a considerable extent abandons the restorative side of the hermeneutic. Secondly, the concept appears to involve the suppression of dynamism ('holds and pins down'), and it is unfair to the masters of suspicion to ignore their commitment to the liberation of life, force, energy. Thirdly, the definition of 'composite discourse' seems to enfeeble the previously ascribed legitimacy of opposed discourses within their own domain. The question still to be answered is, given the tensional character of metaphorical truth, why cannot speculative thought partake of this dialectical openness rather than remain preoccupied with preserving its own segregation from the incursions of the metaphoric. The negative case against Heidegger and Derrida is convincingly made, but the extent to which Ricoeur's own thought might be compatible with such a tensional definition of speculative thought remains unexplored (see Lacapra, 1980).

Ricoeur's response is to appeal to Aristotle's concept of the polysemy of being and, more specifically, the distinction between 'being as potentiality and being as actuality' (*RM*: 307). This seeing 'things as *actions*' (*RM*: 308) could be taken as the dominant preoccupation of Ricoeur's later work; he obviously finds something deeply satisfying in contemplating a structure as both the result of and containing the inspiriting potential of the act. Tragedy, for example, represents, contains, constitutes an action, and is as such the highest literary form (in contrast there appears to be something spineless about lyric mimesis, lacking the solidity of the artefact, a fluctuating mode of being):

> Signifying things in act would be seeing things as not prevented from becoming, seeing them as blossoming forth. But then would not signifying things in act also be signifying potency, in the inclusive sense that stands for every production of motion or of rest? Would the poet then be one who perceives power as act and act as power?
>
> *(RM*: 308)

Thus the ultimate referent of the metaphorical utterance is the power of transformation to which it testifies. This power of redescription demands that the distinction between discourse directed outwards (to facts, things) and that directed inwards (to moods, emotions) must be abandoned:

> Poetic discourse brings to language a pre-objective world in which we find ourselves already rooted, but in which we also project our innermost possibilities. We must thus dismantle the reign of objects in order to let be, and to allow to be uttered, our primordial belonging to a world which we inhabit, that is to say, which at once precedes us and receives the imprint of our works. In short we must restore to the fine word *invent* its twofold sense of discovery and creation.
>
> *(RM*: 306)

'Dismantling the reign of objects' signals a sudden influx of a long-restrained existential vocabulary. Note the recurrent ambivalence of the term 'world' (for detailed discussion of this point, see Gerhart, 1976; and especially Ricoeur's uncharacteristically tart reply, *RM*: 154–5). What seems to be required is a kind of porous quiescence, yet the language of potentialities and projects refuses to be confined to a purely numinous level: a 'specific manner of being in the world' versus 'projecting our innermost possibilities'. What we must do is minimise the 'innermost' and try to restore a certain mundaneness to 'living there'. The fine balance between the existent and the created is crucial: the preobjective world is not one that we passively receive and therefore one open to ideological appropriation, it is one on which we project ourselves, for which we are responsible.

Two serious objections remain to be met: why should we accept that the semantic innovation of metaphor should serve as the model for the second-order reference of the text; and can such an extension be utilised without reverting to the obfuscating and hierarchical language of 'more fundamental modes of being'? These questions will be at the heart of *Time and Narrative*.

7

Time and narrative

NARRATIVITY AND ORDER

One's initial response to *Time and Narrative* is likely to be intimidation. It is difficult not to be overwhelmed by the sheer bulk of this 'long and difficult three-way conversation' (*TN* 1: 83) between history, literary criticism and phenomenology, spread over three books and several hundred pages. These are divided into four volumes: *The Circle of Narrative and Temporality*, which seeks to establish the mutual constitution of the two fields; *History and Narrative*, concerned with the epistemological status of historical discourse; *Configuration in Fictional Narrative*, an analysis of the resources of fiction for structuring time; and *Narrated Time*, split into a detailed exposition of the phenomenological tradition, an account of the 'interweaving' of fiction and history, and a final consideration of the possibility of any overall synthesis. Hillis Miller talks somewhat unkindly of the book's 'mind-numbing slowness and solemnity' (1987: 1104); and it must be admitted that at times one feels Ricoeur's exemplary patience and habitual giving to everyone their due becalms the overall argument almost fatally. Nevertheless this 'reconceptualization of the possible relations existing between the three principal kinds of narrative discourse – mythic, historical, and fictional' has also been hailed as 'the most important synthesis of literary and historical theory produced in our century' (White, 1987: 170).

My own opinion is more hesitant. The ambition of coordination of such a vast field is in itself enormously impressive; and certain self-contained sequences of argument are as subtle and precise as anything in Ricoeur's work. The issue of primary and secondary reference, however, more or less held in check in *The Rule of Metaphor*, here separates out in hierarchical fashion. The immediate referent of human action should perhaps be regarded as a separable tier of argumentation. The 'ultimate referent' of temporality, defined in 'Narrative Time' as 'that structure of existence that reaches language in narrativity' (1980: 169), reverts to Ricoeur's earlier model of dual intentionality in the symbol and generates similar paradoxes of interpretative stance. The symbol does not so much give as withhold: it alludes to mysteries of force, *bios*, the sacred, that can never be fully articulated in language. Therefore the subject of *The Symbolism of Evil* becomes not so much the meaning of primary symbol and mythology as the appropriate relation of understanding to the enigmas they disclose. Similarly, we must not remain on the level of narrative configuration, the organisation of events; this allows us to read time, and by reading our own reading, we may establish an appropriate mode of address to the sacred (see Klemm, 1983: 127–8).

There is obvious continuity with the closing stages of *The Rule of Metaphor*. The idea of split reference and refiguration is here wholly transferred from the level of the sentence to that of text; and the vehicle of transformation becomes the activity of narrative, plot-making. (It is important to keep this sense of the 'faire narratif', the doing of story, with implications for both author and reader: narrative is both the result of an intentional act, that which is made, and that which occasions further action.) The Preface insists that *The Rule of Metaphor* and *Time and Narrative* 'form a pair' in their respective examinations of the 'same basic phenomenon of semantic invention':

> By means of the plot, goals, causes, and chance are brought together within the temporal unity of a whole and complete action. It is this synthesis of the heterogeneous that brings narrative close to metaphor. In both cases the new thing – the as yet unsaid, the unwritten – springs up in language.
>
> (*TN* 1: ix)

The emphasis on 'whole and complete' is perhaps excessive: on Ricoeur's own account, the 'new pertinence' of metaphor emerges from the 'ruins' of previous connections (*TN* 1: 10), and the question of 'temporal unity' cannot be said to arise on the level of the sentence. As the work proceeds, however, the initial claim that the analogy with metaphor is 'exactly parallel' appears less and less binding (*TN* 1: xi; see also 3: 159).

In *The Rule of Metaphor*, the condition of drawing on the Anglo-American analytic tradition was accepting its propositional bias and presupposition of an anonymous linguistically competent subject. Although Ricoeur takes a diversion into psycholinguistics, he is not primarily concerned with investigating a creative faculty: the primary strength of the book lies in its robust insistence on the intelligibility of metaphor at the level of discourse. *Time and Narrative* is centrally preoccupied with questions of temporal and cultural dissociation, and prepared to risk the charge of psychologism in its utilisation of the phenomenological analysis of time as a 'common standard' against which to measure fiction and history (*TN* 3: 100). Metaphor is presented as a unique point of creativity, of innovation of meaning in the utterance of an individual speaker or writer, struggling against the linguistic entropy that produces the polysemy of ordinary language. The 'art of narration' also preserves a 'precariousness', the 'shadow of an eventual death' (*TN* 2: 29). But there is no original story: 'narrative is a redefining of what is already defined, a reinterpretation of what is already interpreted' (*DCCT*: 23). It makes possible a human solidarity through retrieval and renewal of a common past: 'the experience of a shared world', Ricoeur insists, 'depends upon a community of time' (*TN* 3: 113; see also Ricoeur, 1983b; *DCCT*: 18–20).

As always, Ricoeur is contemporary in the best sense, alert and responsive to new areas of inquiry and debate. If *The Rule of Metaphor* culminates in a final confrontation with Heidegger and Derrida, *Time and Narrative* is a powerful intervention in the contemporary preoccupation with primary and secondary narration. Meta-narratives (implicitly Hegel's, but extending to any form of transcendental reason) seek to organise the whole domain of human knowledge. The nature of post-modern understanding is such that an ambition of this kind is not only doomed to failure, but wrong in principle; simply a consoling myth of intellectual mastery. First-order narrative (more simply, stories), with no pretensions to offering more than a contingent and pragmatic verification, are sufficient to keep the conversation going.

Part of the popularity of the idiom lies in the way it can draw support from a variety of intellectual traditions. The heritage of French Nietzscheanism is apparent in many themes in Foucault: the hostility to totalisation, the genealogies of institutions, the rhetoricity of thought. *The History of Sexuality*, for example, tells a story with three beginnings. Sexuality was constructed at the end of the nineteenth century ('a great sexual sermon . . . has swept through our sermons in the last decades' (1979: 7)); in the seventeenth ('then was the beginning of an age of repression emblematic of what we call bourgeois societies' (1979: 17)); and in the twelfth ('the codification of the

sacrament of penance by the Lateran Council in 1215', (1979: 58)).
These represent simultaneous options or perspectives rather than
refutable hypotheses: as always in Foucault, the persuasive simulacrum of explanation seems to have become totally disengaged
from any possibility of verification. (In the above quotation, the very
precision of '1215', one of the few dates in the text, assumes an almost
parodic status.) Another story can always be told, but there can be no
objective criteria for accepting or rejecting it other than interests of
power.

This in turn is strongly compatible with a radical pragmatism such
as Rorty's, whose present position appears to be that narrative connections can be justified by their persuasiveness or charm or revision-
ist provocation or just about anything except a truth-claim. His 1986
Clark lectures at Cambridge (available in Rorty, 1989), for example,
presented the tradition of Hegel, Nietzsche, Heidegger and Derrida
as Bloomian strong poets, seeking self-realisation through trans-
gressing the imposed personality of the precursor. Implicitly, their
work is obsolete if regarded as systematic philosophy, tedious if read
for an immanent historical content: to say that Hegel had something
to do with the Prussian state is not wrong, simply boring – the final
and inexorable court of appeal. Some of the peculiar fluctuations of
Jameson's *The Political Unconscious* can be attributed to this mode of
justification: Marxism is only a story but it is the most adequate and
uplifting story, on grounds of ethical appeal rather than dialectical
necessity.

Similar debates are conducted in post-Heideggerian hermeneutics:
the rehabilitation of prejudice, the insistence on the finitude of understanding, and antagonism towards any form of alienating distanciation from the supportiveness of the linguistic heritage. So arguments
against narrativism tend to follow the contours of those employed
against Gadamer in the previous chapter. It is no coincidence that
Habermas has conducted similarly vigorous polemics against Foucault, Lyotard and Derrida, arguing that without some privileging of
the ideal of critique, post-modernism must relapse into the political
acquiescence labelled by him neo-conservatism.

For Ricoeur, also, there are emphatically no more meta-narratives:
as early as *History and Truth*, he insists on the necessarily fictive status
of any directive idea, and argues for the legitimacy of an eschatological framework to serve as a check on the 'temptation of the completed totality' (*TN* 3: 102). Although the model of rationality
explicitly invoked in *Time and Narrative* tends to be that of a Husserlian

'questioning-back', the actual organisation and progression of argument continues to rely on predominantly Hegelian procedures. The overall structure offers an imposing edifice of interwoven dialectic: the physical time of Aristotle and Kant versus the psychological emphasis of Augustine and Husserl; nomological models of explanation versus narrativist understanding in history; the interplay of concordance and discordance within the configurational activity itself. In the penultimate chapter, 'Should we renounce Hegel?', there is an explicit attempt to exorcise the seductive and, it is insisted, largely unrefuted claim of absolute knowledge; modern thought bypasses Hegel rather than effectively dismantling his system. There is none of the jeering polemic quality of Lyotard's 'incredulity towards meta-narratives' (1987: xiii) (though incredulity, it should be stressed, is not an argument). Instead 'the abandoning of this philosophy' is felt 'like a wound': 'the courage of the work of mourning' must be undertaken to overcome the 'weakness of nostalgia' (*TN* 3: 206). What is urged is an acceptance of 'imperfect mediation' without forgoing the 'impetus' of the 'process of totalization' (*TN* 3: 103).

Within narrativist thinkers, there tends to be a cavalier progression from the collapse of absolute truth to the invalidity of all mediating narratives. What starts off looking like a re-evaluation of the conceptual importance of narrative reverses on itself so that coherence lies in no more than narrative: partial, *ad hoc*, and insusceptible to critical analysis. This is the way things hang together: we had just better get used to it, and renounce any untenable ambitions. A nimble somersault takes place from narrative as a bond of human solidarity – what has been told can and must be retold – to a rather complacent fatalism, just another story.

'The leaving behind of Hegelianism', Ricoeur agrees, 'signifies renouncing the attempt to decipher the supreme plot' (*TN* 3: 206), but the major argument against the ambition of absolute knowledge is its abolition of narrativity through the 'grasping history as the totalization of time in the eternal present' (*TN* 3: 202). Not only, in his view, is narrative susceptible of analysis, but also, in a deeply unfashionable postulate, the 'paradigm of order' (*TN* 1: 38). It provides the interim principle of organisation between the anonymity of linguistic pragmatics, and the unacceptable pretension to recount the 'supreme plot'.

Narrativism tends to say very little about what stories are; reasonably enough, perhaps, given that on its own terms there is no meta-perspective for analysing them. This allows the delivery of its own propositions as a series of virtually *a priori* axioms, question-begging to a quite staggering extent, readily subsumed into either a qualmless pragmatism or a positivist systems-theory of quite dystopic proportions. No adequate or even working characterisation of narrative is offered: there seems to be an undeclared assumption that structural narratology has exhausted that line of inquiry. In addition, there is little or no analysis of such basic questions as how (or if) historical narrative differs from fictional. Lyotard's *The Post-Modern Condition* at least provides some kind of brief characterisation, which will serve to establish some preliminary contrasts with Ricoeur.

First, traditional stories, 'the quintessential form of customary knowledge', are competence-building (1984: 19): they pass on the techniques of knowing how. They are to be judged 'good' in so far as they conform to the relevant criteria in the social circle of the 'knower's' interlocutor. Lyotard's borrowings from analytic philosophy accentuate its much-berated social quiescence. Ricoeur's account of participation raises many of the same problems, but he retains, however awkwardly, the phase of application, the moment 'beyond reading, in effective action, instructed by the works coming down' (*TN* 3: 159). Texts rather than simply reconfirming an existing ideology refigure possible modes of action.

Secondly, 'the narrative form, unlike the developed forms of the discourse of knowledge, lends itself to a great variety of language games'; these 'areas of competence' are 'tightly woven together in the web of the forms, ordered by the unified viewpoint characteristic of this kind of knowledge' (1987: 20). Lyotard talks vaguely of 'clouds of narrative language elements' (p. xxiv), but fails to provide any minimal characterisation of a narrative sentence or account of how such sentences become transformed into a story. The 'unified viewpoint' here seen as a wholly unproblematic attribute is for Ricoeur the whole marvel of story-telling: the 'narrative excess (*surcroît*) of order, coherence, and unity' (*DCCT*: 25). At numerous points, his relative conservatism on this 'exigence for order' (*TN* 1: 63) is apparent: the insistence on wholeness, the fretting over unresolved endings, the excessive alarm at the Bakhtinian polyphonic novel. Texts that orchestrate 'a plurality of centres of consciousness irreducible to a common denominator' are seen as undermining 'the base of the edifice, the organising role of emplotment' by replacing the 'temporal configuration of action' with a 'factor of incompleteness, of remaining incomplete' (*TN* 2: 97) (though novelists such as Dickens and Doestoevsky surely benefit greatly from the periodic breakdown of a

manifestly inadequate authorial commentary). Ricoeur follows Kermode's *The Sense of an Ending* in linking the 'problem of eventual
exhaustion' of the narrative function to 'the abandonment of the
criteria of completeness and therefore the deliberate choice not to end
a work' (*TN* 2: 20). It is an 'effect of closure' that permits the
'transition' to 'openness' (*TN* 2: 20). It is conceded that a 'disappointing ending' may in some cases be 'appropriate', but this is
merely displacing the problem without declared procedures for ascer-
taining what is suitable for a given case. (Can there, for example, be a
frivolous ending?) The threat to narrative, it should be noted, comes
from polyphony rather than the *nouveau roman*: what alarms him is the
equation of sheer discordance with a kind of anarchic liberation, with
the collapse of even the aspiration to order, so powerfully espoused by
Nietzsche. From this perspective, narrative gives illusory form to the
authenticity of chaos, fictions are no more than consolation in the face
of death. The alternative to this voluntary self-deception is the ethic of
Redlichkeit, the 'radical intellectual honesty' that commits itself 'to the
fascination of the absolutely unformed' (*TN* 1: 72).

Composition is allied with control in somewhat unproblematic
fashion: what has been made has been ordered. Ricoeur emphasises
the logical rather than chronological character of a whole, the 'absence of chance and conformity to the requirements of necessity' (*TN*
1: 40). Temporal unity (all that happened within a given time-span)
is explicitly opposed to dramatic unity (a single action with beginning, middle and end). 'To conceive of a causal connection, even
among singular events, is already a kind of universalization' (*TN* 1:
41). Hence the disapproval of disconnected episodes: one thing after
another instead of one thing because of one another (though yielding
so much to internal organisation leaves, as Ricoeur acknowledges, the
problem of specifying its distinctive mode of causality). But there
remains an internal tension within the text as an overcoming of
discordance wholly lacking in the narrativist tradition. 'Narrative
consonance imposed upon temporal dissonance' remains the result of
a 'violence of interpretation' (*TN* 1: 72). There can be no simple
opposition between narrative order and temporal chaos: the dialectic
of order and discord occurs on both sides of the equation. Completion
presupposes resolution of pre-existing conflict, but also demands it.

Thirdly, the narrator's only claim to competence for telling the
story is the fact he has heard it himself. On this model, the reader's
passivity is near-absolute: there are no criteria for a bad or ill-
constructed story, no possibility of doubt or rejection. One must listen

in order to speak, and so preserve a tacit self-interest in acquiescence. Lyotard has an enormously impoverished idea of the 'set of pragmatic rules that constitutes the social bond' (1987: 21) compared to Ricoeur's model,. admittedly theological in derivation, of the development of narrative identity in time through interpretative recovery of a founding symbolism (*TN* 3: 247–49). This preserves at least the possibility of alternative readings, and therefore a political struggle over the right of definition. Furthermore, narrative itself represents a bond with the past, of honouring the dead, of preserving a human continuity between mortal generations. 'We tell stories because in the last analysis human lives need and merit being narrated. The whole history of suffering cries out for vengeance and calls for narrative' (*TN* 1: 75; see also 3: 187–89). Thus far from being a check and a rebuff on the ambition to establish principles of universal morality, a bond and an ethic is located within story-telling itself.

Fourthly, there is the mode of temporality of narrative. Lyotard claims that its 'vibratory musical property' is 'clearly revealed in the ritual performance of certain Cashinahua tales' (1987: 21). The post-modern theorist lapses into a manifestly absurd primitivism. There is no discernible relation whatsoever between 'interminable monotonous chants' and 'immemorial beating' (1987: 21) and the major narrative works of European culture, or even popular story-telling. Nevertheless the supposed atemporality of metre leads to the inference that 'a culture that gives precedence to the narrative form doubtless has no more of a need for special procedures to authorize its narratives than it has to remember its past' (1987: 22). The synchronic model of communications theory is evident in the claim of 'a theoretical identity between each of the narrative's occurrences': in a strongly Platonist aside, 'the people are only that which actualize the narrative'. Jameson's preface rightly describes Lyotard's account as 'a way of *consuming* the past, a way of forgetting' (1987: xii). In contrast, one is struck by the amplitude and dignity, if also the potential circularity, of Ricoeur's commitment to the 'diachronic temporality, that is a memory and a project' (1987: 22) that Lyotard assigns exclusively to the game of science: 'the contemporary search for some narrative continuity is not just nostalgic escapism but a contestation of the legislative and planificatory discourse that tends to predominate in bureaucratic societies. To give the people back a *memory* is also to give them back a *future*' (*DCCT*: 28).

My treatment will necessarily be selective. I hope, however, to give reasonably full accounts of the phenomenological characterisation of temporality, stemming from Augustine's analysis of the soul's experience in time; the counterbalancing ordering principle of Aristotelian poesis, enlarged to cover both fiction and history; and the narrativist versus covering law debate in historiography. I shall conclude with some discussion of Hayden White's suggestive, though undeniably cryptic, contention that the figural structure of Ricoeur's own text serves as a 'metaphysics of narrativity' (1987: 52).

THE APORETICS OF TEMPORALITY

Augustine and Aristotle are aligned as proponents of opposed traditions: one of the paradoxes of time, the other of the intelligible organisation of a narrative. (The failure of Augustine to relate his discussion of time to the narrative structure of the *Confessions*, and the similar absence of linkage in Aristotle between the *Poetics* and the *Physics*, is seen as a positive benefit, guaranteeing the 'independence' of their respective viewpoints.) Augustine's analyses reveal the 'internal multiplicity' of the soul's temporal experience: Aristotle's account of poesis, enlarged to cover both fiction and history, serves as a containment of its internal disruption, highlighting the 'confidence in the power of the poet and the poem to make order triumph over disorder' (*TN* 1: 4).

Ricoeur begins his reading of Augustine with the originary ontological question, as to the being or non-being of time. The capacity of ordinary language to make meaningful demarcations is set against the sceptical paradox: the future is not yet, the past is no longer, the present does not remain. Thus the notion of the present, viewed as a point without extension, is replaced by that of a perpetual passing away. But 'temporal qualities ... can exist in the present, without the things of which we speak ... still existing or already existing' (*TN* 1: 10). The question now shifts to 'where' the location of things past and future might be: this can only be in the present, which now divides into an 'internal multiplicity' (1:10). Thus an extended and dialectical present is constituted out of memory, expectation, and present perception.

Traditional problems remain, such as how does the memory-image present to the mind refer to past or future, and what validity has this quasi-spatial model? What is required is an expulsion of any cosmological basis for extension and measurement. Augustine provides a detailed series of arguments designed to uncouple the time of the soul from that of the heavens: the notion of a day, for example, is totally dissociated from the idea of solar movement. The concept of passing away is re-evaluated so as to reveal 'both the multiplicity of the present and its tearing away' (*TN* 1: 16). Measurement is shown to take place in the mind, and the standard of comparison to be the mental impression. But the passivity of sensory reception must also be contrasted with 'the activity of a mind stretched in different directions, between expectation, memory and attention' (*TN* 1: 18). Thus recitation involves anticipation: the present is changed into a point of forward-directed intention: 'the impression is in the soul only as much as the mind *acts*, that is, expects, attends, and remembers' (*TN* 1: 19). Problems remain with the spatial model of temporal experience and the key metaphor of 'passing away': in addition, to talk of a threefold action both distended and engaged scarcely dispels the enigma. Nevertheless, by tying the extension of time to the distension of the soul, Augustine sees 'discordance emerge again and again out of the concordance of the intentions of expectation, attention, and memory' (*TN* 1: 21). This concept of triple intentionality will form the basis of the phenomenological analysis of introspective time in Husserl and Heidegger.

The Augustinian tradition is contrasted with the definition of time in terms of movement in Aristotle, Kant, and post-Newtonian scientific discourse. The former attempts to expose the mechanisms by which the human mind constitutes its temporality, whereas the latter seeks to establish the objectivity of time in the physical universe. Ricoeur's ultimate purpose is to demonstrate how both traditions are obliged to make covert borrowings from outside their own domain. Thus in Husserl, despite the supposed expulsion of the external world through the epoche, the very status of laws and the idea of succession depends on an implicit analogy with the physical universe. A parallel strategy is adopted with Kant, of demonstrating unacknowledged borrowings from the internal consciousness of time. His propositions are necessarily indirect: time does not appear but makes appearance possible. Certain of its properties, however, are not intuitive but based in the individual subject. It is necessary, however, for the problematic of internal sense to be systematically repressed in order not to be drawn into questions of the noumenal, the internal constitution of the soul. Ricoeur insists, for example, on the challengeable nature of any analogy drawn between the realms of time and space. Nothing justifies the supposition of an organising principle for time equivalent to perspective for space. 'The determinations by which time is distinguished from a mere magnitude must themselves be based on an implicit phenomenology, whose empty place is evident in every step of the transcendental argument' (*TN* 3: 59).

Husserl's major innovations are seen as the identification of mechanisms of retention and protention, and the distinction between retention and recollection (primary and secondary memory). Intentionality is not merely transcendental, directed outwards towards an external correlate, but also addresses the just-gone. It may thus be described as 'longitudinal' (*TN* 3: 28). It is this transgression of the logic of identity by the temporal totality which Derrida pounces upon in *Speech and Phenomena*. The present only exists as such in relation to a past, thus the instant of absolute self-presence, of origin, must presuppose a simultaneous presence and non-presence. But this demand for an absolute present is itself an illegitimately imported abstraction. The objection is only valid against a phenomenology that confuses the opposed traditions of the living present and the isolated instant. The composite nature of temporality simultaneously includes both. The object exists in the flowing of moments of perception as well as in an immediate present: the 'thickness' of the moment exists in both isolation and continuity (*TN* 3: 28). The whole vocabulary – flux, phase, fall, above the pairing living–dead – is acknowledged to be 'irreducibly metaphorical' (*TN* 3: 27). But this dependence on homonyms and ambiguities does not vitiate these insights; 'these metaphors constitute the only language available to the work of returning to the origin' (*TN* 3: 267).

The originality of Heidegger lies in breaking with the priority of perception and the inevitably retrospective orientation of the retention of impressions. Instead the principle of the unity of Dasein is entirely divorced from any standard of measurement of movement and sought in the principle of care. There is no easy definition of this mode of forward-directed apprehension that provides a structural unity for the major existential themes of projection, thrownness, and fallenness. The unity of past, present, and future is 'ecstatic' (*TN* 3: 63), separately externalised but mutually implicated in a continual process of unification and diversification. This permits a hierarchisation of levels of time. Firstly, temporality, the being-towards-death of any individual existent that asserts the primacy of the future over the past and the ultimate closure of that future. Secondly, historicality, the extension of time between birth and death, conceived not as a passage from past to future, but as a re-opening of the past in the future, a re-enactment of the possibilities of the having-been. Thirdly, within-time-ness, a primordial time that must be recovered from the system of dates and its reduction to a mere linear chronology of nows.

The gulf between instant and moment, however, leads to a reactivation of entirely different spheres of time. Heidegger refuses to acknowledge even the possibility of an autonomous level of time such as evolution or geology, which are reduced to mere mechanisms of the physical universe. This split with ordinary time separates the time of individual destiny from that of public history: historicality is separated off from the practice of the historical sciences; and the personal having-been subsumes any separate comprehension of the communal past. This is the context in which de Man's more cryptic assertions on 'the rhetoric of temporality' must be understood. 'Understanding can be called complete only when it is aware of its own temporal predicament' (1983: 38) – essentially that of the internal multiplicity and impossibility of conceptual mastery emphasised throughout *Time and Narrative*. Ricoeur would be obliged to concur with de Man's definition of time as 'truth's inability to coincide with itself' (de Man, 1979: 78); and both thinkers prize an authenticity in declared error, a sombre dignity in defeated illusion. But where Ricoeur's stance of supplication does not preclude a difficult regathering of commitment to achievable aims within the human sphere of culture, de Man repeatedly contrasts 'the temporality of everyday existence that always falls back into estrangement and falsification' with the yearning for 'another temporality that would remain clearly aware of its own mode of being' (de Man, 1983: 45; compare 1979: 44). The division, indeed virtual *epoché*, between the empirical and the ontological self serves to divorce 'the ideal self-created temporality engendered by the language of the poem' (1979: 225) from the experience of any communal history; and de Man clearly inherits all the difficulties arising from Heidegger's insistence on the wholly private nature of the authentic time in which one comes to accept one's own death.

In order 'to disentangle the authentic meaning of this extension', Ricoeur seeks to establish 'the possibility of grounding the possibility of history as a science in the existential structure of time' (1980b: 180–81). This requires establishing some way of moving from a privatised being-towards-death to the multiple characters of history. What is most striking is Ricoeur's attempt to transpose the Heideggerian *Wiederholung*, recapitulation, from a personal to a cultural level: through the mediation of narrative, one liberates possibilities in a communal past rather than a personal destiny through a self-effacing gesture of continuity. He initially notes that 'the exclusive concern for the past which generates history must appear as an intriguing enigma when put against the background of the existential analysis of care and its primary orientation towards the future' (1980b: 181). The span of the individual life must not be treated as a minuscule fraction between two endless spaces of before and after. It is limited from within by being-towards-death: the backward move towards the past is retrieved in the anticipation of a project and the endlessness of historical time is grafted onto the finite structure of being-towards-death. Crucially, however, this experience of death is non-transferable: 'the uncommunicable aspect of dying imposes the primacy of individual fate over common destiny'. Therefore the perspective under which the notion of a heritage is introduced remains 'radically monadic' (1980b: 182). For Heidegger, the transmission of the potentialities of the past occurs from the self to the self rather than from self to other (1980b: 182; *TN* 3: 74–5). Ricoeur contends that 'narrativity, from the outset, establishes repetition on the plane of being-with-others'. It establishes a 'time of interaction' that 'continues beyond the death of each of its protagonists', and so establishes a bridge between 'the private time of our mortality and the public time of our language' (*DCCT*: 20).

Time and Narrative holds the phenomenological account of time in somewhat ambiguous relationship to narrative. Initially Ricoeur clearly feels that categories derived from the existential analysis of time warrant a direct, even formulaic, transposition. Earlier studies, in particular 'Narrative time', and also the introductory chapters of the opening volume, suggest that what is going to be offered is a replacement of the synchronic model of structuralism by a Heideggerian vocabulary. (No intimation is given of the extended detour through phenomenology that opens the third volume, nor the broader meditation of the postscript.) 'Narrative configurations and the most elaborated forms of temporality corresponding to them share the same foundation of within-time-ness' (*TN* 1: 64). Some of this remains, but the increasing stress on the 'aporetics of temporality' (*TN* 3: 4) and the mutual occlusion of the two major traditions of philosophical analysis emphasise the position of time as that by which thought is proved inadequate.

One might have expected a treatment of Augustine's classic exposition of time to serve merely as a prelude to and anticipation of Husserl's more developed phenomenological analysis; and Ricoeur certainly emphasises the breakthrough of the concept of triple present, consciousness being outside of itself through both protention and retention. But equal weight is given to the appropriateness of Augustine's 'highly interrogative and even aporetical' mode of argumentation: each attempt at resolution 'gives rise to new difficulties which never cease to spur on the inquiry' (*TN* 1: 5). Although this 'does not disallow some sort of firm certitude', this 'assertive core can never be apprehended simply in itself outside of the aporias it engenders' (*TN* 1: 6). Instead of the refutation of an opposing position, there is a drama of thought laying bare its own limits, a series of aborted syntheses demanding further inconclusive formulation. But 'unlike in skepticism, the admission that there is an enigma is accompanied by an ardent desire which for Augustine is a figure of love' (*TN* 1: 13). Hence the 'peculiar tone of a "lamentation" full of hope': the appropriate stance for contemplation of time is essentially apostrophic.

The Conflict of Interpretations had previously set up the model of the multi-faceted hermeneutic field internally at variance with itself. There, however, one's impression was of often closely-knit thematic groupings in open and unspecified relation to each other. There is much common ground – symbol, desire, suspicion, faith – but little or no cross-referencing: the essays are presented as sufficient unto themselves while providing separate vantages on the common problem of interpretation. In *Time and Narrative*, we get simultaneously both the patient disposition of three massive fields of study, and a far more explicit acknowledgement of aporia. The major example of this is in the phenomenological analyses of volume 3: the logical exposure of logical impasse. 'The endless aporias of the phenomenology of time will be the price we have to pay for each and every attempt to make time appear' (1:84). But there is also a poignant inconclusiveness on issues of historiography and literary criticism: a willingness to entertain, for example, 'the death of the narrative function itself' (*TN* 2: 4), of there being nothing left to say. And the emotional timbre has changed in line with this. 'The reader will have recognized', Ricoeur observes, 'dissimulated at several places in our text, under the modesty and sobriety of prose, the echoes of the sempiternal elegy, the lyrical figure of the lament' (*TN* 3: 273). The mood is overwhelmingly that the only lesson we can hope to learn is the lesson of humility, resonating through the echoes of Pascal and Kierkegaard, in the concern with the endless debt to the past, and above all in the repeated meditations on the significance of personal death in the context of eternity, 'the contrast between time which remains and we who move on' (*TN* 3: 123). The repeated insistence that the emotions have 'their own *rationale*' (*TN* 1: 44) – for example the justification of 'commemoration and loathing' in historical discourse (*TN* 3: 187) – culminates in the startling rejection of narrative itself in the closing pages: 'the lyricism of meditative thinking goes right to the fundamental without passing through the art of narrating' (*TN* 3: 273).

In the postscript, Ricoeur will draw an explicit parallel between the experience of time and that of sin. Both issues elicit not so much an achieved knowledge as a kind of wounding in the continued incapacity to know. The Socratic wisdom, knowing one's own ignorance, can easily become facile, a pre-emptive abstention from rigorous inquiry: here the humiliation of speculative thought itself represents a kind of piety. Ricoeur's earlier work on the split ontology of the human condition is echoed in his term for this 'slippage', *la faille* (*TN* 1: 12), the discordance that forever denies the soul its desire for unity. The recurrence of this 'insurmountable fissure' (*TN* 2: 110) establishes a continuous opposition between the guilt of finitude, of existing in time, and eternity: 'a temporal rupturing and exploding of the present in contrast to the eternal presence of God' (*DCCT*: 19).

There remains something illicit about the periodic eruptions of the concept of eternity (just as the citation of Augustine's example of anticipation and retrospection, reciting a hymn, as a 'powerful paradigm' for not only actions but for the 'entire province of narrative' seem heavily loaded (*TN* 1: 20)). It is said to give the 'horizon of a limiting idea' that compels thought about what is outside time (*TN* 1: 22); it intensifies the existential experience of *distentio*; and it also encourages thought to 'surpass itself by moving in the direction of eternity' (*TN* 1: 22). There is no attempt to derive eternity from time: 'what is posited, confessed, thought, is in one stroke the contrast' (*TN* 1: 22). Words pass, the Word remains: 'how can a temporal creature be made in and through the Eternal Word?' (*TN* 1: 22).

Eternity becomes an 'experience', the absence of which is 'not simply a limit that is thought, but a lack that is felt at the heart of temporal existence' (*TN* 1: 26). This 'permeation' with negativity compels lamentation at 'the way in which the soul, deprived of the stillness of the eternal present, is torn asunder' (*TN* 1: 27). There seems to be a suspiciously close identification here of 'the sinner and the created being' which Ricoeur so vehemently resisted in his earlier work (*TN* 1: 28). Because the human experience of time is distended, it necessarily carries with it the pain of exclusion from eternity; the implication is that this must therefore have been deserved through some previous transgression. Ricoeur tries to reverse this by joining the 'sorrow of the finite with the celebration of the absolute'; but as always there is a far more potent and immediate language of suffering than of paradise ('recollection, living fullness, being at home and light' (*TN* 1: 28)). There can be listening, firmness, but 'this remains in the future, the time of hope. It is still in the midst of the experience of distension that the wish for permanence is uttered'. Thus a treatment of narrative must remind itself of what it is not before giving 'full justice to human temporality' (*TN* 1: 30) – but also receiving justice, and perhaps condemnation, from temporality as well. But the attempt to posit an upper limit to the hierarchisation of time, a point at which Heidegger's categories might be transcended by reconciliation on a mythic level, and so to break free of the ultimate pessimism of the existential ethic is never convincingly realised. Ricoeur himself concludes, with a kind of ominous poignancy, that 'the most serious question' posed by a 'philosophical reflection on narrativity and time' is the extent to which it may may 'aid us in thinking about eternity and death at the same time' (*TN* 1: 87).

THREE VERSIONS OF MIMESIS

Aristotle serves two functions: firstly, in a comparatively minor role, as the proponent of cosmic time, the pin-point instant defined in terms of movement in the physical world (*TN* 3: 12–22); secondly, as the advocate of the ordering power of poesis over the 'existential burden of discordance' (*TN* 1: 31). Ricoeur's whole approach could be seen as a massively expanded meditation on (or, less charitably, a systematic misreading of) the single dictum: 'the imitation of the action is the Plot'. Muthos or emplotment (the term fiction is avoided because of its variable relation to reality) undergoes a process of 'broadening, radicalizing, enriching and opening up to the outside' (*TN* 2: 4). Thus it expands to include narrative forms in general, including history which Aristotle had explicitly opposed to poesis, and overriding the internal opposition between drama and diegetic narrative ('the first laterally qualifies the second to the point of serving as its model' (*TN* 1: 36)). Ricoeur is equally willing to abandon the theatrical part of tragedy: music and spectacle. Comedy is defined as an imitation of action, involving characters of lower ethical worth; and epic only distinguished by its 'magnitude' which 'in no way affects the basic rules for organizing the events' (*TN* 1: 36) (surely untrue for unity and wholeness). It is obviously debatable whether such elements as perepeteia, anagnorisis and pathos can be

167

transposed onto the entire field of narrative without dissolving the clarity of the model. The question of the intrinsic 'latitude' of Aristotle's work is, however, secondary (*TN* 1: 32): Ricoeur will veer between respectful citation of a classical authority (hence the apparent conservatism in concepts of ordering, character, and ethics), and bold, sometimes unsupported, innovation ('plausible, fecund, – and risky' (*TN* 1: 35)).

The term 'poetic' is initially defined as a 'mark of production, construction, dynamism' which renders muthos and mimesis 'operations rather than structures' (*TN* 1: 33). The activity of making a system (sustasis), composing plots, will be asserted against 'every sort of static structure, achronological paradigm, or temporal invariant' (*TN* 1: 33). This is particularly important in view of the customary translation of mimesis as imitation or representation, which is hard to detach from a Platonic sense of a derivative copy of an ideal model ('things imitate ideas; art imitates things' (*TN* 1: 34)). Ricoeur, in contrast, will never cease to emphasise its role as 'human making'. To imitate an event is wholly different from representing part of physical nature. Action can itself be seen as a kind of structuring, the acquisition of an identity through inscribing oneself into a role in the world. Mimesis duplicates this process of ordering, and so can be regarded as the act specifically appropriate to the rendering of action, the doing of doing. The narrative artefact is related to ethics and politics, practical wisdom (Aristotle never uses the term logic in relation to poetry, presumably because its intelligibility lies in the realm of praxis not theoria). The analogy with metaphor as transformation of past connotation into new meaning is both re-established and displaced in the movement from poetics to ethics. The concept of 'the metaphorical transposition of the practical field by the muthos' (*TN* 1: 46) provides a key area of innovation in *Time and Narrative*: of application, praxis, as a direct response to the experience of interpretation, and so radically opposed to a sacramental emphasis in the treatment of the creative word.

Thus mimesis divides upon itself: an initial familiarity with the semantics of action, the making of a structure interpreting and organising that knowledge, and a reception and actualisation of that structure. (Ricoeur adduces as support the 'double allegiance' of the word praxis: making of structure, acting in the world (*TN* 1: 47).)

The composition of plot is grounded in a 'pre-understanding of the world of action' (*TN* 1: 54). The minimum narrative sentence is always A did X in these circumstances (whereas B or C did Y or Z), thus implicitly referring to a whole semantic network, of goals, motives, intelligible consequences, agents, means, circumstances, help, hostility, and cooperation. Practical understanding must be capable of relevantly posing and answering a whole series of deceptively simple inquiries – what, why, when, and with and against whom. This can obviously be referred back to Ricoeur's discussion of the constitutive nature of ideology. 'There is no lived reality, no human or social reality, that is not already *represented* in some sense.' Therefore 'the referent of narration, namely human action, is never raw or immediate reality but an action that has been symbolized and resymbolized over and over again' (*DCCT*: 23–4). The challenge is not to break with these presuppositions, but to transform them: 'to mediate over and over again in a new and more creative fashion'. Narrative adds discursive unity to a simple sequence of action sentences. Whereas these are paradigmatic, with their relations of inter-signification being 'perfectly reversible', narratives possess an 'irreducibly diachronic character' and so belong to the syntagmatic order (which includes reading backwards). Thus understanding a narrative involves both a preliminary competence in the semantics of action and a familiarity with the rules of composition governing the syntagmatic order. The first acquire actuality (because previously only virtual) and integration (because unified into temporal wholes) through passing through narrative typology.

'These symbolic articulations of action' in turn become 'bearers of more precisely temporal elements, from which proceed more directly the capacity of action to be narrated and perhaps the need to narrate it' (*TN* 1: 54). It is not a question of establishing analogies to the triple present, but exploring the 'exchange that real action makes appear between the temporal dimensions'. The vocabulary of practical articulation always possesses a latent temporality: the unifying power of the story enables 'the present of the future, the present of the past, and the present of the present' (*TN* 1: 60) to be brought into complex and continuously evolving relation with each other.

At this point we move into a Heideggerian idiom, albeit a version stripped of ontological claims. Reckoning with time becomes a prerequisite to measuring rather than vice versa (a day is not tied to the orbit of the earth but is '*time to do*' (1980: 174)). The crucial demarcation between moment and instant must be preserved to prevent the reduction of the present of acting and suffering to an abstract present of linear time. Thus narrative time becomes the time of care, 'the

169

privileged discursive expression of preoccupation and its making-present' (1980: 176). A story is not a chronology of isolated events. Characters themselves undergo change, react to or are reacted upon by circumstances that precede them: a plot is a sequence of predicaments, and so can be seen as 'the time of the now-that wherein a person is both abandoned and responsible at the same time' (1980: 176). Heroes of stories have an imperative of action: their 'reckoning is still visibly rooted in preoccupation' (hence the general irrelevance of precise dating). It is characteristic of a state of inauthenticity to be absorbed by 'the description of the things of our concern'; nevertheless, some existential features are revealed in to-handness (*vorhanden*, *zuhanden*). This makes an interesting contrast with the formalist concept of motivation: an object described in a realist text must necessarily have a subsequent function in the narrative. Ricoeur suggests that they are charged with significance because of this perpetual 'present of praxic intervention'. This temporal dimension is also reflected outwards. The relation with the audience 'retains this public character of time while keeping them from falling into anonymity' (1980: 175); recitation incorporates listeners into audience, creates a bond of narrative identity.

Secondly, emplotment or the formal structure of narrative is the act of configuration which coordinates the multiple vocabularies of action. This draws the chronology of events into the coherence of an intelligible whole, containing the internal tensions of concordant discordance – reversals, pitiable incidents, and so on. It also possesses temporal characteristics that allow it to be called a synthesis of the heterogeneous, a 'grasping together' related to Kantian judgement, an intuitive manifold under the rule of a concept (*TN* 1: 66). The episodic dimension of a narrative resembles linear time: its configurational aspect reveals more complex and flexible arrangements. It is comprehended as a meaningful whole, gives the sense of leading to an end point, and can be understood from the end to the beginning, allowing us to 'read time backwards' (*TN* 1: 68). Ricoeur equates this cyclic movement of return – of initial attraction to the end as 'pole of attraction' (1980: 174), followed by a recapitulation of the end in the beginning – with Heideggerian *Wiederholung*. Hence narrative becomes a communal act of repetition, a public recapitulation that allows 'the retrieval of our most basic potentialities inherited from the past in the form of personal fate and collective destiny' (1980: 181). Crucially this embodies a temporality internal to narrative irreducible to synchronic analysis.

170

The third volume offers detailed analyses of configuration in poetic composition. It begins with the inductive taxonomy of genre theory, mostly modelled on Frye. This is followed by the exposure of a covert semantics of action in the structural analyses of Propp, Bremond and Greimas. Thirdly, the specific resources of narrative voice and viewpoint are discussed, leading to some diffuse observations on point of view, and rather more interesting analysis of the system of tenses employed in fictional narrative. Finally, Ricoeur rounds off the volume with some detailed analyses of the treatment of time in *Mrs Dalloway*, *The Magic Mountain*, and *Remembrance of Things Past*. (The odds appear somewhat stacked by the selection of tales so explicitly 'about time' rather than showing the temporality of narrative to be a factor in a less conspicuous manner.) At this point, I shall concentrate on the first two aspects.

A live tradition is characterised by 'the interplay of innovation and sedimentation': the 'proper function' of criticism is 'to discern a style of development, an order of movement, that makes this sequence of developments a significant heritage' (*TN* 2: 14). Little sympathy is shown for any pre-existent Platonic hierarchy of genres: the singular unity of any individual work may stand as a model. Typology however possesses a kind of residual immunity: innovation remains a form of rule-governed deformation. As always in Ricoeur, imagination 'produces things according to rules' (*TN* 1: x). The canon retains a kind of formal inevitability issuing from 'the sedimentation of a practice with a specific history' (*TN* 2: 14). Ricoeur's explicitly theological studies (e.g. 1975c, 1975d) go into the issue of genre in far greater detail: in his work on literary narrative, the Aristotelian categories of drama, epic, and lyric are overridden, and replaced by narrative (including fiction, history, drama, epic, and novel), lyric (including discursive meditation, the 'pathétique' of *Fallible Man*) and myth (difficult to pin down: perhaps best as that which speculative thought emerges out of and ultimately must return to).

Ricoeur firmly distinguishes 'perenniality' of generic forms from the 'atemporality attributed to essences'. From a structuralist viewpoint, any compromise with an inductive view of tradition must be 'tainted with a thoroughgoing historicism': to find 'achronological constraints ... it is necessary to pass from history to structure' (*TN* 2: 29). Three characteristics of the deductive procedures of structural linguistics are emphasised: the attempt to move from the level of the sentence to discourse *per se*; the range of derivations 'stretching from vague analogy to strict homology' (2: 30); and, most importantly, the 'hierarchizing and integrating resources of a logical model' (*TN* 2: 31).

Narrative semiotics dechronologises and relogicises through subordinating the syntagmatic to the paradigmatic. The text is broken down into a series of nodal points and pivotal options which may be formulated in strictly logical terms. Such a methodology has achieved spectacular results in such fields as the study of the morphology of lexical units and the concatenations of South American mythology. But here structuralism must compete with the claims of an existing tradition of narrative analysis. In a brilliant series of analyses, Ricoeur demonstrates the covert dependence of the work of Propp, Bremond, and Greimas on a more traditional comprehension of story.

Propp's *Morphology of the Russian Folk-Tale* is seen as an uneasy combination of a Linnean taxonomy with a Goethean organicism. Firstly, the tale is divided into functions, segments identified not with characters but with significance for the course of an action; Ricoeur instantly detects the Aristotelian ring of a teleological whole. Secondly, the 'principle of closure' determining the finite number of functions is undivulged. Thirdly, though Propp explicitly retains a time factor, it is on the level of simple chronology, an 'axiom of succession' that signifies no more than the 'absence of arbitrariness': there remains an unstated relation of interconnection (*TN* 2: 34). Fourthly, all tales are regarded as variants of an underlying tale, but the status of this archetype remains undefined. Most significantly, there is an absence of consideration of the initial situation; the quest given rise to by villainy or lack is not regarded as a function but as an 'actual movement' (*TN* 2: 36). Ricoeur argues that the final introduction of the concept of 'move' does not derive from segmentation but 'precedes it': 'no segmenting operation, no placing of functions in a sequence, can do without some reference to the plot as a dynamic unity and to emplotment as a structuring operation' (*TN* 2: 38).

Alternatives and choices are introduced by Claude Bremond into Propp's model 'to substitute for its linear trajectory a map of possible itineraries' (*TN* 2: 39). It is simplified into a 'series of dichotomous options': a situation opening a possibility; entering or not entering an action; completion or non-completion of that action. The problem remains of how to move from such an elementary sequence to more complex argumentation. This is achieved through adaptation of the model so as to include a hierarchy of roles built up on binary terms, defined by the attribution of contingent predicates to a subject-noun: agents/sufferers, subject to information (confirmation/refutation) and affects (satisfaction/dissatisfaction; hope/fear); changes in condition (amelioration/degradation: protection/frustration), and evaluation (esteem/disesteem; benefit/tribulation). Ricoeur pays tribute to 'a more complete formalization and a more complete dechronologization' but somewhat undercuts this by noting 'neither the concept of a role nor the nomenclature of roles as such has any narrative character' (*TN* 2: 42). Lacking this setting within the plot, the logic of roles still depends on 'tacit reference' to a semantics of action. Bremond provides a 'table of action' but simply assumes the mediation of the 'simple cultural archetype' of plot: 'to know all the places capable of being assumed – to know all the roles – *is not yet to know any plot whatsoever*' (*TN* 2: 43). The value of Bremond's work turns out to lie in corroboration of a pre-understanding of a 'lexicon of narrative roles', but it remains incapable of giving insight into how these roles are structured.

A.J. Greimas combines a rigorously achronological model with strict transformation rules in order to account for previously irreducible diachrony; essentially the moves from function to role to actant. It is necessary to ground the combinatory possibilities of action on some 'depth principle' (*TN* 2: 45); Greimas utilises Lucien Tesnière's division of the sentence into verbs, nouns, and adverbs. Three advantages are posited: 'it is rooted in a structure of language' (Ricoeur *qua structuraliste*); it offers stability; and it also offers a degree of limitation and closure. Greimas is prepared to supplement this with an inductively derived inventory of roles. The model combines three relations – of desire, communication and action – each resting upon a binary opposition and fixed transformation rules. Each sphere hinges on an instance of conjunction and disjunction: the establishment of a contract unites mandate and acceptance; breaking it separates interdiction and violation; restoration equals a new conjunction. In line with other schemas, syntagma becomes paradigmatic. Ricoeur insists that such a model merely 'sets into relief the concept of a test' and confirms 'the irreducible role of temporal development' (*TN* 2: 46). The axiological status of contract, violation, restoration, exceeds any formal negation: Greimas himself acknowledges that rupture is an 'affirmation of the individual's freedom'.

Greimas subsequently seeks to extend or reduce the model to a sublexical level by recourse to the simplest possible logical model: the fearsome semiotic square. The condition for grasping any meaning whatsoever is that it is possible to state an elementary system involving three relations: white vs not-white (contradiction), contrariety (white vs black), not-white vs black (presupposition). These are treated as operations, active transformations 'by means of which one content is negated and another is affirmed' (*TN* 2: 49). Above the semantic depth-structures come the intermediary or 'superficial structures of doing something', which are broken down into various spheres – wanting to do, to have, to be, to know, to be able. Each involves a subject and antisubject, with relations of confrontation, domination, and attribution of value, all of which possess 'equivalence' to the square. So the 'topological syntax' of action permits a 'circular transmitting of values' (*TN* 2: 50). All the 'dynamism of emplotment' is located at the level of logical-semantic operations: the narrative configuration is merely a secondary and derivative manifestation (*TN* 2: 51).

Ricoeur makes two claims. Firstly, the surface level is richer than the depth structures and operates according to 'a mixed grammar, a semiotic-praxic grammar' rather than through a strict equivalence (*TN* 2: 58). 'Wanting to', for example, surreptitiously introduces an entire semantic field of volition; struggle and defiance cannot be translated into strict logical relation; and even the categories of transference contain an affective surplus – to deprive someone of something is to render them a victim. Secondly, in so far as the model gets more flexible, it relies on a pre-existent acquired familiarity with following a story. The strong model of elementary structures has to be weakened to accommodate actual stories. Transformations may have permutations according to the rules of the semiotic square, 'but then nothing would happen. There could be no event, no surprise. There would be nothing to tell' (*TN* 2: 56). The gap between the initial situation where all relationships balance one another and the final outcome, and where new values are produced, is concealed in Propp by the restitution of the original state: victory over the aggressor is explicitly paired with initial misfortune, overriding any combinatory sequence. Greimas is obliged to acknowledge that his analysis is teleologically guided by the assumption of the creation of value in the course of the narrative. In pushing forward the logical demands of his model, it is necessary to have had continual recourse to supplements from the field of narrative of a 'clearly syntagmatic order – without which the taxonomic model would remain sterile and inert' (*TN* 2: 60).

Ricoeur continues to attribute 'simplicity and elegance' to the project despite its avowedly 'laborious character' (*TN* 2: 46). But it is difficult to see how a self-proclaimed grammar of narrative can avoid being seriously, perhaps fatally, undermined by such an exposure of covert dependence on extraneous terms. Three conclusions may be drawn from Ricoeur's analysis. Firstly, it gives powerful support to his contention that narrative is made out of (the literal idiom should be retained: see 1980: 171) a complex network of action-sentences. Hence it can be said constantly to test and remake the world of praxis. Secondly, the configurational activity characteristic of narrative involves a specific mode of temporality that cannot be reduced to a model of synchronic analysis. The interpolation of an existential vocabulary has obvious attractions, though Ricoeur is yet to demonstrate that the Heideggerian vocabulary does not bring insuperable problems in its own wake. Thirdly, and more problematically, the value of structural analysis lies not in providing an objective knowledge of a text through application of a scientific methodology as in exposing a diachronic remainder. The immediate referent of both fictional and historical narrative is human action; its ultimate referent, revealed by this symbolic residue, is temporality itself. The first merges with and is supported by linguistic analysis of action, emphasising praxis, intervention in the world; the second demands to be read as a kind of quiescent but implicitly anguished meditation on a mythic level. It is difficult to see how they can be reconciled.

In the third stage of the hermeneutic arc, that of reception, the question becomes particularly urgent. The operation of structuring is simultaneously self-sufficient (though not in a full-blown structuralist sense) and a mere rite of passage between the pre-understanding of action and its eventual assimilation by a reader. The text exists both as a structure and an operation, specifically a summons to action. It will be helpful to consider this in the context of Gadamer's account of application (1975: 274–8), and Ricoeur's own previous essay, 'Appropriation' (*HHS*: 182–93).

For Gadamer, the traditional dichotomy of understanding and explanation must be supplemented by a third category of application. This is not a method as such, but a 'subtilitas', 'a talent that requires particular finesse of mind'. The meaning of the text is to be determined in relation to the present situation of the interpreter: thus a continuous tension is established 'between the identity of the common object and the changing situation in which it must be understood' (p. 276). Immediate analogues are available in theology and jurisprudence: the interpretation of scripture results in Christian proclamation, the interpretation of statute in a legal verdict. These judgements are to be deemed acceptable not in terms of their internal coherence or accuracy of historical reconstruction, but through the concrete validation of a specific intervention. Gadamer's aesthetics, however, lag disappointingly behind the implications of his overall hermeneutic (see Holub, 1984: 43); this force of intervention is dissipated in somewhat trivial invocation of performance in music and drama (thereby merely displacing the question of the response of the audience onto the mediation of the performers). What is strong about this third phase of the hermeneutic circle is its implication in Aristotelian phronesis, practical wisdom, and consequent alleviation of the more quiescent tendencies of this interpretative tradition. Meanings necessarily change, and rightly so, because they must become operative in specific and variable life-contexts.

Ricoeur's hermeneutic essays of the 1970s appear to envisage the interpretative process more in terms of a superimposition of texts rather than a meeting of minds. The ultimate purpose of structural analysis, however, is to reinstate thematic questioning at 'a more radical level'; its insights can be incorporated into interpretation as more or less traditionally understood. Thus understanding culminates in self-understanding. Indeed many incidental formulations suggest that ultimate significance of the formal analysis is to serve as a preparatory rite of 'relinquishment' before submission to the 'revelatory power' of the text. The same problem that Ricoeur detected in Bultmann's work appears to arise here: all the rigour of demystification is concentrated on a preliminary phase, while the final assimilation is exempted from comparable scrutiny. Meaning is transferred from a public sphere into a private dimension where criteria of verification are necessarily redundant. 'What must be interpreted in a text is a proposed world which I could inhabit and wherein I could project my ownmost possibilities' (*HHS*: 142). The idiom of the world opening in front of the text, opposed to the intentions concealed behind it, is undeniably attractive. As always, however, the presence of this vocabulary in Ricoeur pulls two ways: outwards to an inhabitable realm of possible life-options, and inwards to the deepest level of experience, Husserl's *Lebenswelt*, Heidegger's being-in-the-world. 'Exposing ourselves to the text and receiving from it an enlarged self' (*HHS*: 143) can sound suspiciously like undergoing a course in irradiation; and is surely an unacceptably quiescent ideal unless accompanied by a moment of awakening and praxis. It is in this context that Ricoeur's refusal to accept any radical division in 'Heidegger and the question of the subject' (*CI*: 223–35) between the earlier existential analyses and the later meditations on language acquires its greatest significance. While common features may be adduced – notably the structural position occupied by both being-towards-death and *Urdichtung* (primal poeticising) as that which compels an apperception of one's own identity – it is clear that what is desired is a superimposition of practical intervention onto numinal meaning, the union of work and the word. An exploration of the possibilities of the self is regarded as necessarily equally directed towards the world. But the initial stratification inevitably raises the question of the ultimate coherence of a discourse in which ethical and political intervention is superimposed, perhaps conflated, with a sacramental quiescence involving reversion to an uncompromisingly theological stance.

Ricoeur acknowledges that the *Poetics* is a treatise about composition with a disregard of cultural reception except in so far as it provides a negative constraint. Nevertheless he is prepared to elicit hints to support the claim 'structuration is an oriented activity that is only completed in the spectator or reader' (*TN* 1: 48). The 'dynamism of configuration' (*TN* 3: 159) cannot reside in internal finality, but demands the supplement of pleasure 'made actual outside it' (1: 48). The logical criteria of probability have their counterpart in the pleasure of recognition experienced by the spectator. The 'probable impossibility' is linked to the somewhat dubious pleasure of being persuaded. Finally fear and pity (here seen as unequivocally 'pleasurable' (*TN* 1: 50)) are the correlates of incidents internal to the text. The importance of catharsis thus lies not in being the affective response that characterises the highest literary art, but in the testimony that it offers to this outward-directed impulse (*TN* 3: 176); hence the insistence on a sharp distinction in Jauss's aesthetics between aisthesis, repose, and catharsis, repercussions; the response to the work must be 'at once a stasis and an impetus' (*TN* 3: 179). In striking contrast to more orthodox phenomenological accounts of a disembodied reading process, Ricoeur insists that Aristotle's ideal spectator is one of 'flesh and blood and capable of pleasure' (*TN* 1: 50; see also 3: 171), and more importantly, perhaps, capable of action: the reader completes the imperative of the text in an external realm.

It is worth contrasting Ricoeur's stance with the oft-quoted truism: the active production of text rather than passive consumption of meaning. Few states could be more wholly divorced from action in any meaningful ethical sense than the hedonist reverie urged in Barthes's later work; a capitulation to the pre-determination of the public sphere and a withdrawal to a wholly private libidinal space. Ricoeur, in contrast, equates the pleasure of the text with 'learning, concluding, recognising the form' (*TN* 1: 40). One need not wholly endorse the more ascetic tendencies of his exposition to applaud this resolute refusal of any simplistic dichotomy between effort and satisfaction: in *Fallible Man*, one recalls, happiness was defined as an unfinished task.

This initial pledge to explore the power of narrative 'to *disclose* and *transform* the actual world of action' (*TN* 2: 160) through movement into the 'life-world of the reader' is unfortunately not carried through in Ricoeur's more detailed discussion of the conversion of structure into effect. The text's 'power of clarifying, examining, and instructing' (*TN* 3: 176) is diluted into a somewhat unsatisfactory coordination of a theory of reading with one of cultural reception, in which literary history (Jauss) and psychology (Iser) are seen as presupposing and complementing each other. There is a particularly acute contrast between Ricoeur's own account of the aporias of the Husserlian analysis of time and Iser's thesis that the play of retention and protention 'fits perfectly' onto the reading process (*TN* 3: 168). Ricoeur also seems to have undercut his own argument by insisting that the reader 'intuitively apprehends the work as a unified totality' (*TN* 3: 162). If this apperception is immediate and uncontestable, there can be no struggle towards order; the activity of reading consists of the comparatively localised trajectory of the 'wandering viewpoint'. To characterise the activity of reading in terms of plugging zones of endless indetermination, a kind of mental aerobics that requires no further justification, allows a retreat to a more conservative account of aesthetic experience: 'the more readers become unreal in their reading, the more profound and far-reaching will be the work's influence on social reality' (*TN* 3: 179). This is dogmatic, to say the least, and difficult to square with contentions such as 'a life examined in this way is a changed life, another life' (*TN* 3: 158).

> It is the task of hermeneutics to reconstruct the set of operations by which a work lifts itself above the opaque depths of living, acting, and suffering to be given by an author to readers who receive it and thereby change their acting. For a semiotic theory, the only operative concept is that of the literary text. Hermeneutics, however, is concerned with reconstructing the entire arc of operations by which practical experience provides itself with works, authors and readers.
>
> (*TN* 1: 53)

This concept of interpretation represents a major break with the

Arnoldian injunction of 'disinterestedness'; 'let us think of quietly enlarging our stock of true and fresh ideas, and not, as soon as we get an idea, be running out with it into the street, and trying to make it rule there' (Arnold, 1962 3: 282); 'a polemical practical criticism makes men blind even to the ideal imperfection of their practice ... and clearly this is narrowing and baneful to them' (1962 3: 271). This is part of an endemic strategy of authority through disengagement – the capacity of non-partisan far-sightedness over 'ideas transported out of their own sphere, and meddling rashly with practice' (1962 3: 268) – indicative of the incipient elitism and inculcation of social acquiescence running throughout the English tradition: compare 'indeed the difference between the intelligent and refined, and the stupid or crass person is a difference in the extent to which overt action can be replaced by incipient and imaginal action' (Richards, 1925: 85; see also Baldick, 1983). It is striking how immediately compatible this is with de Man's insistence on 'the crucial distinction between an empirical and an ontological self' (1983: 50); 'a certain degree of confusion arises when this knowledge is interpreted as a *means* to act upon the destiny that the knowledge reveals. This is the very moment at which ontological inquiry is abandoned for empirical concerns that are bound to lead it astray' (1983: 48). (There is, of course, a blatant circularity here: the knowledge revealed is that of the inauthenticity of the decisions of the empirical self; consequently abstention is itself a form of acting upon that knowledge, and in itself an ominous political tactic (see Lentricchia, 1985). The ironic subject, deprived of any possibility of 'making this consciousness applicable to the empirical world' is obliged 'at once to ironize its own predicament and observe in turn, with the detachment and disinterestedness that Baudelaire demands of this kind of spectator, the temptation to which it is about to succumb' (1983: 217). It is in this context that what looks most mundane and didactic in Ricoeur's project – the emphasis on the 'practical experience' of the text and its capacity to make its recipients 'change their acting' – could be said to represent a major effort of revisionism.

HISTORY AS NARRATIVE AND EXPLANATION

Ricoeur carefully distinguishes the thesis of the ultimately narrative character of history from a defence of narrative history *per se*. Nevertheless he contends that the discipline would lose its specific character if it broke all links with '*our basic competence for following a story*' (*TN* 1:

91). The constitutive features of the historical field are borrowed indirectly from narrative. Thus they are rooted in the temporality of action and our pragmatic competence for dealing with events in time. Nevertheless the inquiry is designed to enforce a recognition of the 'major bifurcation' of the narrative field as well as its common features: dynamic configuration; order over succession; discordant concordance; narrative schematisation of generalities as laws; and sedimentation versus innovation. Due weight must be given to the special role of circumstances, unintended consequences, and anonymous forces in historiography. At this stage Ricoeur prefers to postpone discussion of the ultimate referent of the discipline. But it should be noted that while history and fiction diverge in their primary referents – fiction may enlarge, recast, transform, but history nevertheless 'did happen', leaves material signs or traces on the course of events – they converge again in their secondary referent. Both find their ultimate purpose in refiguring the field of praxis through temporal configurations of a higher rank.

We are warned in advance of the painstaking and circuitous progress of the argument: the 'respective insufficiency' of nomological and narrativist theses must be demonstrated before the relation between history and narrative can be directly examined (*TN* 1: 93). The overall organisation represents a fine example of Ricoeur's habitual procedure of pushing antimonies to the point of their own breakdown, and offering a series of mediating concepts: every aporia reveals a legitimate question, here brought into a tracking, progression, or a questioning back, rather than the absolute fractures of the final volume. The failures of logical theory and historical practice are used to define a sphere of legitimacy and proven jurisdiction for a narrative configuration: in the subsequent movement, this is shown to be capable of absorbing and retaining the characteristic procedures and epistemological legitimacy of historiography.

Ricoeur's discussion remains on a strictly epistemological level, limiting itself to 'the relations between the writing of history and the operation of emplotment' in order to establish common features of configuration in the narrative field. There are several immediate lines of objection: an over-sanguine acceptance, certainly from an Anglo-American perspective, that 'the history of long time spans has now carried the day and tends to occupy the entire field of historical studies' (*TN* 1: 207); the conservative humanism evident in the insistence that the freedom of the historical is always bound to an ethical responsibility, that makes Ricoeur's project seem more one of

restraint and curtailment than radical exploration; a degree of un-
questioned confidence, even aplomb, that critical philosophy can
fulfil the demands to establish the conditions of historiography; and
the doubt whether such methodological reflection comes any closer to
the operative procedures of the practising historian than some of the
more arcane speculation of the status of fiction is to the process of
reading. The strength of this volume lies in its comparative self-
containment. There has been no consideration of the 'ambition of
truth' of history, its claim to be real (*TN* 1: 226), nor of ontological
status of the past as the having-been. Consequently it is not made to
serve as mediation in the broader dialectical schema – a 'third-time'
permitting the reinscription of lived onto cosmic time – and so
remains separate from such ominous conjunctions as the calendar
and the 'axial moment' of mythic time (*TN* 3: 108), the passing of
generations and 'the mixed, ambiguous notion of death' (*TN* 3: 115),
the historical trace and possible apperception of the wholly other (*TN*
3: 125) – and manages to preserve clear-cut demarcations from the
mythic perceptions that surround it.

The recurrent structure of an interpolated moment of distanciation, 'tying the explanation ... to prior understanding' (*TN* 1: x), is
familiar from the hermeneutic debate, and undeniably possesses a
comparable theological dimension: nomological explanation, like
structural analysis, requires the relinquishing of narcissism. Ricoeur
insists on the continued though relative autonomy of explanation:
'whatever the limits of historical objectivity may be, there is a problem of objectivity in history' (*TN* 1: 176). Far from urging a willing
suspension of disbelief, historians are required to acknowledge and
defend their own intellectual partiality: 'poets begin with form: historians argue from it. The former produce: the latter argue. And they
argue because they know that we can explain in other ways' (*TN* 1:
186). And this may perhaps be seen as the chief merit of this part of his
work: not in breaking down the demarcation between history and
fiction, a fashionable activity over the past twenty years, but in
continuing to preserve a rationality of procedure that provides history
with a different truth-claim and ontological status. Though 'to narrate is already to explain' (*TN* 1: 178), there remains a separate
problematic of adjudication. The practice of history writing may well
feel itself to have sufficient pragmatic warrant to remain in epistemological innocence as to the logical status of the concepts that it
employs. But then it is open to an onslaught from narrativist theses,
which dissolve the discipline into an eclectic relativism or

181

ideological instrument. Ricoeur vigorously contests the assumption of the inevitable complicity of the representation of history in the interests of power, that finds its most powerful ancestry in Nietzsche. (There is, though, surprisingly little direct attention to Foucault, only a brief reference to the ethic of discontinuity in the history of ideas, and a claim that a comparable decentring may be achieved through a hermeneutic concept of the past (*TN* 3: 217–19).) Ricoeur is fighting the corner for a critical rationality, and is obliged to go into some forbiddingly technical areas of debate.

French historiography is presented as 'traditionally and unfailingly distrustful of philosophy', preferring 'strict adherence to the profession of the historian' over any critical self-reflection (*TN* 1: 95). It represents practice, opposed to the epistemological rigour but also aloofness of positivist inquiry. Both, however, repudiate narrative: one in favour of the 'total social fact', the other for a severer model of explanation (*TN* 1: 102).

The 'common-sense' assumptions of the status of historical events – their pastness, their involvement with human action, and their unrepeatability – are subjected to virulent criticism by the Annales school. They are seen as intrinsically complicit in a docile promulgation of the political chronology of the nation state. (The issue of narrative is not directly addressed but subsumed into the attack on political history.) Even the reliance on documentation is condemned on account of the ideological formation of the archive; only that which furthers the interests of the powerful is preserved. The most striking single innovation is the displacement of the idea of the historical event involving identifiable agents by the concept of extended duration (*longue durée*): behind the frenzy of high politics, the rhythm of genuine change may span decades, generations, centuries. But slowness is not synchrony. Historical anthropology and the history of *mentalités*, however attracted to the serial time of economics, demography, and sociology, cannot devote themselves to a state of equilibrium: 'it is through their temporal aspect of stability or mutation or breaking up that structures come into the field of history' (*TN* 1: 110).

The positivist debate starts with the question of the status of general laws in history: what has become known as the covering law model. Karl Hempel urges the bypassing of chronicle, narrative, or documentary mediation 'in favour of a direct relationship between an individual event and the assertion of a universal hypothesis, therefore of some form of regularity' (*TN* 1: 112); the event is removed from a narrative context, defined in terms of particular and universal, and regarded as repeatable through an analogy with physical properties. The shifting semantic criteria of the concepts of law, cause, and explanation are bound together under the single concept of regularity. Explanation and prediction are identified: the predictive value of a hypothesis ensures its explanatory validity. The highly prescriptive nature of the model is the condition of its scientific aspirations: history can offer no more than 'descriptive sketches' which, however, Hempel is prepared to distinguish from pseudo-explanation (*TN* 1: 113). Empathetic understanding is unceremoniously expelled, along with any appeal to narrative. Ricoeur is surprisingly conciliatory to the project of weakening the strong model to 'augment its applicability' (*TN* 1: 115). History does not establish laws, it employs them: they may remain implicit and are permitted a 'diversity of levels of imprecision' (*TN* 1: 116). As usual, the distinctive feature of Ricoeur's hermeneutic is its capacity to accommodate a distinct moment of formal or nomological explanation, though here he concedes that at one extreme of dilution it simply merges with prudential judgement. The basic point is that proponents of a modified form of the covering law model tend to view it as inseparable from the claim to objectivity in history, the 'essential stake' (*TN* 1: 119).

Narrativist theses appear with the break-up of the strong model of historical explanation, and the consequent revaluation of the resources of narrative understanding. The work of W.H. Dray fully recognises the 'logical dispersal of explanation in history' (*TN* 1: 122). Because it does not presuppose a determinate structure, there is no univocal implication in the deduced nature of the event; explanation need not be restricted to laws and instances. The rejection of the model might seem to lead to a return to the uniqueness of each specific instance, and from there to an extreme nominalist view of the world as radically dissimilar particulars. Ricoeur makes the point that there are relative levels of uniqueness, and that it is the task of the historian to establish how events differ rather than how they are the same: an adjudication which follows the 'logic of practical choices instead of that of scientific deduction' (*TN* 1: 125). The language of causality in history is necessarily polysemous: the problem is to 'regulate' it through 'rule-governed usages'. In evaluating a sentence 'because' in response to the question 'why', two criteria justify the factor being 'really necessary'. The first is the pragmatic but 'necessarily incomplete' one of acceptable reason for this selection which Ricoeur compares to Aristotle's narrative probability (*TN* 1: 126). The second, the inductive test, depends on a kind of imaginative variation:

envisaging an alternative scenario and judging the difference of non-occurrence (for example, the progress of the Second World War had Hitler not invaded Russia). These judgement procedures cannot be detached from their immediate context but must be 'interpolated into the narrative fabric' (*TN* 1: 127).

Rational explanation applies to actions performed by agents similar to ourselves, and hence invokes pre-explanation, competence in a linguistic framework. The mixed model of G.H. von Wright moves through propositional logic to an 'approximation' of historical understanding without disputing 'an originary capacity of apprehension as regards the meaning of human action (*TN* 1: 132). Thus it provides a logic of system that demands 'the intervention of free and responsible subjects' as its 'complement' (*TN* 1: 134). Put crudely, this involves the difference between necessary and sufficient cause, the one permitting prediction, the other based on retrodiction. Agents bring about systems which can then be analysed as closed structures: interference equals 'the intersection between one of the agent's abilities and the resources of the system' (*TN* 1: 135). Wright's work provides logical confirmation that agency precedes and eludes causality. Teleology implies action, unified by intention rather than cause: essentially a can only achieve b through c, therefore c must be understood through the intention to pursue b. Nevertheless causes remain too heterogeneous to be incorporated into a practical syllogism: 'the boundary between scientific explanation and ideology is revealed to be a fragile one' (*TN* 1: 142). It remains necessary to unify nomic and teleological elements in a plot.

The question now arises of whether the configurational aspect of narrative can sustain this burden of explanation. Somewhat surprisingly, Ricoeur opts for a criticism of premature narrativist theses, and to this end turns to the work of Arthur C. Danto. This seeks to provide a minimal characterisation of history through study of a specific class of sentences, that will establish the asymmetry between past and future, break with any residual image of the past as receptacle of that which has been, and prevent any extrapolation of concatenations of the past in the direction of that which is to come. Instead 'the whole truth of this event can only be known *after the fact* and long after it has taken place' (*TN* 1: 145). Thus three times are involved: that of the event, of the event in terms of which the first is situated, and of the narrator: historical sentences describe an action in the light of a later event, viewed from a third temporal vantage. So history weakens the intentional component in action, and also the primacy of testimony.

Causality can only be retrospectively inferred; thus there can be no history of the present, above all no prediction of the future, only an anticipation of a future historian. Danto, however, does not enter into what holds sequences of narrative sentences together: on his account they could be regarded simply as a series of points. Furthermore he will accept no distinction between explaining and describing: 'a narrative that fails to explain is less than a narrative' (*TN* 1: 148).

Ricoeur next turns to the work of W.B. Gallie for the concept of 'followability', narrative as 'connection between events'. Explanation is not dismissed but 'in the service of' a prior narrative form (*TN* 1: 149). Gallie approaches the structural constraints of emplotment from a psychological angle. The 'successive actions, thoughts, and feelings' that constitute a story present a 'particular directedness'; this development pulls the reader forward and induces a continually readjusted set of 'expectations concerning the completion or outcome of the whole process' (*TN* 1: 150). Narrative conclusions, though possessing a teleological function, cannot be predicted: the internal coherence of a story must unite contingency and acceptability. There is an additional factor of anticipation: 'the subjective teleology that takes the place of structural analysis' (*TN* 1: 150). History is narrative because it requires a competence to follow stories, and because its interest derives from our shared humanity with its agents. Ricoeur emphasises the importance of blockage of narrative continuity for 'inserting a critical moment into the very heart of the basic act of following a story' (*TN* 1: 157). The somewhat provocative suggestion is made that historians only borrow from the laws of science in order 'to allow us better to follow the story' (*TN* 1: 154). In no way is this a weakened form of the covering law model. Every narrative explains itself: explanation is only a supplement to overcome a blockage. But the process of grafting and interpolating is itself capable of great subtlety and elaboration.

In the work of Louis O. Mink, the configurational act is identified with the Kantian act of judgement, a grasping together combined with a reflective operation. Thus history is seen as a holding together rather than a series of discrete hypotheses, in which conclusions are exhibited rather than demonstrated. While praising the emphasis on the synthetic character of narrative activity, Ricoeur vigorously protests against the reduction of the 'poignancy' of history, its capacity to induce a kind of 'learned wonder' (*TN* 1: 158). Mink is charged with a 'unilateralness' and with misunderstanding the 'specific temporality of narrative' through his removal of contingency (*TN* 1: 160). 'A superior degree of configurational comprehension' becomes 'the mark of its abolition' (*TN* 1: 160). One may wonder whether Ricoeur's own use of the schematism of the Kantian productive imagination escapes a similar charge. The uncompromising insistence on grasping together as a whole certainly seems at odds with the temporal unfolding of understanding always subject to correction through dialogue in the public sphere. The severity of Ricoeur's rebuke seems more motivated by Mink's pretension to master time. Any aspiration to the 'totality' of nontemporal understanding is *per se* arrogant: an aspiration to the divine *totum simul*.

Hayden White transfers history from an epistemology of objectivity and proof to one of poetics, thus bringing it under the same classification as fiction. Thus the writing of history (including the philosophy of history) ceases to be a second-order activity and becomes 'constitutive of the historical mode of understanding' (*TN* 1: 162). The great strength of *Metahistory* lies in its refusal to separate history from other narrative forms or to accept the break between real and imaginary upheld by the majority of literary critics. In both spheres, the act of emplotment invites us to 'recognize a traditional class of configurations' in its narrative ordering (*TN* 1: 164): White borrows, and somewhat unnecessarily complicates, Frye's scheme of genres: romance, comedy, tragedy, and satire. It is assumed, however, that to 'reclassify history as a literary artefact' is equivalent to 'declassifying it as knowledge' (*TN* 1: 162); there is no consideration of the possibility of incorporating nomological elements to enhance its cognitive potential.

One might have expected from White an outright condemnation of Ricoeur's work for pursuing the 'coherence, integrity, fullness and closure of an image of life that is and can only be imaginary' (White, 1987: 24). But instead *Time and Narrative* is applauded for demonstrating the inevitable dependence of history on narrative, which in turn 'confirms the suspicions of those who regard narrative representations of historical phenomena as being inherently mystical in nature (1987: 189). History has failed to achieve the abandonment of narrative necessary for the transition to a genuinely self-constituting discipline: it remains 'proto-scientific, not to mention its manifestly mythical, or ideological, nature' (1987: 189), always in the service of an ethnocentric appropriation. White daringly states his 'personal belief' in the role of the 'socially responsible interpreter' as a preemptive rebuttal of the charge of relativism: '1) expose the fictitious nature of any political program based on an appeal to what "history" supposedly teaches and 2) remain adamantly "utopian" in any criticism of political "realism"' (1987: 227n). There are immediate objections to be raised. If 'fictitious' is synonymous with spurious, self-insinuating, as the context seems to suggest, how does 'utopian' thought differ? And how can a comment such as 'as for revolution, it always misfires' be debated, let alone justified, without some recourse to historical events: the Philippines, the American Revolution, the foundation of the Irish free state? But what undermines White's position most decisively is his dogmatic assumption that the fictional forms are inherently unreal. If 'fictitious' (and also the 'imaginary' that precedes it) are valorised as a positive component, history is restored to its previous authority. Ricoeur stresses the active recovery of tradition in these forms rather than a static taxonomy, thereby enabling him to redefine emplotment as that which 'dynamises' and brings about the transition between narrating and explaining (*TN* 1: 168). The same objection will later be made against White's theory of tropes (*TN* 3: 152–4): not that such a dependence cannot be demonstrated, but that it may be regarded as a means of comprehension of human action rather than a dissimulating pretence to objective authority. Ricoeur alludes back to the tension of the identity and difference in the metaphoric copula with a rather cumbersome schema of same, other, and analogue. The idealist stance of total re-enactment of the intellectual essence of an event (Collingwood) is opposed to a stance of complete estrangement from the past (Veyne, de Certeau); the dichotomy is bridged by the transformative power of analogy. Ricoeur insists on the full force of Ranke's dictum, showing it 'wie es eigentlich war', as it really was, as a constitutive capacity of historical discourse (*TN* 3: 151): the power of seeing-as contains an ontological force, positing a mode of existence other than and so challenging the actual.

Ricoeur now seeks to establish a series of mediating concepts to bridge 'the epistemological break between historical knowledge and our ability to follow a story': quasi-cause, quasi-character, and quasi-plot. (The prefix should have the full-force of the imaginative transformation of 'as if'.)

The essential feature of singular causal imputation (or quasi-cause) is that action cannot be understood through Humean causality, but requires segments of teleological inference irreducible to the reconstitution of a calculation. Such a deontological logic allows reference back to the history of human actions, testifies to the reasonableness of inquiring into the intentions of actors in terms of practical inference, and allows coordination of action with nomological explanation. There is no such thing as an effect separate from a human action: it is part of that action. A logical gap remains between cause and law. Causality only retains a conditional necessity: given these unique conditions it was necessary that x occurred. This only becomes determinism if the universe is regarded as a single system rather than multiple sub-systems subject to individual intervention. Thus the resistance of historical causality to the 'retrospective illusion of fatality' contains a 'moral and a political significance that exceeds its purely epistemological one' in its resistance to 'the retrospective illusion of fatality'. Nevertheless it is 'irreducible to moral imputation' because it 'evaluates intentions not only in terms of aim but also of results' (*TN* 1: 188). It integrates into a meaningful unity, but one that includes the unintended consequences of an action. Although singular, it is not restricted to an individual point of view: it can be transposed from specific agents onto collective entities.

Maurice Mandelbaum argues that 'the irreducible object of history is of a *societal* order' (*TN* 1: 195). Societies are tied to a place for a duration; connected to the individual through the institutional roles they provide; characterised by an uninterrupted existence. This 'semi-autonomy of institutions and activities' permits an analogical transfer that allows them to be referred to as 'quasi-character' (*TN* 1: 197). 'History replaces the subject of action with entities that are anonymous', apparently breaking with 'the time of memory, expectation, and circumspection of individual agents' (*TN* 1: 176). But nothing requires a character to be a human being: odd, but sound. Societies are regularly treated as agents, 'personalities of a higher order', in Husserl's phrase (*TN* 1: 198). Territorial organisation, institutional structure, temporal continuity, all refer back, albeit obliquely, to constituent individuals. In particular, the 'continuous existence' of these first-order entities allows a break with an atomist notion of cause and effect as a relation between two logically distinct events (*TN* 1: 200): the insertion of generalities supplies a kind of cement, adhesiveness, within a historical continuum. It should be stressed that this in no way underwrites the ambition of universal history. 'There is no single plot that could encompass every plot, nor a single historical character who would be the superhero of history': such a denial of the inevitable 'pluralism of peoples and civilizations' would only be 'a reductive operation that can never be actually accomplished in practice' (*TN* 1: 203).

It should be stressed that Ricoeur, having vigorously contested for the relative autonomy of 'the concrete totalities characteristic of first-order entities' (*TN* 1: 206), insists on the derived character of this level as representing a false claim to totality. Lyotard criticises Ricoeur as the representative of a 'contemporary hermeneutic discourse' that is 'incorporated into the metanarrative of a subject ... which guarantees that there is meaning to know and thus confers legitimacy upon history (and especially the history of learning)' (Lyotard, 1984: 35). There is nothing illegimate in a cultural tradition (or, to use another of Lyotard's examples, a social class such as the bourgeoisie) occupying such a narrative function provided the concept is kept at its appropriate level. Lyotard, however, will acknowledge no interim concepts between primary narratives wholly unsusceptible of analysis and grand narratives which ground the very procedures of explanation. The impoverished and self-undermining nature of his position becomes apparent in the role played by science in his own narrative: either this concept operates as a first-order entity through oblique reference back to the activities of individuals or it will assume the kind of meta-historical necessity repeatedly denounced elsewhere in his text.

Once the legitimacy of causal attribution as a mode of emplotment and anonymous entities as forms of characters has been acknowledged, there should be little difficulty with the quasi-event. It no longer need be susceptible to charges of brevity, distortion, an occluding suddenness, but may take the form of a metabole or change in fortune occupying generations. Even in Annales history, 'the event continually reappears in the very midst of structures' (*TN* 1: 217); Braudel's epic account of the Mediterranean world, as Ricoeur demonstrates at length, depends on 'transitional structures that ensure the overall coherence of the work' (*TN* 1: 209). The time of civilisation cannot be dissolved into the time of nature: in so far as it is historical, it is susceptible to particular human interventions. The geographical level is itself permeated by spheres of influence, both in terms of transformations of physical environment and the shifting contours of political entities. Above all the Mediterranean itself assumes the role of principle of continuity and major protagonist: the complex personification of a cultural era.

'The event is restored at the end of each attempted explanation as a remainder left by every such attempt ... as a dissonance between explanatory structures and finally as the life and death of the structures themselves' (*TN* 1: 224). Again we find that explanation through structure results in a 'remainder', the 'supplement and complement' of a diachronic residue that assumes the position of symbolic illumination of the nature of temporality. 'If the brief event can act as a screen hiding our consciousness of the time that is not of our making, the long time-span can, likewise, act as a screen hiding the time that we are' (*TN* 1: 224): attention to this 'dissonance' can enable us to overcome this forgetting of the time of our mortality. One can perhaps overstate the importance of the sombre overtones of 'life and death' – 'something happens to even the most stable structures . . . in particular, they die out' (*TN* 1: 225) – but they point to an important tension within the overall conceptualisation of time. How can the mortal time-span be brought into relation with the mocking impassivity of cosmic time? Ricoeur subsequently offers extended discussion of how devices such as the calendar, the concept of generations, and the trace (in the sense of mark on the course of events, continuing existence of the past in the present) allow 'the reinscription of historical time on cosmic time' (*TN* 3: 100) and so overcome the divide in Heideggerian temporality. But while the general point may perhaps be allowed to pass uncontested – the sense of history links the perspective of an individual life to the larger perspectives of generations, the race, the cosmos – one may doubt whether history can sustain the kind of demands being placed on it. What occurs in the final stages of Ricoeur's argument is a kind of schism between the poignancy of the individual's situation within time and the kind of mythic comprehension that proves most adequate to it: 'death reveals an individual destiny which does not exactly fit within the framework of an explanation that is itself not scaled to the measurements of mortal time. And without death as it seals a destiny such as this, could we still know that history is human history' (*TN* 1: 214). The collective project of humanity, the continuous narrative of which we form a part, cannot ultimately either resolve or console us for this existential plight.

THE LIMITS OF NARRATIVE

Ricoeur's study of metaphor was vulnerable to the obvious but powerful objection that it is meaningless to talk of reference with respect to innovations of meaning that by their very nature cannot be subject to procedures of verification. The generous invitation to enter a 'habitable world' (*TN* 1: xi) must deal with the rejoinder: whose world, and how does it relate to the more mundane environment in which we live and move and have our being? The term 'world' itself conflates what ought to be two separate concepts: the immediately accessible setting, tone and movement of a narrative and the symbolic residue of structural analysis that requires an entirely distinct mode of appropriation. As previously noted, the Heideggerian vocabulary lends itself to a stratification between the undertaking of practical interventions ('the proposing of a world that I might inhabit and into which I might project my ownmost powers' (*TN* 1: 81)), and a somewhat somnolent reverence before the power of the creative word ('a dimension of passivity accessible through poetic discourse, in particular the modes of elegy and of lamentation' (*TN* 1: xi)). Ricoeur repeatedly insists that these are reciprocally illuminating: no action without vision, and no vision which does not intersect at some point with ethical and political concerns. Yet in numerous other contexts it has been insisted that nothing less than the 'abolition' of 'descriptive, constative, didactic discourse' will permit the 'freeing of the second order reference' (*HHS*: 141); and a transcendence of a dispensable level of meaning, similar to that effected in the double intentionality of the symbol, between the primary configuration of action and its ultimate referent of temporality.

The initial premise, 'the world unfolded by every narrative is always a temporal world' (*TN* 1: 3), is unlikely to provoke much dissent: what, after all, would a non-temporal world be like? This is expanded into the claim that 'time becomes human to the extent that it is articulated through a narrative mode, and narrative attains its full meaning when it becomes a condition of temporal existence' (*TN* 1: 52). Ricoeur's assurances that this 'mutual constitution' produces 'not a vicious but a healthy circle whose two halves reinforce each other' (*TN* 1: 3) do not entirely dispel suspicions of a potential tautology: if nothing else, this involves an unfair disparagement of the human achievement of Galilean time, the time of experimental science. Narrative is on some level the manifestation of the human experience of time; a bringing to discourse of the 'hyletic' (*TN* 3: 24), the raw data of 'our confused, unformed, and at the limit mute temporal experience' (*TN* 1: xi). The author produces the text out of his or her own experience utilising the capacity of time to be spoken (without this postulate the whole argument collapses). This is wrought into a structure that possesses both a semiotic coherence and a configurational shaping. The reader in following the story participates in this structuration. But how? Is it a re-enactment of the original authorial shaping or a separate and autonomous act of creation? Ricoeur seems to be saying both: because the human experience of time has discernible common features, narrative provides transferable meaningful organisations of time. The problem here is the inelegant multiplication of categories. In *Mrs Dalloway*, for example, there are monologues composed out of complex interweavings of memory, anticipation, and sensory experience: the present of the past, the present of the future, and the present of the present. So the argument appears to be: Virginia Woolf, out of her own experience of time, produces these linguistic structures, which take on an objective existence of their own. Working from these, the reader does not re-enact an original authorial experience, but responds to a possible arrangement that enhances understanding of his or her own temporal experience; and through a good faith involved in the transaction, a communal bond is established in the narrative realm. But the argument is obliged to presuppose what it sets out to prove, that there is an identifiable public time: the whole process unravels if the premise of common temporal structures is withdrawn. Following '*the destiny of a prefigured time that becomes a refigured time through the mediation of a configured time*' (*TN* 1: 54) can offer little new insight, if both halves of the equation are ultimately interchangeable. A genuine comprehension of temporality may only occur at a secondary level where the structure of interpretation itself illuminates the human relationship to time and, through that, the sacred.

The charge of 'redundancy of interpretation' (*TN* 1: 73) cannot be directed against Ricoeur's discussion of the status of action in narrative. The charge of mentalism, of unverifiable conjecture about necessarily private and incommunicable states of mind, is pre-empted by the insistence on the semantic autonomy of the text. Ricoeur mentions the 'struggle' of the reader with the narrator; and some attention is paid to the implicit 'strategy of persuasion (*TN* 3: 159). But the intentions of an implied author are solely present in and inferred from the text: the biographical figure is merely the means by which the discursive field of human action assumes a specific form. This shaping is not a conscious and voluntarily undertaken option but a primary existential imperative: the making of a plot is parallel to the making of a life, a symbolic representation that renders the self intelligible to itself. Psychoanalysis is defined as a 'quest for this personal identity that assures the continuity between the potential or inchoate story and the actual story we assume responsibility for' (*TN* 1: 74); a second analogy is provided by the legal procedure of disentangling and evaluating a specific life-story out of a background of multiple narratives. Thus on the level of praxis, one can legitimately speak of a psychological and ethical demand for narration to constitute the 'yet untold stories of our lives' (*TN* 1: 76).

This in turn provides a rationale for the use of narrative in historical discourse: 'it is by trying to put order on our past, by telling and recounting what has been, that we acquire an identity' (*TN* 1: 77). Traditional historiography minimises the problems of its own rhetorical constitution by stressing the appropriateness of a narrative form that parallels the intentions of agents who already 'hypotactically figurate their lives as meaningful stories' (White, 1987: 179) (though these 'lived stories' are construed as novelistic in a highly restrictive sense, excluding such modes as myth and folklore). Furthermore, plots not merely represent but redefine human.action by providing 'a critique of social narratives and, in this sense, a rectification of our common memory' (*TN* 3: 119). Our comprehension of praxis is necessarily ideologically embedded: the process of configuration restores malleability and allows the assertion of alternative narratives: 'for history is not only the story of triumphant kings and heroes, of the powerful; it is also the story of the powerless and dispossessed. The history of the vanquished dead demands to be told' (*DCCT*: 17).

There is no undue problem in defining a primary referent for historiography: the past, when all is said and done, 'did happen'. Ricoeur's discussion of its ontological status is primarily concerned with the mediation between personal and cosmic time performed by such devices as the calendar, the passing of generations, and the trace. The status of 'fictive experience', in contrast, is necessarily more 'precarious' (*TN* 2: 6); what comparable status can be claimed for a fictional world?

Two justifications are offered for the 'reality' of literary texts: the first, already encountered, that the 'shock of the possible' brings about an 'augmentation' of an 'impoverished world' (*TN* 1: 79–80); the second, a convergence of many strands of his earlier thought, that 'narrating, telling, reciting is to remake action following the poem's invitation' (*TN* 1: 81). In both cases, fiction is able to explore non-linear arrangements of time in ways that history, bound to the past, cannot. Ricoeur singles out for detailed analysis such resources as the internal differentiation created by the gap between *énoncé* and *énonciation* ('the time taken to narrate and the time of the things narrated' (*TN* 2: 100)); the complex transformations of tense usage that occur in fictional narration; and the apparently limitless flexibility of its deployment of narrative voice and point of view. A further somewhat sophistical argument on which great emphasis is placed expands the unstated conventions of reading to include 'the belief that the events reported by the narrative voice belong to the past of that voice' (*TN* 3: 190): ontologically speaking, fictional characters have real pasts or, at the very least, pasts no less unreal than those of the personages constituted by historical discourse.

There are some fine comments on the paradoxes of literary verisimilitude. Defoe's adaptation of the Puritan spiritual autobiography endows his narrators with an apparently inexhaustible memory; Richardson's use of the epistolary form depends on the possibility of an instantaneous transcription of emotion. Thus the 'always more strongly affirmed aim of faithfulness to reality' leads to 'an ever sharper awareness of the artifice behind a successful convention' (*TN* 2: 13). A sharp retort is also given to the post-modernist demand for 'fragmented, inconsistent fiction' (*TN* 2: 14). Not only does it dogmatically presuppose the ultimate incoherence of reality, but also 'by reduplicating the chaos of reality by that of fiction returns mimesis to its weakest function – that of replicating what is real by copying it' (*TN* 2: 14).

This argument is equally applicable to protests against Ricoeur's insistence on order from a deconstructive perspective. Hillis Miller, for example, insists that the 'intrinsic heterogeneity' of any narrative 'means that there is no such thing as a "reconfiguration" of "lived time" that is not fundamentally inaugural, disruptive' (1987: 1104). Leaving aside the question of how, on his own terms, he can claim to know what is 'fundamentally' anything, what is in effect being proposed is a naïve correspondence theory in which a 'disruptive' reality is mirrored in textual instability. Nevertheless his central charge remains to be met: that Ricoeur's elaborate conceptual schematisation is vitiated by his inability to read any particular text.

This is to overstate somewhat. Ricoeur undoubtedly prefers to rest his case on explicit thematic groupings rather than subversive detail; stress falls on the dominant configuration rather than textual ambiguity. An entirely gratuitous anxiety is voiced, for example, about 'how the same novel can be a novel about time, a novel about illness, and a novel about culture' (*TN* 2: 116). The degree of paraphrase may at times appear cumbersome, but the occasional laboriousness of a reading is no conclusive argument against it. The complexity of relatively minor points of narrative technique is brought out well: the account of the neutralisation of historical time in the use of dating in fictional narrative is especially impressive. The full import of such motifs as the thermometer without markings in *The Magic Mountain* becomes apparent; there is also a fine sense of the 'temporal weight-lessness' of Mann's novel (*TN* 2: 129), and the intricate duplication of viewpoints between its major character, the narrator, and the reader.

Nevertheless it must be conceded that in Ricoeur's dealing with literary texts, there tends to be a holding off, a lack of confidence in their capacity to bear adversarial scrutiny, that is ultimately conde-scending. Granted that 'speculation on time is an inconclusive rumi-nation to which narrative activity alone can respond', the subsequent claim that the aporias uncovered by phenomenology are 'clarified' by 'poetical transfiguration' is notably undeveloped (*TN* 1: 6–7). Per-haps simple rephrasing will help: narrative is a way of dealing with time, perhaps even the primary human resource. But the cross-cutting of different planes of discourse must still appear an evasion of what a theoretical resolution of the issue might involve. In fact, despite the repeated insistence that 'fiction does not illustrate a pre-existing phenomenological theme, but actualizes it in a singular figure' (*TN* 3: 130), there is a persistent shoring up through recourse to philosophical analogies. This at times approaches a bathetic pon-derousness. *Mrs Dalloway*, for example, has 'nothing to do with Berg-son's spatialized time ... that is why I compared it to Nietzsche's monumental history' (*TN* 2: 106). It is not that such parallels are *per se* unilluminating – the Husserlian analogues to Woolf's monologues are particularly apt (*TN* 3: 132–4) – but that they tend to impose a rather leaden immobility onto both terms of the comparison. When reading Augustine for conceptual argument, Ricoeur can readily acknowledge the importance of rhetorical features – aporia, apos-trophe, ellipsis – in the dynamic movement of the text. There is a similar generosity in the interpretation of Heidegger: a great sensi-tivity to pacing, strategies of retardment and repetition. The placing of the analysis of time after that of Dasein and authenticity, for example, implies that it is part of a more general overcoming of forgetfulness. The justification of Heidegger's immense 'labor of language' in the gigantic verbal 'construction site' of *Being and Time* lies in his need 'to provide existential attestation for its existential concepts' (*TN* 3: 65): not merely to explicate the categories of Dasein, but to provide a continuous testimony to the authenticity of the pursuit. In Ricoeur's treatment of Woolf, Mann, and Proust, this sense of concerted interrogation is absent. Because too much is granted, we come away with too little. The real drama of reading comes with the philosophical masters.

It is noteworthy that Ricoeur endorses Wayne Booth's account of friendship as the appropriate ethical attitude to adopt towards a text (echoing his own earlier description of responding to past philosophers with 'a kind of unilateral friendship, like unrequited love' (*HT*: 37)). Although prepared to countenance unstable narrators in principle, Ricoeur at several points denounces the 'more or less perverse pleasure the reader takes in being excited and gulled by them' (*TN* 1: 73), and shows a scarcely veiled distaste for the 'malign delight in disfiguring' exemplified by Joyce's *Ulysses*. The favoured model is very much a 'pact of trust' (*TN* 3: 161), a contract of good faith and polite behaviour, something like the 'tacit clause of sincerity' in Austin's speech-act theory (*TN* 3: 235): in a poignant aside, 'old promises that are not kept' are cited as more convincing proof of our fallen nature than 'fleeing in the face of death' (*TN* 3: 68). The critical moment involves subjecting the text to procedures of objective decoding. But there is little or no suggestion that resistance and repudiation might be part of the pleasure of the text: Woolf's elitism, Mann's ponderous ironies, Proust's aestheticising of personal relations have all to be acknowledged if their work is to be adequately understood. Instead the logical status of each fictional world as 'singular, incomparable, unique' (*TN* 3: 128) (as the product of a techne) is used to exempt them from the purgative scepticism so prominent in Ricoeur's earlier hermeneutic work.

This sacramental immunity is most vividly apparent in the respective treatments of Northrop Frye and Frank Kermode. Praise is lavished on the *Anatomy of Criticism* for its culminating vision of the literary universe as gravitating towards a 'still center of words' (Frye, 1957: 117). The apocalytic imagery which evokes this movement 'testifies to an order we cannot master in its cyclical composition' (*TN* 2: 18); an enigma which compels us to forgo the 'will to mastery in rationalizing reconstructions' and submit to its ultimate mystery (*TN* 2: 18). *The Sense of an Ending*, in contrast, is seen as governed by a 'ceaseless oscillation between the inescapable suspicion that fictions lie and deceive us to the extent that they console us and the equally invincible conviction that fictions are not simply arbitrary inasmuch as they respond to a need over which we are not the masters' (*TN* 2: 27). In an abrupt shift of tone, Kermode is condemned for having 'imprudently posed and prematurely resolved' the problem of the relation of fiction and reality instead of 'holding it in suspense'. Frye seems more 'dogmatic', but is ultimately 'more reserved' because he does not allow 'literature and religion to become mixed or confused with each other' (*TN* 2: 27). Ricoeur's reading of the *Anatomy* as a purely secular work is, to say the least, questionable, though there is considerable plausibility in his view that the 'ambiguous and troubling tone – the *Unheimlichkeit*' of Kermode's work contains a covert theological injunction. The primary importance of this disconcertingly belligerent outburst lies, however, in its being symptomatic of a more general readiness to absolve the creative word from exposure to demystifying interpretation.

Mrs Dalloway is, among other things, a novel of an elitist political culture, of feminist self-assertion, of momentary intangible affiliations between otherwise random human destinies. All these can be accommodated within Ricoeur's initial scheme of mimesis, yet he prefers to centre his analysis on the 'border-line between fable and myth' (*TN* 3: 137) evident in such slight motifs as the chimes of Big Ben and Fidele's dirge from *Cymbeline*. This pursuit of a mythic, or more accurately, allegorical level of meaning (it is no disadvantage for Proust's characters to have 'the phantasmatic dimension of emblematic beings' (*TN* 3: 138)) involves a dismissal of more mundanely human concerns. 'In his madnesss', Septimus (despite, or perhaps because of, his intimations of 'universal meaninglessness') becomes 'the bearer of a revelation that grasps in time the obstacle to a vision of cosmic unity and in death the way of reaching this salvific meaning' (*TN* 2: 109). Maybe so, but to regard his suicide as a 'limit-situation' of existential insight seems to invite an obliviousness towards the political causes of his situation (a shell-shocked war veteran) and the suffering of his loyal, anguished wife. We are back to the problematic of the 'more fundamental level' of reality opposed to the merely (one hesitates to say really) real. Ricoeur's extended meditation on the enigma of temporality as that which both constitutes and contains any individual existent has considerable fascination in its own right. But, as Hayden White warns, such a semi-mystical reverie must necessarily run the risk of becoming a kind of 'dogmatic mythology' in its own right (1987: 184). The vocabularies held together within the internal tension of the utterance in *The Rule of Metaphor* here appear to split apart. Contemplation of the mythic inscrutability of time appears to reduce the primary referent of human action to no more than a kind of preliminary typology whose ultimate value lies in the exegetical self-reflexivity that it provokes.

Many of us may find this unacceptable, and prefer to see the value of the work as lying in its stress on the communalising function of narrative, its infinite resourcefulness in restructuring and comprehending human activity. There may even seem something hapless and forlorn in the incongruous disproportion between the giganticism of *Time and Narrative*, its hubristic aspiration to mediate such vast areas of human thought, and the comparative meagreness of its ultimate conclusions. But at the very least the continuity of this conceptual asceticism with the dominant modes of contemporary thought must be acknowledged; and a peculiar appropriateness in its profound and dignified humility standing as the culmination of Ricoeur's lifetime's work.

Bibliography

The bibliography lists only those works by Ricoeur which are referred to in the text. Please see Vansina (1985) for a full bibliography.

Aarsleff, Hans (1982) *Linguistics from Locke to Saussure: Essays on the Study of Language and Intellectual History.* London: Athlone Press.
Adams, Hazard (1984) *Philosophy of the Literary Symbolic.* Tallahasee: University Presses of Florida.
Althusser, Louis (1969) *For Marx,* tr. Ben Brewster. Harmondsworth: Penguin.
Aristotle (1984) *The Complete Works of Aristotle.* 2 vols, ed. Jonathan Barnes. Princeton: Princeton University Press.
Arnold, Matthew (1962) *Lectures and Essays in Criticism,* vol. 3 in *The Complete Prose Works of Matthew Arnold.* (1960–77), ed. R.H. Super, 11 vols, Michigan: University of Michigan Press.
Augustine (1961) *Confessions,* tr. R.S. Pine-Coffin. New York: Penguin.
Austin, J. L. (1975) *How to Do Things with Words,* ed. J.O. Urmson and Marina Sbisa, second edition. Oxford: Oxford University Press.
Bachelard, Gaston (1968) *The Psychoanalysis of Fire.* Boston: Beacon Press.
Baldick, Chris (1983) *The Social Mission of Modern English Criticism 1848–1932.* Oxford: Clarendon Press.
Barthes, Roland (1976) *The Pleasure of the Text,* tr. Richard Howard. London: Cape.
—— (1982) 'Introduction to the structural analysis of literature', in *A Roland Barthes Reader,* ed. Susan Sontag. New York: Hill & Wang: 251–95.
—— (1985) *The Fashion System,* tr. Matthew Ward and Richard Howard. London: Cape.
Beardsley, Monroe C. (1958) *Aesthetics.* New York. Harcourt, Brace & World.
—— (1962) 'The metaphorical twist', *Philosophy and Phenomenological Research* 22: 293–307.
Benhabib, Seyla (1985) *Critique, Norm, and Utopia.* New York: Columbia University Press.
Benveniste, Emile (1971) 'The nature of the linguistic sign', in *Problems of General Linguistics,* tr. May Elizabeth Meek. Coral Gables, Florida: University of Miami Press.
Black, Max (1962) *Models and Metaphors.* Ithaca: Cornell University Press.

Bloom, Harold (1973) *The Anxiety of Influence.* Oxford: Oxford University Press.

Bonhoeffer, Dietrich (1972) *Letters and Papers from Prison,* ed. Eberhard Bethge. New York: Macmillan.

Booth, Wayne (1980) 'The way I loved George Eliot: friendship with books as a neglected metaphor', *Kenyon Review* 11 (2): 4–27.

—— (1981) *The Rhetoric of Fiction.* Chicago: University of Chicago Press.

Bourgeois, Patrick (1975) *Extension of Ricoeur's Hermeneutic.* The Hague: Nijhoff.

Bowie, Malcolm (1987) *Freud, Proust and Lacan: Theory as Fiction.* Cambridge: Cambridge University Press.

Braudel, Fernand (1972–4) *The Mediterranean and the Mediterranean World in the Age of Philip II,* tr. Sian Reynolds, 2 vols. New York: Harper & Row.

Bremond, Claude (1980) 'The logic of narrative possibilities', *New Literary History* 11: 387–411.

Bultmann, Rudolf (1958) *Jesus Christ and Mythology,* ed. Paul Schubert. New York: Scribner's.

Camus, Albert (1971) *The Rebel,* tr. Anthony Bower. Harmondsworth: Penguin.

Cavell, Stanley (1984) 'Existentialism and analytical philosophy', in *Themes out of School: Effects and Causes.* Chicago and London: University of Chicago Press.

Certeau, Michel de (1975) *L'écriture de l'histoire.* Paris: Gallimard.

Collingwood, R.G. (1946) *The Idea of History.* Oxford: Oxford University Press.

Culler, Jonathan (1975) *Structuralist Poetics.* London: Routledge & Kegan Paul.

—— (1983) *On Deconstruction: Theory and Criticism after Structuralism.* London: Routledge & Kegan Paul.

Dagognet, François (1973) *Ecriture et iconographie.* Paris: Vrin.

Danto, Arthur (1965) *Analytical Philosophy of History.* New York: Cambridge University Press.

de Man, Paul (1978) 'The epistemology of metaphor', *Critical Inquiry* 5: 13–30.

—— (1979) *Allegories of Reading: Figural Language in Rousseau, Nietzsche, Rilke, and Proust.* New Haven, Conn.: Yale University Press.

—— (1983) *Blindness and Insight: Essays in the Rhetoric of Contemporary Criticism,* ed. Wlad Godzich, 2nd edition. London: Oxford University Press.

—— (1984) *The Rhetoric of Romanticism.* New York: Columbia University Press.

—— (1986) *The Resistance to Theory.* Minneapolis: Minnesota University Press: 73–105.

—— (1988) *Wartime Journalism 1939–1945,* ed. Werner Hamacher, Neil Hertz and Thomas Keenan. Lincoln: University of Nebraska Press.

Derrida, Jacques (1973) *Speech and Phenomena, and Other Essays on Husserl's Theory of Signs,* tr. David B. Allison. Evanston, Ill.: Northwestern University Press.

—— (1977a) *Of Grammatology,* tr. Gayatri Chakravorty Spivak. Baltimore, Md: Johns Hopkins University Press.

—— (1977b) 'Signature event context', *Glyph* I: 172–97;

—— (1977c) 'Limited Inc abc', *Glyph* II: 162–254.

—— (1978) *Edmund Husserl's Origin of Geometry*, tr. Edward Leavey. Stony-brook: Hays.

—— (1978a) *Writing and Difference*, tr. Alan Bass. Chicago: University of Chicago Press: 278–93.

—— (1978b) 'Le retrait de la métaphore', *Poesie* 7: 103–26.

—— (1981) *Positions*, tr. Alan Bass, London: Athlone Press.

—— (1982) 'The white mythology: metaphor in the text of philosophy', in *Margins of Philosophy*, tr. Alan Bass. Chicago: University of Chicago Press: 207–73.

Descombes, Vincent (1980) *Modern French Philosophy*. Cambridge: Cambridge University Press.

Dews, Peter (1987) *Logics of Disintegration: Post-Structuralist Thought and the Claims of Theory*. London: Verso.

Dilthey, Wilhelm (1976) *Selected Writings*. ed. and tr. H.P. Rickman. Cambridge: Cambridge University Press.

Dummett, Michael (1973) *Frege: Philosophy of Language*. London: Duckworth.

Dray, William (1957) *Laws and Explanation in History*. London: Oxford University Press.

Eagleton, Terry (1983) *Literary Theory: an Introduction*. Oxford: Blackwell.

Eliade, Mircea (1958) *Patterns in Comparative Religion*, tr. Rosemary Sheed. New York: Sheed & Ward.

Eliot, T.S. (1969) 'Dry Salvages', *The Collected Poetry and Plays of T.S. Eliot*. London: Faber & Faber.

—— (1975) *Selected Prose*, ed. Frank Kermode. London: Faber and Faber.

Ellul, Jacques (1973) *Démythisation and idéologie*. Paris: Aubier.

Flew, Antony (1949) 'Psychoanalytic explanation', *Analysis* 10 (1): 8–15.

—— (1956) 'Motives and the unconscious', *Minnesota Studies* 1: 155–73.

—— (1969) 'Two views of Atheism', *Inquiry* 12 (4): 469–73.

Fontanier, Pierre (1968) *Les figures du discours*, introduced by G. Genette. Paris: Flammarion. Originally published in 1830.

Foucault, Michel (1972) *The Archaeology of Knowledge*, tr. A.M. Sheridan Smith. London: Tavistock Publications.

—— (1974) *The Order of Things: An Archaeology of the Human Sciences*, tr. Alan Sheridan. London: Tavistock Publications.

—— (1979) *The History of Sexuality*, tr. Robert Hurley. London: Allen Lane.

Frege, Gottlob (1962) *On Sense and Reference*, tr. Max Black, in *Translations from the Philosophical Writings of Gottlob Frege*. Peter Geach and Max Black (eds). Oxford: Oxford University Press: 56–78.

Freud, Sigmund (1953) *The Standard Edition of the Complete Psychological Works*. London: The Hogarth Press and the Institute of Psychoanalysis.

Frye, Northrop (1957) *Anatomy of Criticism: Four Essays*. Princeton: Princeton University Press.

Gadamer, Hans-Georg (1975) *Truth and Method*, second edition tr. and ed. Garrett Burden and John Cumming. London: Sheed & Ward.

Gallie, W.B. (1964) *Philosophy and Historical Understanding*. New York: Schocken Books.

Gallop, Jane (1985) *Reading Lacan*. Ithaca: Cornell University Press.

Geertz, Clifford (1973) *The Interpretation of Cultures*. New York: Basic Books.

Genette, Gérard (1980) *Narrative Discourse: An Essay in Method*, tr. Jane E. Lewin. Ithaca: Cornell University Press.

Gerhart, Mary (1976) 'Paul Ricoeur's notion of "diagnostics": its function in literary interpretation', *The Journal of Religion* 56: 137–53.

Goldman, Lucien (1964) *The Hidden God: A Study of Tragic Vision in the "Pensées" of Pascal and the Tragedies of Racine*, tr. Philip Thody. London: Routledge & Kegan Paul.

Goodman, Nelson (1968) *Languages of Art: An Approach to a Theory of Symbols*. Indianapolis: Bobbs-Merrill.

Greenblatt, Stephen J. (1980) *Renaissance Self-Fashioning: from More to Shakespeare*. Chicago: University of Chicago Press.

—— (1988) *Shakespearian Negotiations: the Circulation of Social Energy in Renaissance England*. Oxford: Clarendon.

Greimas, A.J. (1970) *Du Sens: Essais Sémiotiques*. Paris: Seuil.

—— (1983) *Du sens II*. Paris: Seuil.

—— (1983) *Structural Semantics: An Attempt at a Method*, tr. Daniele MacDonald, Ronald Schleifer, Alan Velie. Lincoln: University of Nebraska Press.

Grice, Paul (1957) 'Meaning', *Philosophical Review* 66: 377–88.

—— (1968) 'Utterer's meaning: sentence-meaning, and word-meaning', *Foundations of Language* 4: 225–45.

—— (1969) 'Utterer's meaning and intentions', *Philosophical Review* 78: 147–77.

Habermas, Jürgen (1972) *Knowledge and Human Interests*, tr. Jeremy Shapiro. London: Heinemann.

—— (1987) *The Philosophical Discourse of Modernity*, tr. Frederick Lawrence. Cambridge: Cambridge University Press.

Hartman, Geoffrey (1980) *Criticism in the Wilderness*. New Haven, Conn., and London: Yale University Press.

Heath, Stephen (1981) 'On Suture', in *Questions of Cinema*. London: Macmillan: 76–112.

Hegel, G.W.F. (1975) *Lectures on the Philosophy of World History: Introduction – Reason in History*, tr. Duncan Forbes. Cambridge: Cambridge University Press.

—— (1977) *The Phenomenology of Spirit*, tr. A.V. Miller. Oxford: Clarendon Press.

Heidegger, Martin (1962) *Being and Time*, tr. John Macquarrie and Edward Robinson. New York: Harper & Row.

—— (1971) *Poetry, Language, Thought*, tr. Albert Hofstader. New York: Harper.

Hempel, Karl G. (1942) 'The function of general laws in history', *The Journal of Philosophy* 39: 35–48.

Hester, Marcus (1957) *The Meaning of Poetic Metaphor*. The Hague: Mouton.

Hill, Geoffrey (1985) 'Holy Thursday', *Collected Poems*. Harmondsworth: Penguin.

Hirsch, E.D. Jr (1967) *Validity in Interpretation*. New Haven: Yale University Press.

—— (1977) *The Aims of Interpretation*. Chicago: University of Chicago Press.

Hjelmslav, Louis (1959) *Prolegomena to a Theory of Language*, tr. Francis J. Whitfield. Madison: University of Wisconsin Press.

Holub, Robert C. (1984) *Reception Theory: A Critical Introduction*. London: Methuen.

Husserl, Edmund (1960) *Cartesian Meditations: An Introduction to Phenomenology*, tr. Dorian Cairns. The Hague: Martinus Nijhoff.

—— (1964) *The Phenomenology of Internal Time-Consciousness*, tr. David Carr. Evanston: Northwestern University Press.

—— (1970a) *Logical Investigations*, tr. J.N. Findlay, 2 vols. London: Routledge & Kegan Paul.

—— (1970b) *The Crisis of European Sciences and Transcendental Phenomenology*. tr. D. Carr. Evanston: Northwestern University Press.

Ihde, Don (1971) *Hermeneutic Phenomenology. The Philosophy of Paul Ricoeur*. Evanston: Northwestern University Press.

Irigaray, Luce (1985) *Speculum: of the Other Woman*, tr. Gillian C. Gill. Ithaca and New York: Cornell University Press.

Iser, Wolfgang (1978) *The Act of Reading: a Theory of Aesthetic Response*. Baltimore: Johns Hopkins University Press.

Jakobson, Roman (1987) 'Two aspects of language and two aspects of aphasic disturbances', in *Language and Literature*, ed. Krystyna Pomorska and Stephen Ruding. Cambridge, Mass.: Harvard University Press: 95–114; 'Linguistics and Poetics', 67–94.

Jameson, Frederic (1980) *The Political Unconscious*. London: Methuen.

Jaspers, Karl (1971) *Philosophy of Existence*, tr. Richard R. Grabau. Oxford: Blackwell.

Jauss, Hans Robert (1982) *Aesthetic Experience and Literary Hermeneutics*, tr. Michael Shaw. Minneapolis: University of Minnesota Press.

Kant, Immanuel (1933) *Critique of Pure Reason*, ed. Norman Kemp Smith, second edition. New York: St Martin's Press.

—— (1956) *Critique of Practical Reason*, tr. Lewis White Beck. Indianapois: Library of the Liberal Arts.

Kearney, Richard (1987) *Movements in Modern European Philosophy*. Manchester: Manchester University Press.

Kenny, Anthony (1963) *Action, Emotion, and Will*. London: Routledge & Kegan Paul.

Kermode, Frank (1966) *The Sense of an Ending: Studies in the Theory of Fiction*. New York: Oxford University Press.

—— (1987) *The Genesis of Secrecy: On the Interpretation of Narrative*. Cambridge, Mass.: Harvard University Press.

Kierkegaard, Soren (1941) *Fear and Trembling*, tr. Walter Lowrie. Princeton: Princeton University Press.

—— (1941) *Concluding Unscientific Postscript*, tr. David F. Swenson and Walter Lowrie. Princeton: Princeton University Press.

Klemm, David E. (1983) *The Hermeneutical Theory of Paul Ricoeur: A Constructive Analysis*. Lewisburg–London–Toronto: Bucknell University Press–Associated University Press.

Koffman, Sarah (1973) *Camera Obscura. De l'idéologie*. Paris: Galilee.

—— (1985) *The Enigma of Woman*. Ithaca: Cornell University Press.

Koselleck, Reinhart (1985) *Futures Past: The Semantics of Historical Time*, tr. Keith Tribe. Cambridge, Mass.: MIT Press.

Kristeva, Julia (1982) *Powers of Horror: An Essay on Abjection*, tr. Leon S. Roudiez. New York: Columbia University Press.

Lacan, Jacques (1970) 'Of Structure as an inmixing of an Otherness prerequisite to any subject whatever', in Richard Macksey and Eugenio Donato (eds), *The Structuralist Controversy*. Baltimore and London: The Johns Hopkins University Press: 186–95.

—— (1977a) *The Four Fundamental Concepts of Psychoanalysis*, ed. Jacques-Alain Miller, tr. Alan Sheridan. London: Hogarth Press.

—— (1977b) *Ecrits: A Selection*. tr. Alan Sheridan. London: Tavistock Publications.

Lacapra, Dominick (1980) 'Who rules metaphor?', *Diacritics* 15–28.

Langer, Suzanne (1953) *Feeling and Form: A Theory of Art*. New York: Scribner's.

Laplanche, Jean, and Pontalis, J.B. (1973) *The Language of Psychoanalysis*. London: Hogarth Press.

Larkin, Philip (1983) *Required Writing: Miscellaneous Prose 1955–82*. London: Faber & Faber.

—— (1988) 'Church Going', in *Collected Poems*, ed. Anthony Thwaite. London: Marvell Press and Faber & Faber.

Lemaire, Anika (1977) *Jacques Lacan*, tr. David Macey. London: Routledge & Kegan Paul.

Lentricchia, Frank (1980) *After the New Criticism*. London: Athlone Press.

—— (1985) *Criticism and Social Change*. Chicago: University of Chicago Press.

Levinas, Emmanuel (1972) 'La trace', in *Humanisme de l'autre homme*. Montpellier: Fata Morgana: 57–63.

Lévi-Strauss, Claude (1966) *The Savage Mind*. Chicago: University of Chicago.

—— (1968) *Structural Anthropology*, tr. Claire Jacobson and Brooke Grundfest. Harmondsworth: Penguin.

Locke, John (1975) *An Essay Concerning Human Understanding*, ed. P.N. Nidditch. Oxford: Clarendon Press.

Lyotard, Jean-François (1984) *The Post-Modern Condition: A Report on Knowledge*, tr. Geoff Bennington and Brian Massumi. Manchester: Manchester University Press.

McCarthy, Thomas (1982) 'Rationality and relativism: Habermas's "overcoming" of hermeneutics', in *Habermas: Critical Debates*, ed. David Held and John Thompson. Cambridge: Cambridge University Press: 57–78.

Mandelbaum, Maurice (1977) *The Anatomy of Historical Knowledge*. Baltimore and London: Johns Hopkins University Press.

Mann, Thomas (1969) *The Magic Mountain*. tr. H.T. Lowe-Porter. New York: Alfred A. Knopf.

Mannheim, Karl (1936) *Ideology and Utopia*, tr. Louis Wirth and Edward Shils. London: Routledge & Kegan Paul.

Marcel, Gabriel (1950) *The Mystery of Being*, tr. G.S. Fraser, 2 vols. London: The Harvard Press.

Marx, Karl (1977) *Selected Writings*, ed. D. McLellan. Oxford: Oxford University Press.

Merleau-Ponty, Maurice (1962) *The Phenomenology of Perception*. London: Routledge & Kegan Paul.

Miller, J. Hillis (1987) 'But are things as we think they are?', review of *Time and Narrative*, *The Times Literary Supplement* 9–15 October: 1104–6.

Mink, Louis O. (1965) 'The autonomy of historical understanding', *History and Theory* 5: 24–47.

—— (1968) 'Philosophical analysis and historical understanding', *Review of Metaphysics* 20: 667–98.

—— 'History and fiction as modes of comprehension', *New Literary History* 1: 541–58.

Moltmann, Jurgen (1967) *The Theology of Hope*, tr. J.W. Leitch. New York: Harper & Row.

Nietzsche, Friedrich (1966) *Beyond Good and Evil*, tr. Walter Kaufmann. New York: Random House.

—— (1966) *Thus Spake Zarathustra*, tr. Walter Kaufmann. New York: Viking Press.

—— (1967) *The Genealogy of Morals*, tr. Walter Kaufmann. New York: Random House.

—— (1980) *On the Advantage and Disadvantage of History for Life*, tr. Peter Preuss. Indianapolis: Hackett.

Norris, Christopher (1982) *Deconstruction: Theory and Practice*. London: Methuen.

—— (1985) *The Conflict of Faculties: Philosophy and Theory after Deconstruction*. London: Methuen.

Propp, Vladimir (1968) *Morphology of the Russian Folk Tale*, 2nd edn tr. and rev. Louis A. Wagner. Austin: University of Texas Press.

Proust, Marcel (1981) *Remembrance of Things Past*, tr. C.K. Scott Moncrieff, Terence Kilmartin, and Andreas Major. New York: Random House.

Rad, Gerhard von (1962) *Theology of the Old Testament*. vol. 1 *Theology of the Historical Traditions of Israel*, tr. D.M.G. Stalker. Edinburgh: Oliver & Boyd.

Reagan, Charles (1979) *Studies in the Philosophy of Paul Ricoeur*. Athens: Ohio State University Press.

Richards, I.A. (1924) *Principles of Literary Criticism*. London: Paul Trench Trubner.

Ricoeur, Paul (1947) with Mikel Dufrenne, *Karl Jaspers et la philosophie de l'existence*. Paris: Seuil.

—— (1948) *Gabriel Marcel et Karl Jaspers. Philosophie du mystère et philosophie du paradoxe*. Paris: Temps Présent.

—— (1949) 'Le renouvellement du problème de la philosophie chrétienne par les philosophes de l'existence', *Le problème de la philosophie chrétienne*. Paris: Presses Universitaires de France: 43–67.

—— (1950) *Philosophie de la volonté. I. Le volontaire et l'involontaire*, Paris: Aubier. Translated by E.V. Kohak as *Freedom and Nature; The Voluntary and the Involuntary*. Evanston: Northwestern University Press (1966).

—— (1952a) 'Aux frontières de la philosophie', *Esprit* 20: 760–75.

—— (1952b) 'L'homme révolté de Camus', *Christiasme social* 60: 229–39.

—— (1954) 'Sartre's Lucifer and the Lord', *Yale French Studies* 14: 85–93.

—— (1955) *Histoire et vérité*. Paris: Seuil. Expanded second edition (1964) tr. Ch. A. Kelbley as *History and Truth*. Evanston: Northwestern University

Press 1965) (includes: 'Objectivity and subjectivity in history' 21–40; 'The history of philosophy and the unity of truth' 41–56; 'Christianity and the meaning of history' 81–97; 'Emmanuel Mounier: a personalist philosopher' 122–61; 'Work and the word' 192–222; 'True and false anguish' 287–304; 'Negativity and primary affirmation' 305–28).

—— (1957a) 'The relation of Jaspers' philosophy to religion', in *The Philosophy of Karl Jaspers. A Critical Analysis and Evaluation*, ed. P.A. Schlipp. New York: Tudor.

—— (1957b) 'Les événements d'Algérie devant la conscience chrétienne', *Foi-éducation* 27 (April–June): 105.

—— (1960a) *Philosophie de la volonté. Finitude et culpabilité. I. L'homme faillible.* Paris: Aubier. Translated by Ch. A. Kelbley as *Fallible Man*. Chicago: Henry Regnery (1965; rev. 1985).

—— (1960b) *Philosophie de la volonté. Finitude et culpabilité. II. La symbolique du mal.* Paris: Aubier. Translated by E. Buchanan as *The Symbolism of Evil*. New York–Evanston–London: Harper & Row (1967).

—— (1963a) 'Appel aux protestants de France', *Cité nouvelle* 383 (6 June): 1.

—— (1963b) 'Philosopher après Kierkegaard', 'Kierkegaard et le mal', *Revue de théologie et de philosophie* 13: 292–302, 303–16.

—— (1963c) 'Réponses à quelques questions', *Esprit* 31 (11): 628–53. Debate with Lévi-Strauss.

—— (1964) 'Discussione', *Archivio di Filosofia* 34: 1–2, 5–60, 87–94, 117–20, 223–9, 311–18. Debate with Lacan.

—— (1965) *De l'interprétation. Essai sur Freud.* Paris: Seuil. Translated by Denis Sauvage as *Freud and Philosophy*. New Haven and London; Yale University Press (1970).

—— (1966) 'Husserl and Wittgenstein on language', in *Phenomenology and Existentialism*, ed. E.N. Lee and M. Mandelbaum. Baltimore: Johns Hopkins University Press: 207–17.

—— (1967) *Husserl. An Analysis of his Phenomenology*, tr. E.G. Ballard and L.E. Embree. Evanston: Northwestern University Press. The equivalent French collection is *A l'école de la phénoménologie*. Paris; Seuil (1986) (includes: 'Husserl (1859–1938)' 3–12; 'Kant and Husserl' 175–201; 'Existential phenomenology' 202–12; 'Methods and tasks of a phenomenology of the will' 213–33).

—— (1968) 'Lenine et la philosophie', *Bulletin de la Société française de Philosophie* 62: 161–8. Debate with Althusser.

—— (1969) *Le conflit des interprétations. Essais d'herméneutique.* Paris: Seuil. Translated by D. Ihde *et al.* as *The Conflict of Interpretations: Essays in Hermeneutics*. Evanston: Northwestern University Press 1974) (includes: 'Existence and hermeneutics' 3–24; 'Structure and hermeneutics' 27–61; 'Structure, word, event' 79–96; 'Nabert on act and sign' 211–22; 'Heidegger and the question of the subject' 223–35; '"Original sin?": a study in meaning' 269–86; 'The hermeneutics of symbols and philosophical reflection', I and II 287–314, 315–34; 'Preface to Bultmann' 381–401; 'Freedom in the light of hope' 402–24; 'Religion, atheism and faith' 440–67; 'Fatherhood: from phantasm to symbol' 468–97).

—— (1971) 'Sur l'exégèse de Genese 1, 1–2, 4a', in *Exégèse et herméneutique*, ed. X. Leon-Dufour. Paris: Seuil: 239–65. Debate with Barthes.

—— (1973) 'Table ronde. Philosophie et communication', *La communication II*. Montreal: Montmorency: 393–431. Debate with Derrida.

—— (1974) *Political and Social Essays*, ed. D. Stewart and J. Bien. Athens: Ohio State University Press (includes: 'Nature and freedom' 23–45; 'What does humanism mean?' 68–87; 'Violence and language' 88–101; 'From Marxism to contemporary Communism' 217–28; 'Ethics and culture: Habermas and Gadamer in dialogue' 243–270).

—— (1975a) *La métaphore vive*. Paris: Seuil. Translated by R. Czerny, with K. McLaughlin and J. Costello as *The Rule of Metaphor, Multi-Disciplinary Studies of the Creation of Meaning in Language*. Toronto: University of Toronto Press (1977).

—— (1975b) 'Phenomenology of freedom', in *Phenomenology and Philosophical Understanding*, ed. E. Pivcevic. Cambridge: Cambridge University Press: 173–94.

—— (1975c) 'Philosophical hermeneutics and theological hermeneutics', *Studies in Religion* 5: 14–33.

—— (1975d) 'Biblical hermeneutics', *Semeia* 4: 27–148.

—— (1976a) *Interpretation Theory: Discourse and the Surplus of Meaning*. Fort Worth: Texas Christian University Press.

—— (1976b) 'Entre Gabriel Marcel et Jean Wahl', in *Jean Wahl et Gabriel Marcel*, ed. J. Hersch. Paris: Beauchesne: 57–87.

—— (1976c) 'What is dialectical?', in *Freedom and Morality*, ed. John Bricke. Lawrence: University of Kansas: 173–89.

—— (1976d) 'Preface' to M. Dufrenne, *The Notion of A Priori*, tr. E. Casey. Evanston: Northwestern University Press: ix–xvii.

—— (1976e) 'History and hermeneutics', *Journal of Philosophy* 19: 683–95.

—— (1977a) 'Herméneutique de l'idée de Révélation', *La révélation*. Bruxelles: facultés universitaires Saint-Louis: 15–54. Plus debate with Levinas: 207–36.

—— (1977b) 'Writing as a problem for literary criticism and philosophical hermeneutics', *Philosophic Exchange* 2: 3–15.

—— (1977c) 'Construing and constructing', review of E.D. Hirsch Jnr, *The Aims of Interpretation, The Times Literary Supplement* 3911 (25 February): 216.

—— (1978a) 'Image and language in psychoanalysis', *Psychoanalysis and Language*, ed. J.H. Smith. New Haven and London: Yale University Press: 293–324.

—— (1978b) 'Imagination as discourse and in action', *Analecta Husserliana* 7: 3–22.

—— (1979a) 'Hegel and Husserl on intersubjectivity', in *Reason, Action and Experience*, ed. H. Kohlenberger. Hamburg: Felix Meiner Verlag: 13–29.

—— (1979b) *Rationality Today/ La rationalité aujourd'hui*, ed. Th. F. Geraets. Ottawa: University of Ottawa Pres: 205–12. Debate with Habermas.

—— (1979c) 'The function of fiction in shaping reality', *Man and World* 12: 123–41.

—— (1980a) *Essays on Biblical Interpretation*, ed. Lewis S. Mudge. Philadelphia: Fortress Press.

—— (1980b) 'Narrative time', *Critical Inquiry* 7: 169–90.

—— (1981a) *Hermeneutics and the Human Sciences. Essays on Language, Action and Interpretation*, tr. and ed. J.B. Thompson. Cambridge: Cambridge

University Press. The approximately equivalent collection in France is *Du texte de l'action: essais d'herméneutiques II*. Paris: Seuil (1986); in the US, *The Philosophy of Paul Ricoeur*, edited by Charles E. Reagan and Paul Stewart. Boston: Beacon Press (1978) (includes: 'The task of hermeneutics' 43–62; 'Hermeneutics and the critique of ideology' 63–100; 'Phenomenology and hermeneutics' 101–30; 'The hermeneutical function of distanciation' 131–44; 'What is a text? Explanation and understanding' 145–64; 'Appropriation' 182–96; 'The model of the text: meaningful action considered as a text' 197–221; 'Science and ideology' 222–46; 'The question of proof in Freud's psychoanalytic writings' 247–73).

—— (1981b) 'Sartre and Ryle on the imagination', in *The Philosophy of Jean-Paul Sartre*, ed. P.A. Schlipp. La Salle, Ill.: Open Court: 167–78.

—— (1982) 'The conflict of interpretations', in *Phenomenology: Dialogues and Bridges*, ed. R. Bruzina and Br. Wilshire. Albany: State University of New York Press: 299–312, 313–20. Debate with Gadamer.

—— (1983–6) *Temps et récit*. (1983) *Tome I*. Paris: Seuil. (1984) *Tome II. la configuration dans le récit*. (1986) *Tome III. Le temps raconté*. Translated by K. McLaughlin and D. Pellauer as *Time and Narrative*, vols I, II, III. Chicago: University of Chicago Press (1984–7).

—— (1983a) 'On interpretation, in *Philosophy in France Today*, ed. A. Montefiore. Cambridge: Cambridge University Press: 175–97.

—— (1983b) 'Action, story, history: on re-reading *The Human Condition*', *Salmagundi* 60: 60–72.

—— (1984) *Dialogues with Contemporary Continental Thinkers*, ed. Richard Kearney. Manchester: Manchester University Press.

—— (1986a) *Lectures on Ideology and Utopia*, ed. George S. Taylor. New York: Columbia University Press.

—— (1986b) *Le mal: un défi à la philosophie et à la théologie*. Geneva: Labor et fides.

Rorty, Richard (1982) *Consequences of Pragmatism: Essays 1972–80*. Hassocks: Harvester Press.

—— (1985) 'Habermas and Lyotard on postmodernity', in *Habermas and Modernity*, ed. Richard J. Bernstein. Oxford: Oxford University Press: 161–75.

—— (1989) *Contingency, Irony, and Solidarity*. Cambridge: Cambridge University Press.

Russell, Bertrand (1956) 'On denoting' in *Logic and Knowledge: Essays (1901–50)*. London: Allen & Unwin: 39–56.

Ryle, Gilbert (1949) *The Concept of Mind*. London: Hutchinson.

—— (1971) 'Heidegger's 'Sein und Zeit', *Collected Papers*. London: Hutchinson: 197–214.

Sartre, Jean-Paul: (1948) *The Psychology of Imagination*, tr. Bernard Frechtman. New York: Washington Square Press.

—— (1957) *Being and Nothingness*, tr. Hazel Barnes. London: Methuen.

Saussure, Ferdinand de (1974) *Course in General Linguistics*, tr. Wade Baskin. London: Fontana.

Schaldenbrand, Mary (1979) 'Metaphoric imagination: kinship through-conflict', in *Studies in the Philosophy of Paul Ricoeur*, ed. C. Reagan. Athens: Ohio State University Press: 57–81.

Searle, John (1969) *Speech Acts: An Essay in the Philosophy of Language*. Cambridge: Cambridge University Press.

—— (1977) 'Reiterating the differences', *Glyph* I: 198–208.

Spiegelberg, Herbert (1960) *The Phenomenological Movement*, 2 vols. The Hague: Martinus Nijhoff.

Strawson, P.F. (1950) 'On referring', *Mind* 59: 320–44.

—— (1959) *Individuals: An Essay in Descriptive Metaphysics*. London: Methuen.

Thompson, John (1981) *Critical Hermeneutics: A Study in the Thought of Paul Ricoeur and Jurgen Habermas*. Cambridge: Cambridge University Press.

Tort, Michel (1966) 'De l'interprétation ou la machine herméneutique', *Les Temps Modernes* 21: 1461–93, 1629–52.

Toulmin, Stephen (1948) 'The logical status of psychoanalysis', *Analysis* 9 (2): 23–9.

Turbayne, Colin Murray (1962) *The Myth of Metaphor*. New Haven: Yale University Press.

Turkle, Sherry (1978) *Psychoanalytic Politics: Freud's French Revolution*. London: André Deutsch.

Vansina, F.D. (ed.) (1985) *Paul Ricoeur: A Primary and Secondary Bibliography (1935–84)*. Leuven: Editions Peeters.

Veyne, Paul (1971) *Comment on ecrit l'histoire*. Paris: Seuil.

Warnke, Georgia (1987) *Gadamer: Hermeneutics, Tradition and Reason*. Cambridge: Polity Press.

Wellek, Rene, and Warren, Austin (1949) *Theory of Literature*. New York: Harcourt, Brace & World.

White, Hayden (1973) *Metahistory: The Historical Imagination in Nineteenth-Century Europe*. Baltimore: Johns Hopkins University Press.

—— (1978) *Tropics of Discourse*. Baltimore and London: Johns Hopkins University Press.

—— (1987) *The Content of the Form: Narrative Discourse and Historical Representation*. Baltimore and London: Johns Hopkins University Press.

Wimsatt, William K., with Monroe C. Beardsley (1954) *The Verbal Icon: Studies in the Meaning of Poetry*. Lexington: University of Kentucky Press.

Winch, Peter (1958) *The Idea of a Social Science and Its Relation to Philosophy*. London: Routledge & Kegan Paul.

Wittgenstein, Ludwig (1933) *Tractatus Logico-Philosophicus*, tr. C.K. Ogden, second edition. London: Kegan Paul.

—— (1953) *Philosophical Investigations*, tr. G.E.M. Anscombe. Oxford: Blackwell.

Woolf, Virginia (1924) *Mrs Dalloway*. London: Hogarth Press.

Wright, G.H. von (1968) *An Essay in Deontic Logic and the General Theory of Action*. Amsterdam: North Holland.

—— (1971) *Explanation and Understanding*. Ithaca: Cornell.

Index